# NORTH OF UNKNOWN

# NORTH OF UNKNOWN

## MINA HUBBARD'S EXTRAORDINARY EXPEDITION INTO THE LABRADOR WILDERNESS

# RANDALL SILVIS

THE LYONS PRESS
GUILFORD, CONNECTICUT
AN IMPRINT OF THE GLOBE PEQUOT PRESS

Published in the U.S. in 2005 by The Lyons Press

Copyright © 2004 Randall Silvis

Many of the photographs in this book are reprinted courtesy of The Centre for Newfoundland Studies Archives, Memorial University, St. John's, Newfoundland. The 1903 photos are from the Dillon Wallace Collection (COLL-244) and most of the 1905 photos are from the Mina Hubbard Collection (COLL-241). Additional photographs have been reprinted from *A Woman's Way Through Labrador*.

The Lyons Press is an imprint of the Globe Pequot Press.

10  8  6  4  2  1  3  5  7  9

Library of Congress Cataloging-in-Publication Data

Silvis, Randall, 1950-
    [Heart so hungry]
    North of Unknown : Mina Hubbard's extraordinary expedition into the Labrador wilderness / Randall Silvis.
        p. cm.
    "First published by Alfred A. Knopf Canada under the title: Heart so Hungry"—T.p. verso.
    Includes bibliographical references.
    ISBN 1-59228-755-7 (trade cloth)
    1. Labrador (N.L.)—Description and travel. 2. Hubbard, Mina—Travel—Newfoundland and Labrador—Labrador. 3. Women explorers—Newfoundland and Labrador—Labrador—Biography. 4. Women adventurers—Newfoundland and Labrador—Labrador—Biography. 5. Explorers' spouses—Newfoundland and Labrador—Labrador—Biography. 6. Hubbard, Leonidas, 1872-1903. I. Title.

F1136.S55 2005
917.18′2—dc22
[B]

                                                                        2005044428

as always,
this book is for Rita and Bret and Nathan

ROUTE OF LEONIDAS
HUBBARD'S EXPEDITION, 1903
- - - - - - - - - - - - - - - - - - - - - - - - - -

UNGAVA
BAY

GEORGE
RIVER
POST

FORT
CHIMO

George R.

ATLANTIC
OCEAN

Indian
House L.

DAVIS INLET

George R.

Lake
Michikmats

Seal L.

RIGOLET

Naskapi R.

Naskapi R.

Lake
Michikamau

Lake
Melville

Susan R.    Grand L.
NORTH WEST  ○ KENEMISH
RIVER POST

L A B R A D O R

Q U E B E C

SCALE IN MILES
0    25    50    75    100    125    150

ROUTE OF MINA HUBBARD'S
EXPEDITION, 1905

ROUTE OF DILLON WALLACE'S
EXPEDITION, 1905

UNGAVA
BAY

ATLANTIC
OCEAN

FORT
CHIMO

GEORGE
RIVER
POST

George R.

Indian
House L.

DAVIS INLET

George R.

Lake
Michikmats

RIGOLET

Seal L.

Naskapi R.

Lake
Michikamau

Naskapi R.

Lake
Melville

Susan R.   Grand L.

NORTH WEST   KENEMISH
RIVER POST

LABRADOR

QUEBEC

SCALE IN MILES

0    25    50    75    100   125   150

## ACKNOWLEDGMENTS

A book such as this cannot be written without a great deal of help. Among the many librarians and archivists to whom I am indebted for their research assistance, I extend a special thanks to Gail Weir at the Centre for Newfoundland Studies Archives in St. John's, and Sherri Campbell at the Eccles-Lesher Memorial Library in Rimersburg, Pennsylvania.

As always, I am grateful to my agent, Peter Rubie, for his friendship and faith. And to my editor, Michael Schellenberg, for his insights and suggestions.

This book is a hybrid of fact and fiction. The events and individuals depicted here are a matter of historical record; scenes have been expanded and dramatized based on known facts.

# NORTH OF UNKNOWN

# PROLOGUE

*May 4, 1956*

"I AM GOING TO EXPLORE," the old woman said. The friend with whom Mina Hubbard was visiting cautioned her not to stay out too long, their midmorning tea would be ready soon. The friend would have preferred that Mina not go out at all, for at eighty-six years old Mina had become a bit forgetful of late. More than once she had "gone to explore" the town of Coulsdon, a suburb of London, England, only to lose her bearings and be brought back to Fairdene Road by strangers.

But Mina Benson Hubbard Ellis was not the kind of woman who could be persuaded to pass the day in a rocking chair, especially not a fine spring day like this one, a day that smelled of balsam and spruce and of rivers swift with melted snow. A Canadian who had trained as a nurse in New York City at the beginning of the twentieth century, Mina still possessed the same headlong spirit that had defined her as a young woman, the same iron will that, in 1905, had made her one of the most celebrated women of her time.

Even now that spirit was evident in the quickness of her gait and in the angle, not quite imperious, at which she held her chin. She

came away from her friend's house, paused for a moment to enjoy
the scent of the bright May morning, then strode in the direction
of the Coulsdon South railway station. She crossed the busy street
with barely a glance at the traffic, extending her arms in both directions like a traffic cop, enforcing a path for herself, as was her habit.

Few people if any in Coulsdon were aware of Mina's fame and
accomplishments. Few knew of her lecture tours across America
and England. Few knew that during the Second World War, while
bombs dropped all around her lovely home in London's Hampstead
neighbourhood, Mina, as described by biographer Anne Hart in
the CBC radio program *Through Unknown Labrador*, was "serving up
left-wing causes with the tea, and retiring each night, oblivious to
bombs, to a bed whose silk coverlet was always spread with the grey
blanket she had slept under on the long-ago Labrador trail." Few
knew that at thirty years of age Mina had been timid and indecisive,
that she had considered herself unattractive and of small value
except as a companion to the man she all but worshipped, the hap-
less Leonidas Hubbard Jr., whose ignominious fate would soon
determine her own.

If the citizens of Coulsdon knew Mina at all, it was as a small,
eccentric old woman—a woman who now, on this sparkling spring
day, climbed a grassy bank near the railroad tracks and strolled
along like an explorer on a high ridge, eyes searching for something
or somebody.

According to the *Purley and Coulsdon Advertiser* of May 11, 1956,
Jill Foster, a fourteen-year-old girl, was standing on the platform of
the Coulsdon South station when Mina came down the grassy
bank and walked toward the tracks. Jill wondered where the old
woman thought she was going; she had already passed the pedestrian
walkway that would have brought her safely across the tracks to the
station. Then Mina opened a gate intended to keep pedestrians
away from the tracks, and Jill nudged her companion, fifteen-year-
old Roger Aslin.

Roger cupped his hands to his mouth. "You'd better watch out there!" he called. "Train's due any minute now!"

But Mina paid no attention. Perhaps she did not hear well. Perhaps she assumed that an approaching train could be held at bay by her outstretched arms, just as the cars and lorries were.

Or perhaps she knew full well that a train would never yield, that some things in life remain unswervable. A woman's iron will, for example. A wife's unflinching devotion.

In any case, Mina paid no heed to the warnings. She paid no heed to the rumble of the train as it approached the station, or to the shrill blast of its whistle. Maybe the rumble reminded her of a waterfall's roar, a sound that, in an earlier time, had never failed to thrill her. In those days every new waterfall and every new set of rapids had murmured with the promise of discovery, and she had approached each one with a constriction in her throat and the hope that somehow, miraculously, Leonidas, her Laddie, would be waiting there to receive her, to welcome her back into his arms.

Now, she crossed the first set of tracks and stepped into the centre of the second set, and there paused, lifted her chin slightly, and smiled once more.

The children on the platform screamed to her. Mina turned her face to the sun. Did she hear the shouts of warning? Or were her thoughts attuned to another world entirely, to the perfume of pine in the air, the scent of a misty river a world and a lifetime away? Did she again feel that familiar tightening in her chest and hear in the train's approach the rumble of a waterfall rushing to engulf her on such a fine spring day . . . a perfect day for her journey's end?

# PART I

*How It Began*

WHATEVER MINA'S MOTIVE for stepping onto the tracks that day, her devotion to Leonidas Hubbard Jr. was surely at the heart of it. He was a man whose infectious enthusiasm for adventure altered not only his own life but hers and many others' as well.

As a child growing up in rural Michigan, Hubbard developed a passionate interest in history and geography and a love for the natural world. Mina later described him as an imaginative and sensitive boy who had been reared on stories of travel and adventure. "His imagination kindled by what he read," she wrote, "and the oft-repeated tales of frontier life in which the courage, endurance, and high honour of his own pioneer forefathers stood out strong and clear, it was but natural that the boy under the apple trees should feel romance in every bit of forest, every stream; that his thoughts should be reaching towards the out-of-the-way places of the earth where life was still that of the pioneer with the untamed wilderness lying across his path...."

He brought those same sensibilities to his duties as a reporter for an evening paper in Detroit, where he went to work upon his graduation from the University of Michigan in 1897. A slight man of large ambitions, it wasn't long before he yearned for more challenge and adventure. In the summer of 1899, with less than five dollars in his pocket, Hubbard left Detroit for New York City. New York was throbbing with growth, the perfect place for him to launch himself into the ranks of his heroes. His most fervent desire was to become as famous as Teddy Roosevelt, Robert Peary and Jack London, all bold and independent souls, men with fire in their blood. He considered himself cut from the same cloth.

Unfortunately, Hubbard arrived in New York City with no contacts, no letter of introduction and no job prospects. Armed only with clips of his work in Detroit he trudged from door to door in search of a position. No offers were forthcoming.

All too soon the money ran out. With nothing to eat, his energy faltered, and for two days he staggered from place to place so weakened by hunger that he feared he would be arrested for public drunkenness.

Finally, when it seemed he was destined to collapse and die unnoticed on those friendless streets, an acquaintance from Michigan appeared out of nowhere and forced fifteen dollars into Hubbard's trembling hand. That same day one of Hubbard's stories was accepted for publication. But even better news was yet to come. A few days later he was hired as a staff writer for the *Daily News*. Before long he was getting all the best assignments for that paper and also selling an occasional piece to the *Saturday Evening Post*.

Then, calamity. In early May the headaches began, a pulsing ache like a hammer to his brain. Then the cough and sore throat, the nosebleeds and constipation. That first week he continued to work, doing his best to ignore the pain. But when his temperature rose and would not return to normal and the other symptoms worsened too, a doctor sent him to the Long Island Infirmary. Just like that his job with the *Daily News* was whisked out from under him.

In a few short weeks typhoid fever can rob a man of all dignity. Certainly Leonidas Hubbard Jr. felt he had lost that and more as he lay abed in the quarantine ward. During the long days and longer nights of May 1900, as his body fought off the illness, he wondered anxiously what new misery would befall him.

The only bright spot in his life was his nurse. The comely Mina Benson, shy and petite, was a not quite pretty woman but with a gaze so soft that he had more than once felt himself drifting away on it. And she was a wonderful listener as well. A very good thing, too, considering how much Hubbard loved to talk.

From his hospital bed he regaled the shy girl—and he could not help but think of her as a girl, so deferent and modest, though at thirty she was two years his senior—with the tales he never tired of recounting. He told her of Peary's work in Greenland and among the Eskimos and his plans to conquer the North Pole, "The North Pole! Just think of it." He told her of Stanley's exploration in mysterious Africa, of John Wesley Powell's thrilling one-armed exploits in the American West. The name of Leonidas Hubbard Jr. will one day be added to that list, he told her. Exactly where he would go and precisely what he would accomplish, he did not yet know. But a place in history awaited him.

Mina was certain of this as well. She could feel his greatness when he spoke, could feel her skin flush with the intensity of his passions. That he even deigned to confide in her, a plain and unworldly farm girl from Ontario, this she found amazing and beyond explanation.

It was clear to Hubbard that Mina was smitten with him, and he had to admit that they would make a good pair. But what did he, an unemployed journalist, have to offer other than his stories, the tales he knew by heart of his grandfather's exploits as an Indian hunter in Ohio, his father's adventures as a hunter and trapper in the forbidding wilds of Michigan?

In Hubbard's darkest hours Mina's quiet faith in him became his only strength. She knew in her heart that a man of his talents would soon be on his feet, more successful than ever. "I don't think anything can keep you down," she confessed with a blush. And because Mina believed it—dear, sweet girl—Hubbard believed it too.

After four frustrating weeks he was finally moved out of the quarantine ward. For a man as restless as he, it was like a release from prison. He walked endlessly up and down the hallways, filling the time between Mina's visits to his room. He had never been the kind of man who could sit still for long, not unless he was reliving an adventure through his writing or reading, traipsing through dark forest, paddling against the current up a glittering stream. Besides, he had to toughen up his legs if he was soon to hit the streets again.

He promised Mina that when he was released from the hospital he would take her hiking and canoeing and fishing. They would go on picnics and explore the surrounding woodlands together. Mina happily agreed to accompany him wherever he wished to go.

In the meantime Hubbard walked the halls. During one of these strolls he noticed a man seated at the bedside of a pale but pretty woman, holding her hand in both of his. The man, who appeared to be maybe ten years older than Hubbard, heavier and with thinning hair, was dressed in a good suit, a suit far more fashionable than any Hubbard could afford. But the man's face was drawn, his eyes clouded with grief. And on the cheeks of the pale woman whose hand he clutched was the telltale bloom of consumption.

Hubbard felt compassion for that man, and a strange kind of kinship. He considered approaching him, offering his sympathies. After noticing the gentleman on a few more occasions, always seated at his wife's bedside, looking so utterly alone, that was what Hubbard did. The husband, after a moment's hesitation, seized Hubbard's hand. His grip, Hubbard later told Mina, was as desperate as that of a man "about to drown in the ocean of his grief."

The man's name was Dillon Wallace and he worked as a lawyer in Manhattan. He and his wife, Jennie, had been married only three years. And now she would soon be gone from him. It was so cruel and unfair, he confessed; too much for a man to bear.

Hubbard and Wallace spent many hours together in the hospital. Hubbard spoke of his own misfortunes, if only to demonstrate that Wallace was not the sole recipient of raw treatment from the fates, and as evidence that tragedy can be overcome—"Must be overcome!"—lest one wishes to linger forever in the fog of despair.

They talked of the activities they had once enjoyed, found they each longed for the pleasure of a hike through woods where no sound of man intruded, for the accomplishment of filling a creel with sleek trout pulled from a sun-spangled stream. In their shared miseries and common pleasures they took strength and comfort.

Not long after meeting Wallace, Hubbard was released from the hospital. But no longer was he alone in New York. He had made many friends through his work at the *Daily News* and the *Saturday Evening Post* and he had developed a deep bond with Dillon Wallace. His most devoted friend by far, however, and now also his sweetheart, was Miss Benson. All readily assisted Hubbard every way they could, with money, letters of introduction, and with a confidence in him to match his own.

To get his strength back that summer, Hubbard spent some time camping in the Shawangunk Mountains in southern New York state. It was precisely what he needed, a medicine taken in the whisper of a breeze through the branches, the call of crows in foggy treetops, the scent of a campfire, the delicious puck and sibilance of rain pattering on a canvas tent. His new friend Dillon Wallace sometimes accompanied him on these trips. The long hikes and quiet evenings were salubrious for Wallace, a widower now. In fact it was only at these times with Hubbard or when buried in work at his Manhattan office that the lawyer could step away from his grief for a while.

That August Hubbard armed himself with a packet of articles and a letter of introduction and called on Caspar Whitney, editor and owner of a popular outdoor magazine called *Outing*. Whitney, like all who met Hubbard, could not help but be impressed with the young man's enthusiasm and confidence. Though slight of stature, Hubbard projected a powerful presence, a charisma. There was always a smile on his handsome face, and his sharp, finely chiselled features, especially those eyes bright with the spirit of adventure, commanded attention.

The man has energy and ambition, Whitney thought. Why not give him a try? Whitney offered an assignment, an article about the Adirondacks. Hubbard turned it in under deadline, a fine piece of writing.

"All right," Whitney told him. "I'll take you on."

And suddenly all past miseries fell away from Leonidas Hubbard Jr. Not only was he a salaried writer again, but his work would appear in the same pages as that of Peary and Teddy Roosevelt.

Early the next year, Hubbard decided that the time was right for him to act upon his "firm resolution" that "a certain portion of Canada be annexed to the United States." He travelled to the farming country of Bewdley, Ontario, to request permission for that annexation. Mr. and Mrs. Benson were delighted by his proposal, and they granted their approval.

Hubbard returned to New York City an exultant man. All the pieces of his life's dream were falling into place. A plum position with a prestigious magazine and a lovely, sweet woman who had agreed to be his wife. It was everything he had ever hoped for.

Within days he was assigned a series of articles that would take him through the southern states. Neither he nor Mina could abide the notion of being separated for the months it would take to complete the assignment, so arrangements were quickly made for what Mina would describe as "a quiet wedding in a little church in New York." On the last day of the first month of 1901, they began their life together as husband and wife.

For the next five months theirs was a transient life. From the mountains of Virginia they travelled through the backwoods and along the dusty roads of North Carolina, Tennessee, and Mississippi.

Hubbard not only gathered research and filed articles for *Outing*, he sold freelance pieces too, one on moonshining and one about an old pirate hangout, both to *The Atlantic Monthly*.

Mina served as his assistant, eagerly pitching in at every turn. Whether hunting, hiking, researching, writing, or simply talking of his plans for their life together, Hubbard was indefatigable, and his optimism was contagious. Mina had never felt so alive nor so loved.

After their southern trip the couple rented a house in Wurtsboro, a village in New York's scenic Mamakating Valley, from which Hubbard could commute to work in Manhattan. The hunting and fishing in the Mamakating Valley were excellent, and the Hubbards' friends visited them regularly. Especially Dillon Wallace. Mina found the lawyer to be a quiet man and sometimes a bit too sombre, but of course she forgave him his melancholy air; he had every right to it.

Mina frequently cooked for her Laddie and their guests in Wurtsboro, veritable feasts praised by everyone who sampled them—roasts of lamb or beef, mountains of mashed potatoes, honey-glazed carrots, cakes and puddings and coffee and brandy. Sometimes the Hubbards and a friend or two would venture forth on a camping trip into the mountains, and these were the suppers Mina most enjoyed, communally prepared over a campfire for appetites so huge after a day of tramping and canoeing that even the simplest of fare—fried trout and bacon, tea with biscuits and marmalade—satisfied as no banquet ever could.

But Mina did not always accompany her husband on his camping trips. In November 1901 he travelled to the Shawangunk Mountains with Dillon Wallace, and it was on this trip that Hubbard first articulated the dream he had been harbouring since just a boy. A dream to lead an expedition of his own into uncharted territory, an exploration of unknown lands that would forever after link the name of that land with his own.

The announcement took place after supper one evening. The men, sweetly exhausted from a day of snowshoeing through the woods, fired up their pipes and leaned back on the pine boughs in the lean-to they had built. Hubbard sat for a while staring at the camp-fire, all but motionless. At these times Wallace was content to empty his mind of all practical concerns, to allow the gathering night and the flutter of flames to work their magic on him.

But Hubbard's was a restless mind, never at peace. Abruptly he said, "Wallace, how would you like to go to Labrador with me?"

Wallace sucked on his pipe, then blew out a lazy stream of smoke. Another camping trip, he thought. Somewhere new.

"And where might Labrador be?" he asked. He had a vague knowledge of the area's whereabouts, knew that it existed some-where in the northeast corner of the continent. He imagined the fishing would be good there.

Hubbard grabbed his knapsack, produced pencil and notebook. With excited strokes he sketched an outline of the island of Newfoundland. Above its northernmost point he drew a wavy line. "The Strait of Belle Isle," he said. And just above the strait, like a tri-angular piece of lace attached to the side of Canada, was Labrador. Hubbard wasn't surprised that Wallace knew little about the place. Little was known of it. And that, precisely, was why Labrador called to him.

"Don't you realize it's the only part of the continent that hasn't been explored? John Cabot claimed the land for England back in 1497, but all he explored was the coastline. The interior is virtually unknown."

In 1901 most of the Labrador-Ungava peninsula's 500,000 square miles were still a mystery to all but its indigenous population. Bordered on the west and south by Quebec and on the east by the waters of the Atlantic Ocean, Labrador is a rugged and forbidding territory made up primarily of some of the oldest rocks on earth.

Its deep valleys, ancient mountains, high cliffs, and scoured plains were shaped by the Laurentide Ice Sheet some eighteen thousand years ago. The climate is marked by long, harsh winters and short summers. In the north, summers are too cool to support full tree growth; the terrain there and along the coast is mainly tundra. In the interior valleys, protected from the brutal winds, copses of balsam fir and dense forests of black spruce grow, but just as common are vast boglands, barrens, and valley floors covered in lichen and moss.

In 1534 Jacques Cartier deemed Labrador "the land God gave to Cain." Even so, whalers and fishermen and explorers from Spain, France, Portugal, and England were drawn to the Labrador coast, as were Moravian missionaries beginning in 1752, nine years after a French trading post was established at Davis Inlet. Here the indigenous peoples came in the summer to trade furs and fish for sugar, tobacco, tea, and other items.

It wasn't long before the coastline had been well mapped. Not so the interior. Europeans found little reason to venture far inland. In the winter of 1838, a Hudson's Bay Company agent named John McLean made a dogsled trip from Fort Chimo south to the North West River Post, and at some point travelled on the Naskapi River. But, as Dillon Wallace would later point out in his book *The Lure of the Labrador Wild*, "The record left by him of the journey . . . is very incomplete, and the exact route he took is by no means certain."

The interior was well known to the indigenous peoples, however, who moved about nomadically as hunters, trappers, and fishermen. The Innu and Inuit both claim Labrador as their home, but though they share a coincidental similarity in name they are unrelated. The Inuit (Eskimos) are the descendants of the Thule, an ancient whaling culture from Alaska. The Thule originally settled along the northern coast. Over time, as they followed the movements of whales and seals down the eastern shoreline, they migrated as far south as the Strait of Belle Isle.

While the Inuit depended largely on whales for their survival, the Innu depended on caribou. The Innu are an Algonkian Indian nation who had once been thought to be two separate groups, the Naskapi and the Montagnais. Both spoke dialects of the Cree language, though the dialects were dissimilar enough that early white explorers mistakenly identified the groups as separated by more than distance. The name Montagnais comes from the French word for "mountaineer" and was applied to the Innu first encountered along the northern shores of the Gulf of St. Lawrence. The Montagnais in turn referred to their southern neighbours as Naskapi, which has been variously translated as "the interior people" and "shabby dressers."

Both the Naskapi and the Montagnais possessed an intimate knowledge of the maze of waterways and footpaths that criss-crossed inland Labrador. This knowledge was passed down from generation to generation but never recorded. So in 1717 the French geographer Emanuel Bouman could accurately observe, on behalf of all Europeans, "We have no knowledge of the inland parts of this country."

In Hubbard's day, the best extant map of the interior was one made by A. P. Low of the Geological Survey of Canada. But much of that map remained blank space. And some of it, as Wallace would write, "proved to be wholly incorrect, and the mistake it led us into cost us dear."

On that November evening in 1901, as Wallace sat before a campfire with his friend, Leonidas Hubbard Jr. could still proclaim without much exaggeration, "It's terra incognita!"

With that exclamation Hubbard leapt to his feet, unable to sit still any longer. He searched the ground for a good piece of wood, found a log nearly three feet long, heaved it onto the fire. Then, even as he continued to speak, he poked and prodded at the log with a long stick, sending one swirl of embers after another into the night sky. Perhaps he did not view those dancing sparks as fireworks to his words, but Wallace did. It was as if the sparks were coming from Hubbard himself, an emanation of his passion.

"Just think of it!" he said. "A great unknown land right at our fingertips! I've been to the edge of Labrador already for that article I did on the Montagnais trappers. But what I want is to get into the really wild country. I want to have the same experience the old fellas had when they first opened up the very country where we now sit."

Wallace nodded and sucked on his pipe. He did not wish to smile too broadly lest Hubbard suspect he was amused by these ambitions. "Just how would we go about it?" he asked.

"What I propose is to set off north across Grand Lake by canoe. Grand Lake is some forty miles long. You don't have to go much beyond it, only as far as the Naskapi River, to be into virgin territory. Land no white man has ever seen, Wallace. And I mean to claim a piece of the unknown, just as Boone and Crockett and all the others did before us. Just as Peary is doing. Man, I've been dreaming about this kind of thing all my life. And now—don't ask me to explain it because I don't think I can—but now, at last, I know that Labrador is the place for me. And furthermore, I know without a doubt that we can pull it off."

Wallace lifted his pipe away from his mouth. He considered the crackling log, the sputter of boiling sap. "I'm not as confident as you are that I would be up to such an adventure."

"You say that every time I suggest another outing. But you always come with me, don't you? Last time, you said you really didn't have time any more for these trips of ours, yet here you sit, looking happy as a clam."

"True enough," Wallace admitted. "But this isn't Labrador."

Hubbard jabbed at the fire. Sparks shot into the air. "I thought my Lake St. John trip might be enough for me." He smiled wistfully. The scent of wood smoke always filled him with a strange longing. "And for a minute or two, it was. But as I stood there gazing ever deeper into Labrador—*looking into the unknown, Wallace! Can you imagine what that was like?*—I knew then that the mere beginning of the unknown would never be sufficient. I have to go. I have no choice but to do it."

He sat motionless for a minute or two, his gaze going over the fire and beyond Wallace, into the unfathomable darkness.

He spoke softly now. "The city is like a poison for me. Sure, I go there every day, I do my work, same as everybody else. But I'm not alive there. Not the way I am out here. That's why we make these trips, isn't it? To make us feel alive again? I challenge you to tell me it's not the same with you, because I know it is. Back at the office you feel like little more than a machine, don't you? But out here with the elements, out here where you have to catch your food and blaze your own trail, don't you feel like more of a man than at any other time? Really, Wallace, isn't that why you keep coming back for more?"

And there it was, in words too bald for Wallace to articulate himself, words too honest for him to utter. Since his wife's death he had tried to numb himself with work, yes, but he did not love the work any more, he did not awaken to it each morning with a sense of renewal and expectation. He threw himself into it because it deadened him.

But out here . . . How good he had felt traipsing through the snow this afternoon. These expeditions were tiring, yes, but the exhaustion was satisfying somehow, far more satisfying than the dull fatigue of office work could ever be. Here every morning he awakened fully alert, eager for a glimpse of the sun as it poured its first pink light through the trees. Here the raucous call of ravens and the chatter of jays was a music purer to his ears than the orchestrated boom of any symphony. And here even his grief released its weight on him, the grief that at other times so sapped his strength, weakened his legs and put a tremble in his hands. It was not that his grief lessened here—it never diminished—but there was a peculiar kind of lightness to it when he came into the woods. When he waded through knee-deep snow and thought of Jennie he was not depleted by bitterness but felt instead—and this he finally admitted to himself—he felt closer to her out here.

As for Hubbard, well, he was just a boy really. He'd had some rough times of his own, certainly, but of real loss, of life's blackest and deepest despair, what scars did he bear? Still, the boy was bold and reliant, no one could claim otherwise. Hubbard was, in truth, a splendid companion. Wallace had never known another man young or old with Hubbard's verve. He had *joie de vivre* and he wasn't the least bit shy about sharing it.

Truth be told, Wallace thought, where would I be now without him?

A minute or two later Wallace picked up one of his mittens, wrapped it around the teakettle's smoke-blackened handle, filled first Hubbard's cup, then his own. He picked up his mug of tea and smiled across the campfire. "All right," he said. "I'm with you."

"You'll go?" Hubbard leaned forward; his eyes reflected the fire.

Wallace leaned toward him. "To Labrador," he said. And they clinked their cups together.

"To the great unknown!"

For all of Hubbard's enthusiasm, his plan to conquer Labrador remained an elusive one while he tended to the business of making a living, turning out one assignment after another. This continued until April 1902, when he was promoted to assistant editor at *Outing*. He revelled in the chance to have a real influence on the magazine but regretted that the office work left less time for his own writing. But never did he lose sight of his lifelong goal. And in January of the following year, by which time he felt he had proved his worth to the magazine and justified Caspar Whitney's faith in him, he approached his editor.

"What I propose is this," he told Whitney. "I and a small party shall proceed from the head of Grand Lake up the Naskapi River, exploring and charting the territory north to Lake Michikamau. Thence to the headwaters of the George River, and down the river until I make contact with the Indians. No white man has ever visited the Barren Ground Indians at their inland camps. But I will. After which I mean to either continue north to Ungava Bay or else return south by the same route, depending on the weather and the season."

Whitney was anything but sanguine about the magazine acting as sponsor for the expedition. "And you will make the trip by canoe all the way?"

"No doubt there will be a good bit of portaging. The trappers around Grand Lake make mention of an Indian trail."

Whitney, who was more than ten years Hubbard's senior, pulled at his chin. "To be honest with you, Leon, it doesn't strike me as much of a challenge."

"Six hundred miles through uncharted lands!"

"But if I'm not mistaken, you intend to travel through the summer. And return before the snow falls."

"Even so," Hubbard said, and struggled to come up with a convincing argument, "by all accounts it is a bleak, unforgiving place. There are sure to be dangers and hardships aplenty."

But Whitney was not easy to persuade. He was determined not to waste the magazine's money on a trip that might result in less than thrilling copy. Although *Outing* regularly published articles on all manner of recreational activities—hunting and fishing, bicycling, boxing, and football—he was wary of throwing his magazine's support and money behind a summer-long project that required little more of its participants than a strong back. When it came to wilderness adventures, he had only to look at his own experiences as exemplars of dangers faced and hardships endured, with compelling stories as the result. Whitney had trekked two thousand miles across the Northwest Territories in 1895, for example, not in summer but in the frozen heart of winter, and not gliding along by canoe but trudging along on snowshoes, accompanied by mutinous Indians so starved he had been forced to guard the rations at knifepoint. Now *that* had been a challenging adventure. Hubbard's, in comparison, promised to be little more than a camping holiday.

"What kind of provisions would you take?" he asked, if only because he held Hubbard in high esteem and did not wish to dismiss him without a fair hearing.

"We would travel light," Hubbard said, "to facilitate quickness. Caribou and other game, as well as fish, will provide for most of our needs."

"Game is abundant in the area?"

Hubbard recognized the question as a trap. If game was indeed abundant, where was the challenge? "Not overly so," he answered. "Uncertain at best, I'd say."

Whitney's instincts told him to back away from this endeavour. Normally he would have had no difficulty doing so, for he was a forthright man with strong opinions seldom kept to himself. Some of his staff found him brusque, even abusive, and more than one had suffered a lashing of sharp words from his quick, thin lips. But Whitney did not mind if others considered him harsh. It was what the job demanded of him.

His problem was that he liked Leon Hubbard a great deal, both as a writer and as a man. He knew him to be unselfish and loyal, generous to a fault. But too much equanimity out on the trail could rapidly turn from a virtue to a liability. The wilderness called for a taskmaster unafraid to be dictatorial, prepared to push his crew to its limits. Beyond them, if necessary. Whitney doubted that Hubbard had even a drop of the tyrant in him. He would be solicitous of every thorn-prick and blister.

Even so, Hubbard was among the most popular of the writers on the magazine's staff. Any dispatches from him in the field would make for hot copy. Moreover, if denied this opportunity to fulfill a lifelong ambition, he might grow dissatisfied with his editorial duties, and might seek support elsewhere.

"If you go to Labrador," Whitney told him, "I cannot keep you on salary here."

Hubbard felt the wind go out of his sails, felt his chest grow leaden.

"I will, however, be happy to consider all articles and photographs that result from your adventure, and to pay you your usual rate for them."

Well, it was something, at least. Enough to bring a smile to Hubbard's mouth. And it was that look, at once humble and without a trace of resentment, that nudged Whitney toward another concession.

"And perhaps *Outing* can see its way clear to providing a bit of additional support as well. So as to ensure adequate provisioning."

Hubbard was as close to ecstatic as he had ever been. At home that night in the village of Congers, some thirty miles north of New York City, where he and Mina had rented a cottage, he pinned a Geological Survey map of Labrador to the wall of his study. To Mina it seemed a mere outline of the peninsula, its perimeter sketched in detail but much of its interior only empty white space.

"Here is where I expect to find the George River," Hubbard told his wife, laying his finger to the map. "And somewhere in here I hope to encounter the caribou as they make their migration eastward. Here, reportedly, we shall see the Indians. And here the Height of Land, whence our canoes will be carried northward with the current rather than having to fight against it."

Mina did her best to conceal the tentativeness of her smile, the quiver in her voice. A whole summer without her Laddie? How could she bear it? She could not return to nursing for a mere two months; no hospital would take her on knowing it would soon lose her again. So what would she do with herself? There was a garden to put in, yes, but by June most of the work would be done. She could not pull weeds from daybreak to dark. If Laddie would write to her daily, that would be something, but months would pass before he could post the letters. No, his summer of adventure would mean a summer of emptiness for her. Long, long days and even longer nights. How do you masquerade as happy when the focus of your life is taking itself away from you?

She kept her dread to herself, bit down hard on every selfish thought.

In February Hubbard placed a call to Dillon Wallace's office. "Bully news!" he said. "I've got bully news today!"

"Is that so? What's up?"

"We leave for Labrador this summer."

Wallace could do little more than blink. What had been a mere idea, and one he had never entertained with as much zeal as Hubbard did, loomed on the threshold of actual deed.

"Come out to Congers tonight," Hubbard told him, "and I'll tell you all about it. Mina will make something special for our celebration."

Over the course of that evening, as Mina doted and served, her stomach fluttering with trepidation, Hubbard's exuberance eroded away Wallace's doubts. Yes, they would have a grand time conquering the wilderness together. They would both be famous men.

At evening's close the Hubbard exploration into unknown Labrador was christened with a glass of sherry and a handshake. The men plighted their troth, as Wallace would later write in the dedication of his first book. The phrase made Mina grit her teeth in silence—this allusion to marriage—an allusion that might have been altogether ridiculous except that she, indeed, was to be left behind.

Such desolation, inside and out. Mina's first good look at the Labrador coastline, seen through the weak light of a coastal dawn and the grey of a bone-chilling drizzle, perfectly mirrored the anguish of her heart. It was July 5, 1903, and ahead in the mist lay Battle Harbour, a small settlement on Labrador's southeastern shore, and the place where she would be put ashore to return home alone while Laddie and his crew continued.

Over the past two weeks Mina had known little else but anguish, all of it suffered in silence, as was her duty as an explorer's wife. Then yesterday the lurching motion of their steamer, the *Virginia Lake*, had got the best of her, and she had spent most of the afternoon and evening with her head in a bucket. Laddie had stroked her hair and called her his "dear, brave girl" and assured her repeatedly that they would reach calmer waters soon.

The vomiting had stopped but the sickness had not left her. Somehow she knew it never would. The forebodings had begun in earnest on June 20, when she and Laddie had first stepped aboard the steamer *Sylvia* in New York harbour. With them had been Wallace and a half-Cree, half-Scottish woodsman from Ontario named George Elson.

Mina had liked Elson at first sight, and not merely because he was a fellow Canadian. A small measure of reassurance was accorded her in the knowledge that Laddie would be guided through the woods by this robust, quiet man. George was taller than either Wallace or Hubbard, broad-shouldered and deep-chested. With his thick moustache he looked a bit like Teddy Roosevelt, as strong and solid as an ox. But there was a gentleness to him as well, and just the hint of Scottish music in his speech.

Hired by letter out of the Hudson's Bay post at Missanabie, Ontario, Elson had arrived in New York City a couple of days before the *Sylvia* was to sail. He had travelled those thousand miles on his own, though he had never before visited a city of any kind— only to find no one to meet him at Grand Central Station. But instead of wandering around hopelessly George had commandeered a cab and in short order gotten himself to Fifth Avenue and Hubbard's office.

But even George's solid presence could not quiet Mina's dark forebodings. The passage from New York to St. John's, Newfoundland, where they had arrived on the twenty-sixth after a short layover in Halifax, had in no way been enjoyable for her, despite her husband's and Wallace's increasing excitement. Not long out of New York the rain had begun, and the *Sylvia* had bucked and lurched its way through a steady headwind.

In St. John's they were to transfer at once to the steamer *Virginia Lake* but, to Hubbard's vexation and Mina's secret relief, the ship was overdue and not expected for several more days. This delay gave Hubbard time to purchase and pack more provisions, and provided Mina an interlude from the fears that gnawed at her. To pass the time the entire party travelled to the village of Broad Cove, where, they had been promised, the trout fishing would be excellent. There Mina did her best to pretend that at the end of their short holiday she and Laddie would return to Congers and life would go on as usual.

But she could not slow the hours no matter how tightly she clung to her Laddie each night, and just before noon on July 1 the party was again aboard ship.

The *Virginia Lake*, overbooked and crowded even before they boarded, stank of spilled fuel and seal blubber. The ship functioned as a mail boat, a freighter and a passenger ship, and every spring it hauled a cargo of slaughtered seals from the Labrador coast to St. John's. Its decks had not been adequately cleaned and were still foul and slippery. In comparison with the *Sylvia*, the *Virginia Lake* seemed tiny and repugnant.

With its five small staterooms already claimed, the Hubbards were forced to settle for a cramped cubicle. Wallace acquired a berth only after browbeating a steward into relinquishing his own cabin. George, without complaint or expectations to the contrary, lugged his duffel to steerage.

One of the worst moments for Mina during the entire passage occurred in the open air of the deck, on a grey afternoon when icebergs could be seen rising and falling in the open sea. Smaller chunks of ice that the men called growlers scraped past the hull with a prolonged squeak and an awful moan. Mina had gone top-side with Laddie for one of his frequent inspections of the gear. He was met there by William Brooks Cabot, a former acquaintance who had also travelled north on the *Sylvia*. Cabot was embarking on his own canoe trip, this one a solitary paddle along the Labrador coastline, in hopes of encountering Naskapi Indians when they came to the trading posts. Cabot, an engineer and gentleman explorer from Boston, had been making annual treks into northern Canada since 1899. He would spend months at a time travelling alone or with a few friends, hiking and canoeing.

Cabot would later explain his passion for the wilderness in his book *In Northern Labrador:* "My objective was Indians. They were people in the primitive hunter stage . . . living substantially in the pre-Columbian age of the continent. . . . They lived under their own law, in their old faith unchanged." It had been Cabot who, when he and Hubbard had first met in Quebec during one of Hubbard's early writing assignments, had planted in Hubbard's brain the notion of following the Northwest River into unknown Labrador.

Now, on the deck of the *Virginia Lake*, Cabot cast a critical eye at Hubbard's canoe as it lay surrounded by other gear. "An eighteen-foot Old Town, I see. Canvas-covered. Same as mine."

"A good choice for both of us," Hubbard said.

"Except that I will be travelling alone. Yours will carry three men and all your gear. Through some reportedly tempestuous waters, no less. Personally I would be concerned about swamping. Too much weight for one canoe to carry."

"I've been assured that it will more than suffice."

It wasn't long before George Elson joined them on deck. He stood off to the side, smoking his pipe but taking in every word of Laddie's conversation with Cabot. Mina now and then looked to

George to see how the exchange was striking him. For her part, she did not appreciate the critical tone of Cabot's observations.

"You've weighed everything, of course?" Cabot asked.

"It comes to approximately five hundred pounds."

Cabot cocked an eyebrow. "And three men add what, another four hundred fifty?"

Hubbard laughed good-naturedly and slapped Cabot on the shoulder. "Don't worry, we'll all fit in quite nicely. I've checked and rechecked a dozen times."

Mina could have vouched for that, had anybody asked. She had listened to the litany so many times, had checked the items off on Laddie's list so frequently that she knew every item in the outfit: One miner's tent, six and a half feet by seven, six pounds. Five blankets, seventeen pounds. Two six-by-seven-foot tarps, three pack straps, two waterproof bags each containing forty pounds of flour. Twelve smaller waterproof bags containing sugar, chocolate, notebooks, and other supplies. Kodaks plus thirty rolls of 120-exposure film packed in tin cans. Four thirty-five-pound sacks of flour, thirty pounds of bacon, twenty pounds of lard, thirty pounds of sugar, fourteen pounds of salt, four pounds of dried apples, ten pounds of rice, twenty pounds of erbswurst, ten pounds each of pea-flour and tea, five of coffee, six of chocolate, ten of hardtack and ten more of tea.

"Where are your firearms?" Cabot asked.

"In our cabins. Wallace and I each have a lightweight .45–70 rifle."

"For the caribou."

"Precisely."

"Good choice there. What else?"

"A pistol each for partridges and such."

"That's it?" Cabot asked.

"Wholly sufficient, I should think."

"No shotgun?"

"Too heavy."

"You won't bring down many geese or ducks with a rifle."

"Merely enough to feed us," Hubbard said, and he gave a wink to George.

George waited for Cabot to ask his opinion on the matter, even formulated what he thought was a tactful response: *Being as how I don't have Mr. Hubbard's skill with a rifle,* he would answer, *a shotgun wouldn't be a bad thing to have.*

But of course Cabot would never turn to a half-breed for corroboration. "Even a small-bore shotgun would be preferable to none," he said.

"The ammunition alone would tip the scales. My aim is to travel as lightly as possible."

"But at the expense of practicality?" Cabot shook his head. "Even if I had to carry reduced-shot charges, I wouldn't think of going into the bush without a shotgun."

"Reduced-shot? You know, I hadn't considered that." But Hubbard continued to smile, unperturbed by Cabot's criticism.

Mina studied George's frown and wondered if it was an indication of uncertainty. It was true that Laddie had never solicited George's expertise in outfitting the party; nor had he sought advice from any of the more experienced personnel at *Outing*. But why should he? This was Laddie's expedition from beginning to end. Surely he knew what he was doing.

"Where is your gill net?" Cabot asked.

"I plan to pick one up at the North West River Post. The locals will know better than I what size fish we'll be taking."

Cabot offered a nod of approval. But Mina's relief was short-lived. "You've written ahead to order it, of course."

"I've been too busy with other details. But what kind of post would it be that has no gill nets available?"

At this Cabot lifted his gaze to the sky. Was that barely audible grunt a suppressed sigh of exasperation? Mina wondered. How dare he criticize, if only by implication, her husband's choices? Laddie had been planning the trip for months! He knew everything there was to know about it.

Yet even as Mina's face flushed with anger over Cabot's impertinence, her stomach fluttered with anxiety. The sickness of dread was as strong as it had ever been. Had her stomach not been so empty she would have had to rush to the rail. As it was, she felt hollowed out by fear, a brittle shell about to collapse.

Later that day the coast of Labrador appeared off to their left, a hazy adumbration. Mina stood at the rail with her Laddie, Wallace and George, a driving rain stinging their faces. The sea was a violent churning of opposing colours, of whitecaps smashing over black water. As for the rocky coast of Labrador glimpsed through the rain, it seemed to Mina the embodiment of bleakness, a line of sea-pounded, wind-scoured rocks, lifeless and black.

Wallace said, "It appears brutally inhospitable, wouldn't you agree?"

Laddie laughed, revelling in the challenge, enjoying even the rain. "We'll have a bully time of it, boys!"

Mina gripped his arm. *Don't go*, she thought.

That night, her last aboard ship with her husband, she clung to him in their narrow bunk. She lay with her face pressed to his neck so that her every breath inhaled the scent of him. And for the first time, she hinted at her fear.

"What Cabot said earlier," she told him. "I have to admit that it worries me."

Laddie stroked her hair. "He's never been to the interior, only up and down the coast."

"But isn't the interior a harsher place than the coast? So perhaps his concerns are not so unwarranted after all."

"I've been advised to expect a plenitude of wild game," he assured her. "Don't be surprised if I gain a few pounds while I'm there."

"But what if—?"

"Shhh," Laddie told her. "Don't worry, beloved. I am not a reckless man."

She slept little that night. Instead she watched her husband sleep. She listened to his breathing. She laid her hand upon his heart and felt its rhythm in her fingertips.

She tried with all her might to will away the dawn, but a grey light eventually came seeping into the cabin, a light as sickly as she felt. Some time before six A.M. Laddie walked her onto the deck. Though the sea was calmer there in Battle Harbour, an icy drizzle was falling, making the deck even slicker—a good excuse for holding desperately to Laddie's arm. In the weak light of morning, while her insides thrashed and heaved, Mina pulled off her gloves and wove her fingers between Laddie's. She had so much to say but she choked down every word. She was determined not to cry, not to taint his departure with her misery.

"Will you miss me, sweetheart?" he asked.

What answer could possibly encompass the extent to which she would miss him? She could only lay her head against his chest and suggest, with the grip of her fingers, how mightily she would feel his absence.

Then Captain Parsons was there beside them. Mina had thought him a somewhat nervous man throughout the trip, though rightfully so, responsible as he was for manoeuvring the *Virginia Lake* through a maze of icebergs, fog, and frothing seas. He appeared much calmer now that the ship was at anchor, even merry as he raised a hand to point ashore.

"If you look halfway up that hill there, Missus Hubbard, you can see the Grenfell Mission house. That there is where you'll be staying till I come back down the coast to fetch you home."

Mina nodded, unable to respond, her throat constricted, eyes blurring.

"Soon's you're in the jolly boat, ma'am, we can lower it down and set you ashore."

George was the first to bid her goodbye. He stepped up shyly, moved as if to reach for her hand, then thought better of it and drew back, clasped his hands at his waist. "Have a good trip home," he told her. "I'm glad you was able to come along this far."

She gave him a look he understood well. *Please take care of him,* her eyes begged.

Next came Dillon Wallace. "Don't you worry now," he said. "And try not to miss him too much. George and I will see that he doesn't get into too much trouble."

"Only enough to make it interesting!" Laddie answered. And when Mina looked up at him she saw that his cheeks too were streaked with tears.

George and Wallace remained behind as Laddie walked her to the jolly boat. "My lovely sweet girl," he whispered, and held her close a final time. "You will try to enjoy the summer with your sister, won't you? Will you promise to do that for me?"

When she looked up she could see nothing but his face, her world gone black all around the edges. Next thing she knew she was seated in the jolly boat, his hands slipping away from hers as they lowered the boat away.

"I will dream of you every night!" he called down to her. "You'll think of me too, won't you?"

She could barely get her breath now, felt the sea coming up to her and then suddenly there, cold and hard and as black as the Styx, bucking her up and down. She wanted to call to Laddie but she had no breath, no words, only choking sobs as the oarsman splashed his paddles down and, with a few quick strokes, began to carry her away.

"Goodbye, beloved!" her husband called, but before she could find her voice again, the morning haze gathered around him as he stood leaning over the rail, hand raised in farewell.

"Laddie!" she cried at last, but he looked little more than a ghost now, a small grey figure enveloped in grey, her husband of thirty months, her life, enshrouded and fading, and gone.

———

In frozen January the telegram came. *Mr. Hubbard died October 18 in the interior of Labrador.*

Mina was staggered by the blow, though she had been anticipating such a message since the morning of their last embrace. A vague fear had become suspicion when, that fall, no word had come from him, and the party was unaccounted for at the posts they might have reached, should have reached by the last of August. And with each passing day she had become more certain of it, had read it in the distant emptiness of the stars she gazed at each night.

Yes, she had known it long before the telegram came. But hope, sometimes, is our only defence against knowledge, and since August Mina had been wielding hope like a stick to beat the wolves away.

Now she stood with the telegram trembling in her hand, the words swimming before her eyes. All this time, she thought. He has been gone all this time. October 18. Three months. He has been gone three months now. All of winter. He has been gone all winter.

Not until May 27, a Friday, was his body returned to Brooklyn, packed in salt in a lead-lined wooden coffin accompanied by George Elson and Dillon Wallace. Two months earlier the story of the men's ordeal had appeared in the *New York Times*. Much of the article was given over to a long letter Wallace had written to his sister in December from the North West River Post, where he and Elson had remained for a while to recuperate from their brush with death. From this article, which included heart-rending passages from Laddie's journal, Mina learned the haunting details of her husband's death. She read how, on October 18, Wallace and Elson had left her Laddie alone at the campsite because he was too sick to travel farther; how they had then separated, Wallace marching off to recover some cached flour for himself and Laddie while Elson retreated in search of rescuers. After ten days George had finally succeeded in sending a small party of men back to the campsite. They had come first upon Wallace, wandering around in the snow "in stocking feet and underwear, hatless and coatless." He had found the flour but never managed to get back to camp with it. The rescue party then located Laddie's tent, but too late. By all appearances he had died on the very day Wallace and Elson departed from him.

And now, a full seven months after his death, he was being returned to her on the *Sylvia*. Mina shuddered with the memory of how vibrant, how alive he had been last June when they boarded that ship hand in hand for his journey north.

She told herself that she should feel some pity too for George and Dillon because of their terrible ordeals. But how to pity the survivors? All she could think was that Laddie was gone. According to Wallace's letter to his sister, George had struggled valiantly for ten days, wading through deep snow with nothing but rags wrapped around his feet, fording icy streams, even building a raft with his bare hands and then nearly drowning when it broke apart, all to send help to her husband.

But too late, too late.

And Dillon, her husband's best friend. He too had set off for help but, half-starved and frozen, his weight down to less than a hundred pounds, he had ended up wandering aimlessly in a blizzard. He too, he told his sister, would surely have perished had it not been for the rescue party George had dispatched.

But Dillon Wallace had not perished, and by now he was fully recovered from the ordeal. "I will say that I am in perfect health," he wrote to his sister on December 3, "better health, I think, than ever before in my life—with the exception of a frozen toe that has taken long to heal. . . . Am very contented and happy here with my good friends." So how could she feel sorry for him? She had no pity to spare.

As painful as it was to read Wallace's delineation of the tragedy, other more hurtful criticisms of the expedition followed. In April *Forest and Stream* printed a letter from Robert T. Morris, a reader who apparently considered himself an expert woodsman. "It would seem as though the [Hubbard] party was not quite sufficiently skilled in woodcraft," Morris wrote. He then went on to chronicle the bounty of wildlife and edible flora available in Labrador, with instructions as to when and where to find them:

> Assuming that bears, beavers, and caribou were not easily obtainable, although all are inhabitants of the region until the caribou move southward, one would expect to find the following supplies: Porcupines, woodchucks, hares, red squirrels, lemmings and several smaller rodents . . . trout and chars will bite at any time of the year . . . one can find almost anywhere collections of ferns . . . the fruit of the curlew berry and of two cranberries remains upon the plants all winter and in such abundance that one need not go very far without getting a supply . . . the young tops of caribou moss . . . poplar buds . . . the yellow water lily . . . ptarmigan or spruce grouse. . . .

Morris ended his report with what Mina considered unforgivable pomposity:

> If some of us were going over the country traversed by the Hubbard party we would take no provisions at all excepting enough seal oil, salt and pepper, for flavoring the luxuries that we could pick up. . . . Some of us do not believe that "sad tales of privation and hardship" are often necessary. . . . Some of us have been in the wretchedest country in the north, with no dry clothes for two weeks at a time . . . sometimes with not a thing to eat all day long, because the storms were too furious, or no time to stop to get food. . . . Personally I would rather be there now than to have the best bed and board at the Waldorf-Astoria, although I dine there tonight.

As infuriating as this armchair criticism of her husband was, it didn't go as far as the editorial that followed it in the periodical a week later.

It is not unfair to compare the members of the Hubbard party with little children lost in the woodlot next to the farmhouse, perishing of hunger, while, as Dr. Morris showed in his letter last week, meat and drink were all about them. . . . Since these young men started off with insufficient food . . . and since they failed to provide themselves with the knowledge and the means necessary to procure that food . . . it was a foregone conclusion that if they left the beaten paths they must perish. Of the uncertainties of travel in a wild country they were apparently quite ignorant. . . .

Mina read these articles with a cold, stunned outraged. How could strangers who had never met her husband utter such misleading cruelties? So no, she could not meet the *Sylvia* at the dock, how could she? She could barely breathe. Could scarcely set one foot before the other.

For over four months now, ever since the telegram, she had known with a horrible certainty that her life was over, gone with Laddie. And not for a moment had the agony of this knowledge subsided. If anything, it swelled with the *Sylvia's* arrival. The next day, Saturday, she forced herself to dress for the funeral, shrouded herself in black, and allowed friends to escort her those few miles to Mount Repose in nearby Haverstraw.

George and Dillon were there, along with Caspar Whitney and some of Laddie's writer friends, acquaintances from the city. Mina's friends from Congers. High above the west bank of the Hudson River they stood, all made awkward by their grief, all those wordsmiths tongue-tied. Below lay the Nyack Valley, the forested green and the winding blue.

A beautiful place, Mina told herself, knowing that Laddie would approve.

Reverend Howland droned on, and Mina looked from one face to another and felt apart from it all. When people spoke to her it was as if from a distance. Her field of vision was reduced to a tunnel's view, telescopic, charcoal-black around the edges.

They will miss him, she thought. Everybody here will miss him. But none like me. Because all of them have survived. All but Laddie and me.

Somehow the hour passed. She found herself at home again in Congers, accompanied there by a handful of her and Laddie's friends. A light meal had been served, though she could not remember who had prepared the food or how any of it had tasted. She was alone now in the small room where Laddie's map of Labrador still hung, the room where he had planned everything, where they had gone over it all a hundred times. She held a cup of tea in her hand, a white china cup with a pattern of tiny blue flowers, Buffalo china. She sat waiting for George to come into the room; she had sent her sister to the parlour to fetch him. And when he knocked lightly at the door, two shy taps, she heard her voice answer, hoarse and unfamiliar, "Come in, George, please."

He entered with head lowered, hands hanging low and clasped. But he came directly to her and without hesitation he leaned down to wrap both hands around hers. His face was wet with tears and his nose red, and she was so grateful to him for that, for not hiding his sorrow.

He said, "He was a fine, fine man, Missus Hubbard. As good a man as any I have known."

Better, she thought, but with no resentment toward George. She nodded once, and smiled, then glanced at the tea cart. "Please help yourself to some tea, George. I'm afraid I'm not much good at pouring right now."

He poured a bit of tea into a cup, added sugar, took a sip. "I'll never take sugar and tea for granted ever again," he told her.

She asked him to sit. He turned the adjacent chair to face her directly, then waited, gave her time to choose her words. When the question came it was as candid as she could make it.

"How could it happen, George?"

"We got lost right at the start," he told her. She deserved honesty and, besides, it was all he had to offer. "Right off Grand Lake. Took what we thought was the Naskapi but it turned out to be the Susan instead."

"And who made that decision?" she asked.

"It was what we all agreed to. We was told at the post we'd find the Naskapi there at the end of the lake, plain as day. And that's how it was marked on Mr. Hubbard's map too. So when we come to what we thought was it, we took it, no questions asked."

She nodded. "And in your own mind," she said, "that one mistake accounts for the tragedy?"

"We made plenty enough mistakes. All along the way. But most of them, far as I can figure, all come back to that first one."

She held the teacup atop one knee but never raised it to her lips. George waited for the next question. He would answer whatever she asked.

But she could hold only two questions in her mind. She already knew a great deal about the trials the men had suffered, the sickness and hunger, because yesterday Laddie's journal had been returned to her, delivered by Dillon Wallace himself. She had spent the night reading and rereading every word of it, especially the final passage, Laddie's final goodbye to his crew.

*George said, "The Lord help us, Hubbard. With His help I'll save you if I can get out." Then he cried. So did Wallace. Wallace stooped and kissed my cheek with his poor, sunken, bearded lips—several times— and I kissed his. George did the same, and I kissed his cheek. Then they went away. God bless and help them.*

So there were only two things she needed to know right now. The first—who was to blame?—had been answered to her satisfaction.

"It was you who made it out," she said, not an accusation but a statement of fact. "You who sent the rescue party back. But if you were able, George, why did Mr. Wallace not also succeed?"

George was not clear on what she was asking. "Missus?"

"I am asking you if, in your honest opinion, Mr. Wallace did his utmost to assist my husband in his final hours."

"It was me supposed to go for help," George answered. "Mr. Wallace's job was to go back for the flour we left behind."

"And to return with it to my husband. A task he did not fulfill."

"No, ma'am."

Now it was Mina's turn to wait. Her question had not yet been answered.

Carefully, occasionally pausing to search for words, George told her, "We figured it was some fourteen miles or so back to the flour."

"Less than half the distance you yourself were to travel."

"Yes, ma'am. Mr. Wallace promised to try to get there and back to the tent in three days, whether he found the flour or not. The thing is . . . we was none of us healthy. Mr. Hubbard had the worst of it, being too played out to even stand. But Mr. Wallace wasn't much better off."

He paused, stared at the map on the wall as if seeing again the little tent by the stream, a frail Hubbard seated in the tent's opening while George and Wallace made their preparations to depart. "We each of us took but half a blanket," he told her. "All the rest we left for Mr. Hubbard. And we made him as comfortable as we could, laying in some extra wood and filling the kettle with water and all."

"Yes, he wrote about all that in his journal. He also wrote that he gave you the last of his pea meal." A moment later she regretted the bluntness of her statement, for the tears welled again in George's eyes, and soon they slid down his cheeks.

"And every minute since then, Missus Hubbard, I have wanted to throttle myself for letting him make me take it."

Her tears came now too. "It was so like him to do that, George."

"Yes, ma'am, it truly was. He wouldn't take no for an answer."

"Because he knew that you needed it more than he did. You would be doing all the work. He would simply be waiting for your return."

"I only wish it was me been left behind to wait. Maybe then I wouldn't be feeling any of this now."

"But as to Mr. Wallace," she said gently. "He had less than half as far to go as you."

"It rained all that first day," he told her. "And the rain was icy cold. Next morning there was half a foot of snow on the ground. And all along Mr. Wallace was having a hard time keeping up. Him not being used to the country and all, and being so weak himself by then."

Again he paused. His throat was dry, lips parched, and he raised the cup to his mouth. The tea had gone cold.

"That second night, after we found the bag of flour, we built a big fire to warm us up a bit. But Mr. Wallace got too much smoke in his eyes and went blind from it. We figured he'd be fine come morning but he wasn't. He could see but everything was in a haze, he said. But it was fixing to snow again, and I had to be off for Grand Lake, and that's where we parted company."

"I understand," she said. "But he never made it back to Mr. Hubbard with the flour. And all he had to do was retrace the path that got you to the flour in the first place."

George nodded. Yes, she was right. It might have made all the difference. Still, unless you were out there with them, unless you knew the cold and the weakness and the debilitating hunger . . .

"It snowed for ten days straight," he told her. "By afternoon on the day we split up he couldn't of seen our trail even if his eyes were working good. By the next day the snow was knee-deep. Plus, once when he was crossing a stream he broke through the ice and got soaked up to his armpits. It wasn't an easy walk for him, missus."

"Nor was it for you. But the fact remains that you succeeded and he didn't."

"From what he tells me, he got sick from eating some of that mouldy flour we found. So now besides being half-frozen and half-blind, he starts vomiting too. But he says he kept looking for the tent, missus. He kept walking and looking for the next seven days."

With that George seemed to be finished. But Mina Hubbard was not.

She leaned toward him. "George, I want you to give me your honest opinion on this. Did Mr. Wallace lose his senses out there? Is that why he wandered around lost for seven days?"

It took George a while to answer. When he finally did, his voice rose barely above a whisper. "When Donald and Bert and the other fellas found him, Mr. Wallace didn't even have his moccasins on. He was walking around in his stocking feet. He said later that the moccasins kept clogging up with snow, and that was why he took them off. I don't know what become of his hat either, but he had lost it somewhere too."

"Is your answer to my question *yes*, George?"

"He talked about hearing his wife out there. Her that's been dead some three years by then."

"In his letter to his sister he referred to it only as a woman's voice. But he told you otherwise?"

George answered with a sad smile. "There was this one time, he said, when he had just about decided to lay down in the snow and go to sleep, when she come and told him to build a fire. So that's what he did. There was other times too when he wanted to quit. But she wouldn't let him."

Mina was shaken by this report. It altered her perception of Wallace somewhat, awakened her to the truth and depth of his suffering. "Thank you, George. Thank you for telling me this. And thank you for answering all my questions."

He sat motionless for half a minute or so, then pushed himself up and bent to take her hand again, and again the tears came to both of them, a prolonged and awkward goodbye.

The next day George went to Grand Central Station and boarded a train for Montreal. Soon he would be home in Missanabie again, back to his life. Except that now, he knew, nothing would ever be the same.

As for Mina, she met with Dillon Wallace on Sunday morning. He arrived at ten to find her dressed in yesterday's clothes, draped in black. She did open the curtains in the front room, however, and seated Wallace on the sofa with his back to the bright window. The sunlight on his shoulders and on the back of his skull was warm, too warm, and the small room seemed stuffy to him, overheated and smelling faintly of coal smoke.

Mina poured a cup of tea for him and another for herself. Seated in the armchair, she stared into her china cup for a while. She hardly knew where to begin. Without Laddie there to guide the conversation, without Laddie as her buffer, every human interaction felt off balance to her, every movement seemed broken. To live without him was as awkward and impossible as reading the time on a clock whose hour hand was missing. After all these months she had not grown accustomed to his absence. Sometimes, as now, she experienced it so keenly that it all but paralyzed her.

It was Wallace who broke the silence. "You cannot know," he began, then stopped himself when he recognized the speciousness of the cliché. Of course she knew. Better than anyone.

He tried again. "I will never forget how he came to me in the hospital in Long Island. How he walked right up to me as if we were old friends, and reached out to me in my misery. We were utter strangers, and yet . . . I truly believe that he saved my life that day,

Mina. Saved me from the abyss that . . . well . . . I don't need to explain it to you, I know."

She sat so quietly and without movement, he could only wonder what she was thinking. Her pale face was splotched with red. He knew how easily she blushed with embarrassment, but what had he said to embarrass her? Was she angry with him? For saying something improper? Or perhaps for saying too little?

"After that day," he continued, "I always felt that I owed Leon my very life. And I would have given it gladly, Mina, I want you to know that. It is important to me that you know it. No man has ever been closer to me. And after what we went through together up there . . ."

The flush spread over her forehead, widened on her cheeks. And the set of her jaw—she *was* angry! But what had he said?

"I will not abide," she said evenly, her voice hoarse from lack of sleep, "what the critics are saying of him."

With her first few words Wallace had sucked in a breath, anticipating an attack. But now he exhaled slowly, and covered his relief with reassuring words. "The newspapers, you mean? No, no, you mustn't let any of that bother you. Anything they say is mere speculation. It has no importance whatsoever, no relationship to the truth."

"They are saying he was inexperienced. That he didn't prepare properly."

"It's all nonsense, Mina. Every word of it."

She fixed him with a gaze he had never seen from her before, so hard and hot it made his own face burn. "You must never add a single word of support to what they say. You must never vouchsafe their claims."

"You know I never would."

"In fact you must refute them. It is up to you to prove them wrong."

"And I do," he told her. "At every opportunity."

"I am speaking of the story Leon would have written. The chronicle of his expedition. True and complete."

Wallace nodded his approval. "I will help in whatever way I can. As, I'm sure, will George. Our recollections, along with Leon's diary—"

"I would like for you to write the book," she said.

Wallace drew in another breath, sat back against the sofa.

Mina saw him framed in bright sunlight, and the light was painful to her eyes. Backlit by the morning sun he appeared little more than a shadow, his features softened and indistinct. She could not help but compare his nondescript face to Laddie's, to Laddie's sharp chin and angular nose, his eager, intelligent eyes that could blaze out even from such darkness. And now Wallace spoke in a way Laddie by nature could not, stammering with uncertainty.

"But I am . . . I am not a writer, Mina. That isn't my trade. I lack Leon's talent . . . his gift for words."

"You are a man of education. You will not find it difficult once you begin."

"But Mina, really, quite honestly I haven't any notion about how to construct a book. I'm sure it's not simply a matter of . . ."

"Of telling the truth?" she asked. "I am sure that it is."

Now he leaned forward again—sagged forward, she thought—almost appearing to collapse in upon himself.

"I am prepared to pay you, of course. And with that money you can, if need be, hire a professional writer to assist you. You will have Leon's field notes and photographs and his journal as well. These, along with your own and George's recollections, should more than suffice."

He was shaking his head now; he looked up at her with plaintive eyes. "My education is not—"

"Your education," she said, and her voice grew unsteady, quivering as it rose in pitch, "is of secondary concern here, wouldn't you agree? Secondary to your obligation to my husband and your friend? The man to whom you claim to owe your life?"

Wallace closed his eyes. The sunlight pressed upon his back and made his spine ache with the weight of the inevitable.

"He must be remembered appropriately, Dillon. You know that I am right."

Still he could not open his eyes. She was crying now, he knew it though she made not a sound, knew it by the sting of tears behind his own eyelids. He had come to the cottage hoping that after this morning the ordeal would be behind him, the whole regrettable experience, nearly a full year of his life. After this morning he would return to his practice and the unchallenging routine of a lacklustre existence. But the grip of Leonidas Hubbard was too strong. It held Mina fast and always would. And now it was taking hold of him again. It was pulling him into what felt, for all the world, like another kind of abyss.

"You owe him your life, you said. Or did I mishear?"

When Wallace finally opened his eyes again the room seemed too bright, too small. A small woman dressed all in black sat staring at him. He held a white china cup of cooling tea, blue enamelled flowers beneath his hand.

It was unavoidable, all of it, and he knew it. The request she was making of him. The demand. He had no choice but to surrender to it.

And with that decision came a semblance of peace. A phrase came into his mind then, recited in Leon's voice, four lines from Kipling's "The Young British Soldier." The words smelled of a chilling stream and willow brush and the smoky fragrance of a campfire. Wallace spoke the words out loud, smiling, strangely calm now:

> When first under fire, if you're wishful to duck,
> Don't look or take heed from the man that is struck;
> Be thankful you're living and trust to your luck,
> And march to your front like a soldier.

His voice was breaking by the time he finished, his heart was breaking, and Mina was sobbing, doubled forward over her teacup, pinning it in place so that the tea did not splash out, her entire body shaking.

Wallace leaned over and clasped her hands in his. She raised her head, looked up at him. In this manner, their contract was made.

The months passed, every minute a trial of endurance. The pleasure Mina had once taken in simple things had vanished. Reading and gardening no longer distracted. Cooking held no delight when it was for herself alone. Just to peel a potato was a chore.

She had related to the world through Laddie, had felt no shyness when at his side, no uncertainty. But now that nexus was gone and she trudged through each day like a sleeper struggling to wake herself. In Laddie's presence life had glistened with clarity and freshness. Now all was obscured, every breath sour with grief.

All summer long Mina admonished herself to get on with her life. That fall she registered for classes in nearby Williamstown, meaning to finish her high school degree. But still she dressed in the black of deep mourning. And still she wrote long letters to her Laddie, still she prayed to him nightly.

In daylight hours she felt besieged by vultures. Scarcely a week passed that some journalist—the very profession her husband had so respected—did not publish his malicious opinion as to Laddie's lack of fitness as an expedition leader. Such writers were to her no better than parasites. When they attacked her husband they were tearing away at her own heart.

Even Laddie's so-called friends could not resist the temptation toward self-aggrandizement at his expense. Did they think that by questioning Laddie's choices they made themselves appear wise?

Caspar Whitney got into the game through his columns in *Outing*. He first wrote a piece called "An Appreciation," in which he praised Laddie as unselfish, brave and cheerful, "a manly man and a good friend." But he could not leave well enough alone, and in a later piece he absolved himself of all responsibility for Laddie's death.

"His equipment, party, and arrangements," Whitney wrote, "were not only entirely of his own choosing, but even unknown to us. In this respect Hubbard took neither *Outing* nor its editor into his confidence."

Most galling of all was a contradiction Mina detected in Dillon Wallace, the very man she had commissioned to memorialize her husband. The letter he had written to his sister while recuperating in Labrador, published in the *New York Times*, gave her no little cause for concern. This letter had been the first full report of the tragic expedition, and Mina did not pick up on the contradictions it contained until well after speaking with George and Dillon following the funeral.

During her conversations with Wallace he had remarked upon his disorientation throughout his final days alone in the wilderness, how he had become delusional when searching for Laddie's tent, how he had walked in circles, out of his head with hunger, cold and exhaustion. George too had told her the story, for it was the one Wallace had told him. But in Wallace's letter to his sister the account was far less dramatic. " . . . after walking up and down several times where I thought the camp must be," he had written, "I was at length compelled to give up the search, and headed toward Grand Lake."

According to his verbal rendition, he had never given up but had been rendered ineffectual by a temporary insanity produced by the adverse conditions. According to the letter, he had tried several times to find Laddie's tent but then, flour bag in hand, had made a conscious and deliberate decision to give up. Not until later had he become delusional and started hearing "a woman's voice."

Moreover, in his letter Wallace seemed to go out of his way to identify Hubbard as the weakest member of the party. He wrote, "Before we began our retreat from the big lake I had lost thirteen inches in waist measure. Our bones were sticking through the skin. We had not shaved or cut our hair, and our appearance must have been pitiable. I know the others looked, especially Hubbard, like walking skeletons."

*Especially Hubbard.* Mina knew how her husband would have hated being described as pitiable. Worse yet to be singled out as the most pitiable of the group.

"We had several miles to run on a small river with dangerous rapids," Wallace wrote. "Hubbard tried to manage one with George, and nearly wrecked it. Then George and I ran the rest, and took desperate chances, always, however, with success."

And more: "At length one day Hubbard could not carry his little pack into camp, and I made him put it down and follow without any load. I returned and got his pack."

At the end of that same paragraph: "Hubbard gave out."

And later: "I sat up nearly all night keeping the fire going to warm Hubbard."

It seemed to Mina that throughout his letter Wallace portrayed Laddie as a pathetic creature who required caretaking, but painted himself as the strong, devoted friend who uncomplainingly shouldered the burden.

Most infuriating of all, and the baldest of his criticisms, was this, early in the letter:

> I will merely say that we plunged madly into the interior of an unknown country, into regions never before trod by white man, with almost no provisions. For our trip we should have had 550 pounds of flour—we had 120 pounds; we should have taken 200 pounds of bacon or pork—we had 20 pounds; and so on all down the line.

How easy it was to say, at the end of the journey, how the venture could have been improved. But had Wallace voiced any of these concerns before the expedition began? Had he predicted the especially brutal weather or the atypical lack of game? Each time Mina read his letter, her feelings for him darkened a little more.

Mina and Wallace met again a few days after Thanksgiving. He arrived at her door a changed man, all eagerness and grins and several pounds heavier than when last he had visited. She found his ebullience more than a little repugnant, but he was beside himself with "happy news." He had finished the manuscript, the book about Leon. Here it was, hers to read. The writing had gone much more easily than he had expected, he said. It had been just as she had promised; once he got started it all came back to him, every snowflake and gust of wind, every ripple on the water.

He placed the manuscript in her hands as if it were something precious, something miraculous. But no, he could not sit still while she read, he would take a walk into town, have some lunch, allow her adequate time to work through it.

And when he returned hours later, cheeks glowing, wearing a grin of anticipation, he found Mina's cheeks flushed as well, though not a hint of smile graced her mouth.

"Kindly explain to me," she said, even as he was taking his seat on the sofa, "kindly explain to me how it serves my husband's memory to give voice to his critics."

Wallace was momentarily stunned. All he could think to say was "I beg your pardon?"

"Right here," she said, and jabbed a fingertip on the manuscript's final page. Both her finger and her voice quivered. "The critics," she read, "said that 'Hubbard was foolhardy, and without proper preparation he plunged blindly into an unknown wilderness.'"

"But Mina—"

"'Others tell how fish-nets might have been made from willow bark.'"

"But if you read further—"

"'It has been said that, even had Hubbard succeeded in accomplishing everything he set out to do, the result would have been of little or no value to the world.'"

"I only point out the criticisms so that I can refute them."

"'Doubtless some will see in his life's struggle only to win for himself a recognized place as a writer and expert upon out-of-door life.'" Her voice was high and tight as she read, her face ghostly pale where not splotched scarlet. The irises of her eyes were wide and dark.

"Mina," he said, and considered reaching out to her, calming her with his touch. But the rigidity of her posture kept him at bay. "How can I refute the criticisms if I do not first acknowledge them?"

"To acknowledge them at all is to give them credence!"

"I cannot agree. It is my duty as a writer to—"

She laughed out loud, an explosive syllable of derision. A writer, indeed! How dare he think of himself in those terms? Her Laddie was a writer, but this hackneyed thing she held in her hands, this was the work of no writer.

She drew from beneath the manuscript a piece of folded newsprint, which she unfolded and held up for Wallace to see. "This," she said evenly, "this, I have come to realize, was the beginning of the problem. There would not now be such an onslaught of criticism against Laddie had you not propagated it yourself."

Wallace leaned forward to better see the newsprint, his brow knitted. "I assure you that I said nothing to disparage him. I never would."

"Have you forgotten the letter you wrote to your sister? The one that appeared in the *New York Times?*"

"I haven't forgotten it, no. But I said nothing—"

"' ... *we plunged madly* into the interior of an unknown country,'" she read. "For our trip we should have had 550 pounds of flour ... 200 pounds of bacon or pork ...' and so on all down the line."

"That isn't criticism, Mina, it's ... it's hindsight."

"'Hubbard tried to manage the canoe through one with George *and nearly wrecked it.* Then George and I ran the rest, and took desperate chances, *always, however, with success.*'"

Wallace looked at his hands. "Again, Mina, it was never intended as criticism."

"' . . . Hubbard could not carry *his little pack* into camp, and I made him put it down and follow without any load. *I returned* and got his pack.'"

"It's what happened. I wrote about what happened, that's all. Naturally, if you emphasize certain words, it is going to sound like something other than it really was."

"The *Times* referred to your letter as 'the first authentic information of the death of Leonidas Hubbard Jr.' So when you, in your own words, condemn Laddie for a lack of preparation, then portray him as an incompetent canoeist and a weakling whom you, the brave, successful canoeist and devoted friend, were forced to coddle . . . how could you not foresee the kind of public criticisms that would follow? Every one of them merely echoes what you yourself have said!"

"Perhaps, when I wrote that letter . . . I don't know, maybe I merely wanted to reassure my sister of my own well-being."

"Then here," she said, returning her attention to the manuscript, thumbing quickly through the pages. "Here you write, 'He was just a boy, really.' A *boy*, Mr. Wallace? You dare to call a man of his accomplishments a boy? Was that for your sister's benefit as well?"

"I only meant that, him being ten years my junior—"

"What you meant is certainly not what you wrote. Is that how a writer functions?"

"If I failed to make myself clear, I will certainly take all necessary steps . . ."

She flipped the pages over, returned to the beginning of the manuscript. "'It will have to be taken into consideration how hard pressed Hubbard was by the fear that the short summer would end before he had completed his work.' By this statement you imply that the Naskapi River was missed because my husband failed to take proper time to survey the lake."

"Nothing could be further from the truth. Why, just a few lines earlier I make it perfectly clear that the—"

She strode forward and dropped the manuscript onto his lap. "It will have to be redone, Mr. Wallace."

Again he found himself at a loss for words. "If there are a few places, a few phrases you object to—"

"There are numerous places! Dozens of ill-chosen words! You will find each and every one of them marked with my pen."

He leafed through the manuscript. At least one of her marks— an underlining, a circle, a comment scribbled in the margin, a whole paragraph crossed out with an X—could be found every few pages.

"You can begin with the dedication," she told him.

She had circled the entire thing, then drawn an X through it, then driven a thick blue line from start to finish. *Here, b'y, is the issue of our plighted troth.*

He tried to explain himself. "It harks back to the toast we made one another in your presence, Mina. When Leon and I first agreed to undertake the venture together."

"I thought then and I think still that your words were poorly chosen."

"How so?"

"I am his betrothed, Mr. Wallace. Not you."

"I only meant that we made a pledge to one another, that we . . . entered into a partnership as . . ."

"As enduring as marriage? *As sacred as the vows of matrimony?*"

He could not bring himself to look at her. Her voice was like a knife in his ear, an ice pick, so cold and sharp. He stared at the first page of the manuscript on his lap. The words swam before his eyes, broken bits of blackened leaves aswirl on frothy water. Mina turned and crossed to the door, threw it open and stared out across the empty yard, the long and empty horizon, her heart beating wildly, the blood hammering in her head. Never in her life had she raised her voice in this manner.

It seemed to her an eternity before Wallace finally pulled himself to his feet. With the manuscript tucked under an arm, he came to stand beside her. "I think, Mina, that when you have had an opportunity to reconsider your remarks today—"

She glared at him. "Your last line," she said. "Exactly what did you mean by that?"

He knew it by heart, had laboured over it for quite some time. *Perhaps it is God's will that I finish the work of exploration that Hubbard began.*

"It was his suggestion."

"You intend to make the trip again? The trip that *he* conceived of and planned?"

Not for my glory, Wallace thought. For his.

But before he could find his tongue she told him, "I wish to have his notes and photographs returned to me at the earliest opportunity."

As a lawyer, Wallace knew well the advisability of a measured response. He took two steps past her, across the threshold, out onto the small covered porch. Then, only half-turning, refusing to meet her gaze, he said, "I'm sorry, Mina. I have need of those."

Her hand tightened around the glass doorknob. "I will look forward to a revision of the manuscript."

He was about to say *I have no intention*, but she stepped back and closed the door, careful to close it softly lest the entire planet be made to rattle with her rage.

Only when she heard his footsteps going down off the porch, slow and halting, did she unlock her fingers from around the faceted knob and place those stinging fingers to her mouth and allow the flood of tears to come again.

Mount Repose Cemetery in mid-December was grey and cold. The trees were bare and the only scent carried up from the river valley was that of chimney smoke. Gusting winds blew swirls of snow along the hillside. Behind a fir tree near the top of the hill Mina stood huddled in a long black woollen coat, her hands in a fur muff, a cloth hat pulled low over her forehead. The spreading branches of the fir tree, its needles frosted with snow, shielded her not only from the wind but from the eyes of any passersby on the road below.

The Reverend Dr. Sawyer, who these past months had been doing his utmost to comfort Mina, waited in the open beside Leon's grave, several yards lower on the hill. His carriage, an economical Dearborn, was parked along the side of the road. Mina could see the sorrel's breath each time the mare snorted, could see her own exhalations one white puff after another. She wondered if that was what the soul looked like when it floated free from the body, a wisp of breath invisible in an instant, suddenly freed.

Finally there came the sound of another carriage, the muted clop of hooves on snowy ground. Mina peeked around the tree. A hack, rented in Williamstown, pulled up behind Dr. Sawyer's carriage. A moment later George Elson climbed out, dressed in his brown, rough clothes, the heavy trousers and jacket. His hands and head were bare. He came straight up the hill toward Dr. Sawyer. And that was one of the things Mina liked most about George, the way he could take one glance at a situation, size it up, then act decisively and without hesitation.

He came to the graveside and shook Dr. Sawyer's hand. The reverend spoke briefly. George turned just enough to look uphill toward the fir tree, and nodded once. But before walking up to meet her he faced the grave, stood there motionless. And Mina was grateful for that as well, that George felt the need for a few moments with her Laddie. The two men had obviously been very fond of one another.

Eventually George came up the hill and walked around to her side of the tree. She pulled both hands from the muff and grasped his hand in hers. "Thank you so much for coming," she said.

"Thank you for sending the ticket money."

She could feel the strength in his hand, the cold, hard, callused palm. Her hands seemed tiny in comparison, he thought, and so warm. Softer than any woman's hand on his had ever been. Back home he could never dare to hold a white woman's hand in a public place, but here in the cemetery, with the reverend tactfully averting his gaze, George allowed himself to savour her touch.

"Don't you want to know why I asked you to come all this way again?" she asked.

"I'm sure you'll tell me when you're ready to."

"I want you to write something for me," she said.

Something like panic tightened his throat. "I don't write all that good, missus."

"I don't want it to be fancy or writerly. I want it in your own words."

The way she smiled up at him and stood so close, that look of trust in her eyes, it was all very unsettling for George. He drew his hands away and slipped them into his pockets. "I'll do my best for you."

"What I want," she told him, "is for you to tell the story of what happened up there. I want you to write it all down for me, everything you can remember. You can stay with Dr. Sawyer while you work on it. You will be paid for your time, of course."

He did not know how to respond to this. Initially he had assumed that she wanted him to write a letter of some kind, a page or two. But now it seemed she intended for him to write about the entire trip, every arduous day of it. He doubted he was up to such a task.

"I am writing a book about the expedition," she said, "based on Mr. Hubbard's journal. And I would like very much to include your information as well."

"The way I write ain't fit for a book," he told her.

"It will be fine, George, trust me. Between Mr. Hubbard's notes and your remembrance I will be able to provide a complete and honest accounting."

Something about the way she emphasized *honest* troubled him.

"And when the book is published, you will be in it too. How will your friends back home like that?"

He could scarcely guess how his friends would react.

"And I have something else to ask you as well," she said. "There is something important I've been trying to understand."

He said nothing, only waited.

"It concerns Mr. Wallace."

Aha, George thought. But he said not a word.

"Can you tell me now," she asked, "just as you remember it, about the day Mr. Wallace was found? After you and he discovered the flour, I mean, and he then headed back toward camp with it?"

"I wasn't with him then," George said. "So I don't know what all I can tell you."

"But you know the way it happened."

"I know what Duncan and Donald and Allen told me about it."

"Then that's what I want to hear."

"What part exactly?"

"What I am most curious about is how close Mr. Wallace got to the tent. What was his nearest distance to it, I mean."

"Well, from what the fellas say, maybe two hundred yards or so."

"He didn't walk past it in the night, possibly?"

"Oh, I don't think so, no. The fellas said that after they found him and got him settled by the fire, then they went looking for the tent themselves, Donald and Allen did, following Mr. Wallace's tracks, more or less. And what they told me is that those tracks come to a stop somewhere about two hundred yards shy of the tent."

"They simply came to a stop?" she asked. "The tracks didn't go all around the tent in a circle, or anything like that?"

"Not from what I was told, they didn't."

"Tell me exactly, George. Exactly what did the tracks suggest to Donald and Allen?"

"Well," George said, feeling the cold now, a shiver in his spine, "from what the boys said, it looked to them like Mr. Wallace just come to a stop. He maybe stood there awhile, but that's something you can't tell from tracks most of the time. But then it looked like he'd just turned around and come back a ways and made himself a little camp."

"What was his camp like when they found it?"

"Well, he had a nice fire going, they said. And a nice place to lay down where he'd piled up some pine branches."

"And he was able to walk all right?"

"He was cold and all, and fairly weak from not eating. But they said he walked into their camp with them just fine."

Mina nodded. She was no longer smiling.

"That's what the boys told me anyways," he said. "We've talked about it quite a bit since then and that's always the way they tell it."

"Would it surprise you to know that Mr. Wallace is telling a different story?"

"He is?"

"According to his latest version, he became so delirious that he walked past the tent without seeing it. He says he camped within a stone's throw of the tent and spent his last hours walking in circles, completely out of his senses, until his feet were so frozen he could walk no farther. That's the story he's telling now. Though in the letter to his sister, the one he wrote from Labrador, he said something different. He said then that when he felt the search was hopeless, he gave up and turned toward Grand Lake. Does it surprise you that his story has changed?"

"I suppose it does," George said. "Who's he telling this new story to—the newspapers?"

"He has put it into a book. The book I commissioned him to write. But it is filled with exaggerations and untruths, George. You would be ashamed of some of the things he says, I'm sure. That is why we must write an *honest* account of what took place up there. You will help me, won't you?"

He said what he always said. "I'll do the best I can."

She smiled and reached for his hand again. "And we must be careful to tell no one about our plans. If word gets out that you are staying in town, the newspapers will surely be after you for an interview. It is important that you refuse to speak with them. Will you agree?"

It seemed a small thing to George to keep his mouth shut on the matter, the least of her requests. He would not be comfortable telling a lie but he was used to being stingy with his words. The best course of action, he decided, was to write down the story just as quickly as he could, then get back to Missanabie before the local folk, especially Mr. Wallace, even knew he had been in town.

Mina and George met several times over the next two weeks, always in the privacy of Dr. Sawyer's home. Early on it was decided that George's narrative should focus on the final days of the expedition. "Those are the important days," Mina told him. By which George understood her to mean the days when Wallace's behaviour was in question.

George resolved to be scrupulously honest in what he wrote, putting down the events exactly as he remembered them. And apparently that was what Mina expected of him, for each time she reviewed his progress she praised his memory and his eye for detail. She never told him what to write nor suggested he employ a different word or phrase than the one he had chosen. She did sometimes show him the proper spelling for a word, or suggest where to place a comma or the even more mysterious dash or semicolon. And he was eager for the assistance. He had no wish to appear illiterate.

She was especially touched by those entries that spoke of Laddie's affection for George. "Mr. Hubbard tells me he will get a room for me in New York. He again that night asked me to stay with him a couple of months in Congers before I go home to Missanabie, and also to pay him a visit real often, and also that he would never go out doing any travelling without me."

Tears sprang to her eyes and her breath grew short when she read of the men's hardship, and how, on October 11, they found some old caribou bones. "The bones were full of maggots, and when it boiled for some time the maggots would boil out. It just looked like it had been a little rice in it. We drunk it up, maggots and all. It was pretty high, but found it good. Nothing was too bad for us to eat."

The following day, a "fine day," brought no relief from their hunger. "We ate one of Mr. Hubbard's old moccasins, made out of caribou skin, that he made himself. We boiled it in the frying pan, till it got kind of soft, and we shared it in three parts."

But most affecting of all was George's passage for October 16, the day salvation came so close to hand. The three men had trudged to a stream where, weeks earlier, they had caught several fish. Now the stream was dry. But then, as if by miracle, a caribou came walking toward them.

*We all fell flat on the ground, but he was on the lee side of us and soon found out we were there. He stood—behind some little trees and had his head up looking towards where we were, and all of a sudden he was gone, and we didn't have the chance to fire. I got up. A swamp I knew of. I made for that swamp thinking I would cut across him. I tried to run, yet I was very, very weak. Oh! how hard I tried to run. But when I got out there he was across on the other side. I was away for some time, yet when I came to the boys, they were still lain in the same way, and their faces to the ground, and did not move till I spoke to them.*

So much of what George wrote brought tears to Mina's eyes. She had thought she must surely be empty of tears by now, but still they came. And each time George witnessed this, whether her eyes merely glistened or the tears ran freely over her cheeks, he ached for her. He ached with a deep, bruising pain that went all the way through him. He ached with the knowledge that a bit of luck here or there might have made all the difference for Mr. Hubbard, but that George, for all his trying, had never been able to force that luck upon them. He felt responsible for all the mistakes, though none of the decisions had rested with him. But Mina never accused him of failing her husband, never once allowed him to assume any blame.

During Christmas dinner at Dr. Sawyer's, after the good pastor's excruciatingly long blessing of the food, Mina insisted on thanking the Lord personally, not just for the pastor's hospitality but for George's friendship and loyalty. George got so choked up by her words that for the next ten minutes he was unable to speak without a quiver in his voice.

After Christmas, George did not see Mina again for several days. It was late in the first week of 1905 when she finally called on him to inquire if the narrative was finished. But from the very first minute of this meeting he suspected that her mind was on something other than his manuscript. He was sure he detected a change in her, a quality of inner repose. He thought, *She seems like she's made her mind up about something.*

She read his new pages and pronounced them very fine. But afterward she sat with the pages on her lap as she gazed into the fireplace. The pastor had laid on several logs of applewood, and the room was warm and smelled vaguely of autumn. And there was such a stillness to Mina that day; George was mystified. Until finally she turned to him and spoke. The calmness of her voice unsettled him as much as the words.

"I have decided to go to Labrador, George. And I would like very much for you to go there with me."

At first he felt dizzied by her remarks, cold-cocked by an unexpected blow. The pastor's parlour suddenly shrank and darkened and began to spin. He had nearly died in Labrador! Mr. Hubbard *had* died! Why would George, or anyone, for that matter, ever wish to go back?

"Mr. Wallace, as you know, has already announced his intention of fulfilling my husband's plan. But I am a Hubbard and he is not, and if any name is to be attached to the successful completion of that journey, it shall be my husband's name."

"Missus," George began, having no idea what he would say, "it can be a miserable place."

"But you know the way now, don't you? You've seen where the Naskapi enters Grand Lake?"

"That's just the beginning of the trip. There's another six hundred miles—"

"Moreover," she said, smiling serenely, "we will complete Mr. Hubbard's mission exactly as he planned it. Mr. Wallace intends to outfit his expedition more amply and to turn it into what he calls a scientific expedition. He has even persuaded *Outing* to support his efforts. Do you not see the ignominy in this, George? The disrespect to my husband?"

What could he say? It was unthinkable that he, a half-breed, an unmarried man, should accompany her into the wilderness. And anyway, she was completely inexperienced in the trials they would face. It was unheard of for a woman to embark on such an adventure—a white woman accompanied by a half-breed and, by necessity, a few other males? It was scandalous. And it was inconceivable that he could agree to this plan.

When he looked at her he could see the flames from the fireplace dancing in her eyes. Softly she told him, "I want you to think about the consequences, George, if we do not go to Labrador. They will be far more severe, I think, than if we go."

"How's that, missus?" he managed to ask.

"If Mr. Wallace completes his journey, everyone will believe the lies he has written. They will believe that the first expedition failed because of my husband. That it was his own shortcomings—not the weather nor the unusual absence of game nor even simple bad luck, but his personal shortcomings—that brought about his death. Is that what you believe, George?"

"No," he said. "It was all those other things."

"Precisely. But we are the only people who can prove that. Mr. Wallace will not. His only ambition is to prove himself the better man."

Never before had George felt such a sense of suffocation. He felt utterly boxed in by her logic. Nor did he possess the words to refute her, or the strength to try. It would be easier to die in Labrador, he decided, than to argue with her.

"When did you figure on leaving?" he asked.

"In June," she told him. "Just as Mr. Hubbard originally planned."

All through the winter and spring they kept their secret. It was harder than George had thought it would be, especially after he returned to Missanabie at the end of January and went back to working for Mr. King at the Hudson's Bay Company. Offers came in requesting his services as a guide for hunting and fishing excursions planned for the summer, but he turned them all down as politely as he could. His friends wanted to know why. *You got something against making easy money?*

What could he say? The art of deceit eluded him. "I've had my fill of that kind of work for a while, I guess." And it was true, as far as it went. He certainly had had his fill of the kind of work that could starve a man, steal his strength, rob him of his life. His closest friends, those who knew how the experience with Leonidas Hubbard had changed George, thought they understood. But others continued to badger him. Here he was a famous man, written up in papers from St. John's to New York City. *What's the matter, George? Afraid to go into the bush again?*

Plus there were all those letters from Mrs. Hubbard to explain. In a place like Missanabie, if a letter arrived from the States, everybody in town soon knew about it. Mina wrote frequently to tell George about the plans she was making, the provisions she had ordered, the contacts she had made with a publisher eager for a book about her expedition. Now and then she included a newspaper clipping about Wallace's preparations. From these George learned of Wallace's attempt to give his trip the imprimatur of science. He had signed on a young geologist to help him scout the area for mineral deposits, a young forestry student and an Ojibway guide.

Mina also wrote to ask George's advice. Should she order this or that? How many of each? Could he fill out the crew with a couple of good men who could be counted on to hold their tongues about the plans?

She wrote to inform him that certain people, the necessary people, had been informed of her expedition—friends of hers or Mr. Hubbard's who could be relied upon for financial support. But she had been careful to tell them something less than the full truth. A dissimulation, yes, but unavoidable. She had told them that she planned to visit Labrador for the purpose of gathering information for her book about Mr. Hubbard, that she would travel only as far as the North West River Post to conduct interviews. She seemed, in her letters, to take some delight in this charade, and in the admonishment of her friends that even a modest foray into that brutal peninsula might well prove the undoing of such a delicate lady.

But George's worst moment came the day he received a letter from Dillon Wallace, a letter he had been expecting. He and Wallace had not been what George would have called friends, had never shared the depth of affection and respect George had had with Mr. Hubbard. In fact, there had been times on the trail when Wallace's bossy tone had rubbed George the wrong way. Even so, it always made sense that Wallace would want George to accompany him on this second journey. After all, George now knew as much about the interior as any man. Moreover, he and Wallace had lived through the ordeal together, and that fact alone created a bond between them.

So George had been dreading the appearance of Wallace's letter, had prayed more than once that the letter would get lost in the mail. But it did not, it found its way to Missanabie. And that very night

George wrote his reply, not even allowing himself a full day to think about it, lest he lose the resolve to tell his biggest untruth yet.

"I'm sorry," George wrote. "But I'm getting married in the Spring. So it wouldn't be right for me to go off with you."

The remaining days passed in a kind of blur. For George to escort a white woman into the wilderness was simply madness. Who had ever heard of such a thing? If anything happened to her out there—and a hundred different things could happen—he might as well just take out his knife and slit his own throat. Every white person north of the border would assume that either he had been too foolish and incompetent to protect her adequately, or else he had let his animal nature get the better of him. He didn't want to think about what might be done to him afterward. Even so, most times, it was all he *could* think about.

In early June, Mina travelled to Halifax, dressed all in black, and met again with George. He brought not only the gear Mina had ordered but also two strapping fellows to accompany them. Joe Iserhoff was half Russian, half Cree, and Job Chapies was a full-blooded Cree. Like George, they had been born and raised in the James Bay country and were expert hunters and canoemen, and each possessed the quiet dignity of those whose daily lives are lived to the rhythms of nature.

Joe, despite his Russian name, spoke with a soft Scottish accent that Mina found almost musical. Job, on the other hand, did not speak much English and, at least in Mina's presence, was very reserved. But from the beginning the men were gentle and considerate not only toward her but toward each other as well, engaging in none of the tiresome rodomontade so common among more civilized men.

Somehow, all three of Mina's crew had managed to make it to Halifax under the veil of secrecy. But it did not take long for the veil to be whisked aside. While they waited for the ice to break so they could set sail for Labrador, an observant reporter from the *Halifax*

*Herald* put two and two together and eventually harassed Mina into admitting that, yes, all that gear did belong to her. Yes, those three men with Indian blood were with her too. And yes, if you must know, she was about to set forth on an expedition of her own, not merely to the Northwest River but all the way to Ungava Bay, just as her husband would have done had misfortune not befallen him.

She was aware, of course, of Dillon Wallace's expedition?

On that matter, there was nothing she cared to say.

Was it her intention to beat Wallace to Ungava?

She did not care to discuss the matter further.

What were her feelings toward Mr. Wallace? Was she bothered by the insinuations he had made against her husband?

She had nothing to say. Please, not another word on the subject.

On June 13 the *Herald's* headline blared, "Hubbard Expedition Is Rival of Dillon Wallace." "Mrs. Hubbard is a slight woman," the reporter wrote, "with a delicate pale face, lighted up by a very fine pair of brown eyes, whose expression is distinctly indicative of tenacity of purpose. She wears deep mourning. She objected to give out anything whatever as to her plans or to state whether or not there had been any difficulty between the original exploring party and herself."

Two days later the same paper carried another inflammatory headline:

MRS. HUBBARD DOUBTS WALLACE'S STORY OF TRIP
HIS BOOK AND HER HUSBAND'S DIARY VARY
ON ONE OR TWO POINTS
AND MRS. HUBBARD IS DETERMINED TO FIND OUT
THE TRUE FACTS OF HER HUSBAND'S DEATH

The reporter, unable to get any further information from Mina, had gone to S. Edgar Briggs, the manager of Fleming H. Revell Company, publisher of Wallace's first book. "It is no secret among the publishers," the reporter noted, "that the relations between the widow and the man who succoured her husband until he himself almost lost his life have been strained." He quoted Briggs's adamant affirmation of Wallace's integrity, but also his concession that Mina "could not reconcile the apparent discrepancy between the diary of her husband and that of Wallace."

The story that Mina was in Halifax with a crew at the ready created a sensation all the way down to New York City. Wallace got wind of it in St. John's from the editor of that city's *Evening Herald*, who fanned the flames by repeating the rumour that Mina had accused Wallace of hastening her husband's death. Wallace was infuriated.

And so the veil of secrecy surrounding Mina's expedition was not only lifted, it was shredded to pieces.

The race was on.

# PART II

*Into the Wild*

*Mina Hubbard's expedition, June 1905*

MINA HUBBARD SAT ALONE in her cramped cabin, a dismal little cubicle stinking of grease and dirt, as the *Harlow* steamed west across Lake Melville out of Rigolet in eastern Labrador. Nearly two years had passed since her husband's death but she remained dressed all in black. As on her previous steamer trip to Labrador, she felt sick to her stomach—maybe because of the *Harlow's* lurch across the bay, maybe because of the same malady that had laid low Joe Iserhoff. Like Joe, Mina felt feverish one minute, chilled to the bone the next. Fortunately, she had not yet developed the chest cold that kept rattling young Joe with violent coughs, so maybe her illness was of a different nature. Maybe she was sick because of what George had told her not long ago—that Dillon Wallace and his party had come aboard.

Or perhaps it was a different kind of dread that made her legs weak and her stomach queasy—the fear of what lay ahead, beyond Grand Lake. The conviction that she was doomed to fail.

How could she possibly succeed when her beloved Laddie, so courageous and capable and bold, had been defeated by the very task she now set for herself? No, she would fail, of this she was certain—though in truth a part of her was looking forward to that inevitability as the only sure way to put an end to her misery.

To make matters worse, she now sat doubled over with nausea. The disquiet had been building in her stomach ever since she set foot aboard the *Harlow*, but the pain had doubled with word of Wallace's arrival. He was up there on deck somewhere, no doubt strutting around as if he owned the place, playing the hero.

The fear in her was as cold as the chill Atlantic, but the rage in her burned. One minute her skin was on fire, eyes stinging, breath coming in gasps, and the next minute she felt small and trembling and terrified.

Wallace and his party had arrived in Rigolet with only minutes to spare before the *Harlow* weighed anchor, and now their gear lay piled above her on the foredeck. George, wonderful George, had immediately reported the news to her. He had described each man in Wallace's party, offered his assessment of how fit or unfit each appeared for the trials ahead. Mina had listened stoically, holding everything in check, giving no indication of the roil of emotions at work in her.

Wallace would later describe his crew in this manner:

*After careful investigation, I finally selected as my companions George M. Richards, of Columbia University, as geologist and to aid me in the topographical work, Clifford H. Easton, who had been a student in the School of Forestry at Biltmore, North Carolina (both residents of New York), and Leigh Stanton, of Halifax, Nova Scotia, a veteran of the Boer War, whom I had met at lumber camps in Groswater Bay, Labrador, in the winter of 1903–1904, when he was installing the electric light plant in the large lumber mill there.*

To round out the crew, "It was desirable to have at least one Indian in the party as woodsman, hunter, and general camp servant."

This was to be Peter Stevens, a full-blooded Ojibway from Minnesota who spoke only halting English.

Richards, like Easton, was a student and therefore some twenty years younger than Wallace, and he was an eager, and strong-looking fellow. Easton was much thinner but no less eager, and he had had some experience as a wilderness canoeist. Stanton, in his late thirties, was the oldest man in the crew next to Wallace. Though Stanton couldn't lay claim to much wilderness experience, Wallace thought of him as a friend in light of the time they had spent together in Labrador two years earlier, when Wallace was recuperating from the ordeal of his first expedition.

That Mina had once thought of Wallace as a friend, had welcomed him into her home, had fed him at her table, this galled her more than she dared express to George or anyone else. She suspected that, even if Wallace had not directly caused her husband's death, he had at least abetted it by doing less than he might have to prevent it—far less than her husband would have done had their positions been reversed. Furthermore, Wallace had publicly besmirched her Laddie's reputation. And why? So as to make himself appear wiser, more capable than the man who had befriended him? It seemed to her that the only purpose to Wallace's expedition was further self-aggrandizement, carried out under the guise of completing Laddie's work. If Wallace was successful, it would utterly destroy her husband's name.

How dare he? she asked the empty room, her stomach suddenly gripped by cramps. *How dare he?*

She could picture Wallace and his party topside, either strolling about or stretched out on deck chairs, bundled up against the fog and chill, sucking their pipes. Wallowing in arrogance.

She pulled herself to her feet, braced herself against the bunk. No, she would not cower like a mouse in this cabin, no matter how ill she felt. Wallace was the interloper here, not she. It was her duty to fulfill her husband's mission, not Wallace's, no matter how much noise he made about his and Laddie's bond, their "plighted troth."

So no, she would not change out of her mourning clothes, not just yet. She had read the looks that met her all along the way from New York City to Rigolet, she knew the thoughts behind those looks. She defied each and every suggestion that she had mourned long enough. How dare anyone question her grief?

Out into the corridor she went, pulling herself along, up onto the deck. She would go wherever she pleased on this ship. Let anyone try to stop her. Maybe Wallace had caught up with her in Rigolet, erasing her slim lead, but it would make no difference. Neither he nor the gossipmongers nor the icebergs nor an army of judgmental looks would deter her. Laddie was hers and hers alone, and he was with her, always with her. He would show her the way.

A pewter sky, a chilling blast of air. Mina stood at the rail and looked down at black water. The wind buffeted her, blasted straight through her coat. But the air was bracing as well. The scent of a frigid sea stripped the nausea out of her, washed the sour taste from her mouth. Such bleakness wherever she looked, such desolation. Still, she could not help but acknowledge something exciting about the challenge of this place, something elemental, almost primeval. Maybe that was why Laddie had been so drawn to the wild. Challenge and risk brought out the best in him, he always said; made him feel wholly alive. Perhaps they would do the same for her.

She heard voices, a broken conversation, words muted and scattered by the fog. She turned mid-ship and peered through the haze. A pair of figures stood some thirty feet away. The scent of pipe smoke hung in the air. She knew without being able to see him clearly that one of the men was Wallace. She knew too, because the moment held that breathless quality of the preordained, that he would turn and come toward her.

A minute or so later he did just that, though apparently unaware of Mina pressed against the rail, half-concealed in fog. He covered

most of the distance between them before he noticed her and came
to a halt. Neither could see the other's face, only a silhouette, grey
upon grey. But Mina would not allow herself to cower. She reached
along the rail, pulled herself forward, set herself in motion.

As Wallace's face came into view, and as he too stepped forward,
a sudden flutter knotted her stomach. She almost jerked away. But
no, she must not. Laddie would never have flinched and neither
would she. Her gait stiffened but she refused to shorten her stride,
refused to turn away by so much as an inch. Instead, she marched
toward him, her eyes locked on his now but seeing nothing, only
greyness all around.

When they were but steps apart, Wallace drew his pipe from his
mouth and wet his lips, was about to speak. A hand came up toward
his hat. Mina's gaze drilled into him. And at the last moment he
looked away, he averted his eyes as she strode past.

She continued on with the most forceful strides she could manage, another six feet, then six feet more. Then one knee buckled and
she gripped the rail and held herself in place, hand to cold metal.
Her legs were trembling, a shiver was building in her chest. Yet she
could not help but smile. Wallace had been the one to falter, not
she. Might it be a harbinger of what lay ahead? Was it conceivable
after all that, with Laddie's help, her Laddie's strength, she might
actually succeed?

She drew in a slow, full breath. Looked out across black water.
No, Wallace could not stop her. Nothing short of death could stop
her now.

Around six P.M. on the evening of June 23, the *Harlow* dropped
anchor near the southern end of Lake Melville, where the lumber
camp of Kenemish was located behind a cove on the eastern shore.
Immediately Wallace and his crew started loading up their canoes,
eager to paddle the twelve miles across Lake Melville to the
Hudson's Bay Company post at the mouth of the Northwest River.

Before launching into the interior by crossing Grand Lake and heading up the Naskapi River, they intended to complete their provisioning from the post's stores and repack the canoes a final time.

Wallace's frenzied if somewhat disorganized activity disconcerted Mina. If she allowed him to take the lead now, right out of the gate, she might never catch up with him. But Joe Iserhoff remained ill and she could not very well force him into a canoe to start paddling.

George suggested that he and Job go ahead in one of the canoes. At the French trading post, across the river from the Hudson's Bay post, they would gather up the last of their provisions and make everything ready for a plunge into the unknown. Mina agreed. With a mix of relief (that at least part of her party was underway) and frustration (that it was not the whole party), she watched as George and Job set off, their paddles chopping rhythmically at the dark water, flinging up glimmering drops in the cool evening light. Wallace's crew, yet to lower their canoes into the water, continued to debate the proper positioning of their packs.

Mina knew that at this point in the race hers was a merely symbolic lead of a few minutes, not significant enough to elicit a smile from her lips as she watched from the rail. But she revelled in the triumph of having a canoe underway before Wallace did, and in that secret place inside where no one but Laddie could see, she was clapping and laughing with delight.

It was a long two days for Mina. She nursed Joe Iserhoff back to health and, in her spare time, walked all about Kenemish, too restless to sit still for long. So near to setting off on a venture that, one way or the other, could only bring her husband closer, she found the wait excruciating. Yet even through the grey rains and the heavy fogs that came and went over that bleak landscape, she felt her husband near. And she could sense his eagerness too, his excitement at the prospect of a second chance. From time to time, in rare and wonderful moments, she would notice a dog trotting through the street, tail whipping back and forth, or see a chevron of geese flying overhead, honking directions to one another, and suddenly she would feel the warmth of Laddie's body as he walked beside her, the flush of joy he took in such simple observations. But these escapes from reality were all too brief, and when they ebbed it was always abruptly, like a hammer blow to her chest, a staggering return of awful knowledge.

Not until late Saturday night did George return to Kenemish. Mina was packed and waiting. Joe, despite his wan appearance, vowed that he could make the twelve-mile paddle to the French post without breaking a sweat. So off they went in the second canoe.

In the dark hours of early morning, Monsieur Duclos, the agent in charge of the French post, finally welcomed Mina into his home. The house was warm and comfortable, and the food Mina was served seemed, in comparison to the fare she had suffered for the past several days, exquisite. Still, she had no wish to linger. From behind the windows of Monsieur Duclos's home she gazed out at the lake to where the land began its rise toward a range of blue mountains capped with snow.

On the opposite shore of the Northwest River was a scattering of low white buildings, those of the Hudson's Bay Company, and from time to time Mina watched anxiously as one or two of Wallace's men wandered down to the docks. Are they starting out? she asked herself, and held her breath as she waited to see if the canoes would be carried down to the water now, fully loaded and ready to launch. But no, it was only George Richards, the student of geology, scuffling along the shore, picking up stones. Or it was Pete Stevens, the Ojibway guide, sniffing at the wind.

A final man had been added to Wallace's crew at the North West River Post, but George kept this information to himself as long as he could. George needed four strong men, including himself, to man his outfit's two canoes, and he had hoped to find Duncan McLean at the post and hire him to join them. Duncan was one of the men George had dispatched two years earlier to rescue Wallace and Hubbard, and one of the men who had hauled Hubbard's body out of the wilderness. But Wallace had gotten to Duncan first, before Duncan even realized that his old friend was in the area. So instead George persuaded Monsieur Duclos to grant a leave of absence to one of his employees, a boy named Gilbert Blake. He was only nineteen but a hard worker and a merry-hearted lad. More important to Mina, Gilbert had also been a member of the party that recovered her husband's body. She could not resist posing the same questions to Gilbert that she had already asked a dozen times of George.

"When you first found him, Gilbert, when you first looked inside the tent . . . how did he appear to you?"

"Just like he was sleepin'," Gilbert told her. He considered informing her that he preferred to be called Bert, which was how the men addressed him. But he let the opportunity pass. And as time wore on he came to enjoy her more formal use of his name. It made him feel that he was no longer a boy.

"He hadn't been disturbed in any way?"

"No, missus, not a bit."

"No signs of animals having been about?"

"There was some caribou tracks close around the tent, but nothing else. No signs of anything trying to get at the tent, if that's what you mean."

"So he appeared peaceful to you?"

"Like he had just gone to sleep and hadn't waked up. His hand was on this little book he had been writing in."

"His journal."

"That's the one. His hand was on it like he'd just finished writing something. But other than that his blankets was pulled up around him and he looked for all the world like he was just having himself a good long sleep."

Gilbert did not tell Mrs. Hubbard that her husband's skin had been as blue as six-inch ice, and he did not tell her about the crust of ice on her husband's moustache and eyebrows. He did not tell her that he was afraid of death and had refused to touch Mr. Hubbard or even get inside the tent with him. Instead, he smiled gently and told her, "When I go, missus, I hope I look as peaceful as your Mr. Hubbard did."

It was what she needed to hear, not once but again and again. In the weeks ahead Gilbert would repeat his answers many times, but never grudgingly. The repetition of soothing words helped him to sleep a lot better too.

On Friday, June 27, at three in the afternoon, George knocked on the door of Mina's bedroom in Monsieur Duclos's house. "We're loaded and ready," he told her through the wood.

"I'll be right down!"

"You want me to take your pack?"

"I'll bring it, George, thank you. Just give me a minute."

She sat at the foot of the feather bed with her ankles and knees pressed together, hands clasped close to her stomach. Again she closed her eyes and summoned Laddie's smiling face. She did not pray for success in the days ahead, because what good was success without him there to share it? She only prayed that she would not be weak or cowardly and that she would not be the cause of any harm to the men.

She came downstairs then and walked outside and toward the water, where not only her crew was gathered and waiting but also Monsieur Duclos's entire household. Mr. Cotter and his entire household from the rival Hudson's Bay post were there as well. Plus, it seemed, every other resident of the village.

When she approached the dock, George was busy checking, for the fiftieth time, the straps binding their packs to the canoes. He looked up when a murmur went through the crowd, and he could hardly believe his eyes. Mrs. Hubbard was wearing not the relent-less black garb, her unvarying dress for the past two years, but a long brown skirt that swept back and forth at her ankles, a black sweater and a narrow-brimmed hat of soft brown felt. She wore leather moccasins that reached nearly to her knees, and on one hip, strapped to a broad leather belt, a moleskin pouch and a hunting knife in its sheath. On the other hip she wore a revolver in a holster. She was carrying two cameras, a folding Kodak and a larger one for panoramic shots. Tucked close to her body, in a waterproof bag in the moleskin pouch, was Laddie's Labrador journal.

It was all George could do to keep from whistling in approval. He and the other men of his crew exchanged nods and smiles.

Young Gilbert Blake spoke up just as Mina reached the water's edge. "It's a fine day for starting out, Mrs. Hubbard."

She gazed across the water, which was calm for a change, then slowly took in the sky, a bleached-out blue with a slow, soft scroll of clouds. In the distance the blue mountains crowned with snow seemed almost to glow in the afternoon light.

"I do believe this is the sunniest day we've had so far," she said. "It's an absolutely perfect day."

George told her, "Monsieur Duclos offered to take us as far as the Naskapi in his yacht, but there's not enough wind for the sails."

She thanked the agent for his offer and his hospitality. "But I think it's better this way, don't you? We shall begin and end under our own power."

Duclos and several others crowded around Mina to wish her well. They had every confidence, they said, that she would succeed in her endeavour. Even Mr. Cotter told her, "You can do it, Mrs. Hubbard. And without any trouble too."

She turned away as quickly as was possible without appearing rude. The good wishes made her chest ache and her eyes sting. "Are you ready for me, Mr. Elson?" she asked.

"Whenever you are," he said.

She came forward, one hand to her hat, the other reaching for George's arm as she stepped carefully over the stones. While she settled herself in the middle of one canoe, between George in the stern and Job sitting forward, Gilbert climbed into the bow seat of the other. Joe pushed that canoe off, then hopped into the stern seat. A cheer went up from the shore as the paddles dipped.

Mina did not look back nor say another word until certain that her voice was out of range of the shore. "I noticed nobody watching us from the other side of the river, George. And Mr. Cotter had come over to our side."

"They left last night," George told her.

Her breath caught in her chest. "What time?"

"After supper, Mr. Cotter said."

She nodded. She sat stiffly, her back as straight as a board. George wondered if she would sit like that for the next two months.

Minutes later she said, "I'm glad to see the water so calm."

Job said, "It's fixin' to roughen up some. And a little wind going to turn that lake into trouble."

George winced when he heard this, though not because it was new information to him. In Cree he said, "From now on let's keep that kind of thing to ourselves."

Job dipped his paddle, pulled and dipped. "Sorry. Wasn't thinkin'."

"That's a beautiful language," Mina told them. "What did you say?"

George answered, "I'll teach you some words if you like."

"If you teach me too many, you won't be able to keep your secrets."

"I'm not a man that has any secrets."

She turned at the waist, cocked an eyebrow when she looked at him. "How far ahead of us are they?"

"According to Mr. Cotter they was only going the three miles to Tom Blake's place. They'd of spent the night there, then would've got off sometime this morning."

She faced forward again. "Is there anything else you haven't told me?"

"They signed up Duncan McLean to guide them as far as Big Lake. He's one of the two fellas rescued Mr. Wallace that first time. They got to Duncan before I had a chance."

She said nothing, only sat very straight.

The other canoe glided alongside theirs. Joe said, "Which leaves me to wonder who'll be left to rescue Wallace this time around."

Gilbert flashed Mina a grin. "Won't be that Stanton fella, I can tell you that. Man's so skinny, I'm afraid somebody's going to mistake him for a fishing pole and dunk his head in the water."

"What about that Easton?" Joe said. "Nearly drowned once already so far, and that was in St. John's harbour!"

The men chuckled and shook their heads. Gilbert asked, "How's a fella go about fallin' off a iceberg anyway?"

"You start," George answered, "by being foolish enough to climb one in the first place."

Now even Mina could not help but smile.

George told her, "We'll catch them, Mrs. Hubbard. Don't you worry about that."

"All I can say," said Gilbert, "is we better do it quick. Else who they gonna have to show them the way?"

The men laughed and nodded and dug hard with their oars. Mina said, in a voice that feigned exasperation, "I am surrounded by joke-makers."

"True enough," Joe answered. "But none that ever fell off a iceberg."

The sun was just coming up the next morning when George called out, "All aboard!" and woke Mina from a restless sleep. She rolled over in her tent, wrapped like a mummy in her blankets. The grey light of early morning lay across the balloon-silk canopy, providing just enough illumination that she could see the hands on her watch. Three A.M.! She had crawled into her tent less than two hours earlier. There had been a light supper after midnight, then a short nap, and now here was George calling her to breakfast already. There was going to be a lot to get used to on this trip.

Not that she minded getting up and moving again. Maybe the long hours of daylight in these latitudes, even if it was generally a weak daylight, were the cause of her restlessness. Or maybe it was her eagerness to keep moving, to pass beyond not only Wallace but her own doubts and fears.

After supper the previous night, when the men had stretched out on their blankets before a roaring fire, not even bothering to erect their own tent, Mina had retired to her portable little house to write in her diary. But all she had been able to think about was Laddie and how sweet the night would be had he been with her in the tent. They had shared so many nights like that, and in every season. She remembered the cool nights in upstate New York, nights so quiet she could almost hear the stars twinkling. The string of sultry nights on their southern trip, when crickets and buzzing insects and bullfrogs sang so loudly that their cacophony set her teeth on edge—until Laddie taught her to hear them as a symphony, every croak and buzz a love call, a thousand Romeos declaiming to their radiant Juliets.

No matter the weather, Mina had never felt uncomfortable when lying next to her husband. Often they had slept holding hands. Now all she could do was try to reach for him with her nightly prayers and with the words of her journal. It helped a little, but it was never as comforting as his flesh against hers.

She pulled on her moccasins and joined the men outside at the fire. After a quick breakfast of tea, fried bread, and bacon, they climbed into the canoes again. The rhythm of the water had not left her in the night, the steady beat of the paddles dipping and pulling, the gentle back-and-forth rock of the canoes. The wind was up a little this morning, riffling the surface, so no mist lay across the water, and the men paddled hard right from the start, eager to get off the lake and onto the river, where a wind as light as this one would have little effect on them.

They spoke mostly in Cree as they paddled, though nobody was especially talkative. Already the land was beginning to rise toward the plateau far away in the middle of the peninsula, toward that summit near Lake Michikamau known as the Height of Land. There, on the northern slope, the waters would run northward rather than southward, and from that point on they would ride with the current instead of working against it, a fast slide all the way to Ungava. But the Height of Land was still a long way off, and Ungava even farther, more than six hundred miles away through a maze of uncharted swamps and streams and rivers and lakes, past rapids and waterfalls and nobody knew what else.

It was some time after seven when Mina felt a subtle change in their movement, almost like a shift in barometric pressure. But George's paddle was the cause of it; the paddle had gone still and dragged through the water like a rudder. Mina turned to look at him. He was sitting motionless, the paddle held against the side of the canoe as he stared off to the west.

Mina followed his gaze. Then she too spotted the narrow channel where it entered the lake. It was not easy to pick out between the sandhills and, farther back, the dark green firs, and she would have missed it for sure had not George's gaze directed her to it. "Is that the Naskapi?" she asked.

All George said was, "The Susan."

Her breath caught in her throat. She looked again. The Susan's water was not as dark as the lake's but deep green and glinting with sunlight. Just looking at it made Mina's throat thicken and her eyes sting. She hated the Susan River, hated the very sight of it. Still she could not look away, not even as George dipped his paddle again. She could very nearly see another canoe pausing there at the mouth of the Susan, an eighteen-foot Old Town. George sat in the stern of that canoe, just as he did in hers. Wallace held the middle seat. And there was Laddie in the bow, sitting as tall as he could, hands resting on the paddle as it lay across the gunwales. Between the thumb and forefinger of each hand he held the only known map of the area.

"That's got to be it," Laddie said.

Wallace asked, "Does it correspond to Low's map?"

"The Naskapi's the only river he shows." Then, a moment later, "George?"

And George said, "It's what everybody told us back at the post. The Naskapi flows into the end of the lake."

Laddie grinned and folded the map. "It's the Naskapi for sure, boys. Onward and upward we go. Excelsior!"

Mina wished with all her heart that she could call them back. But her voice would not carry that far, two years into the past. Laddie had written about the Susan in his journal, mistakenly referring to it as the Naskapi. A rock-strewn bottom too shallow for paddling. Laddie and his crew would lose valuable time fighting against it, they would use up too many provisions, get hopelessly lost.

Mina sat with her head down as the men paddled, staring at her hands, holding everything inside. The men said nothing to disturb her until, an hour or so later, George broke the silence. Softly he said, "Here we are."

She looked up to see the Naskapi burbling into Grand Lake, wider and deeper than the Susan, unmistakable once seen. She did not know how to feel about being there. This should have been her husband's river, but he had never even seen it. Its emerald water spilled into the brown of Grand Lake and spread out in a wide, rippling fan. The bay was wide too and surrounded by high sandhills, and there were several wooded islands clustered around the mouth of the river, crowding close as if to drink from the Naskapi's green water.

It was a lovely spot, and Mina ached with the unfair beauty of it all.

———

The next day. Thirteen miles above Grand Lake, Mina and her crew pulled ashore for an early lunch. Job, Joe and Gilbert busied themselves with gathering wood and building a fire, unpacking the frying pan and kettle, the tea and bacon. George took up his rifle and said, "I'll see if there's any game about."

"Shall I come along?" Mina asked.

"It's not easy walking on these stones. And I don't think you want to be crawling through the willow brush with me."

"I wouldn't mind at all, really. I've been sitting and doing nothing for too long now."

George thought about it for a moment, searching his mind for a tactful response. "One person can move quieter than two, missus. You'll be more comfortable here. You can even catch yourself a little nap in the shade there."

But she was in no mood for napping. So after George walked off downstream, Mina headed upstream along the rocky shore.

Gilbert was the first to notice. "Missus Hubbard? You want me to come along with you?"

She continued to pick her way across the stones. "I do not, thank you."

Joe and Job both gave Gilbert a look. He hesitated, then broke into a trot to catch her. Not loud enough for the others to hear, he told her, "We're not supposed to let you go off on your own, missus."

"Oh? And is that what you discuss all the time in your language I can't understand?"

Gilbert blushed and looked at the ground.

"Very well, then," she told him. She started walking again, and Gilbert soon fell into step behind her. She asked, "Will this be the first time you've accompanied a lady to the necessary room?"

Gilbert stopped walking. "I'll just wait here," he told her.

"Suit yourself." She dared not look back, lest he see the smile she could not suppress.

The young nurse Leonidas Hubbard Jr.
fell in love with, 1900.

Hubbard, a man with a vision, at
Northwest River Post, July 1903.

Hubbard and Dillon Wallace, hale and hearty, prepare to depart Rigolet for the great unknown, 1903.

George Elson, 1905.

Gilbert Blake, 1905.

Job Chapies, 1905.

Joe Iserhoff, 1905.

Elson in the stern and Wallace in the bow
paddle over calm water, 1903.

Wallace and Elson begin another portage, 1903.

George Elson hangs meat on a drying rack while Dillon Wallace watches, 1903.

Leonidas Hubbard, still strong enough to scrape a caribou hide, 1903.

Hubbard (foreground) and Elson at their last camp together,
1903. Hubbard will not leave this camp alive.

The plain truth of it was that the lack of activity was beginning to grate on her. The men allowed her to do nothing. Oh, she could sit in the canoe and write in her journal all she wanted. She could make sketches of the hills and streams they passed. She could take readings with her sextant and compass. But she was not allowed to handle a paddle. And in camp, if she so much as reached for a stick of wood to lay it on the fire, one of the men would jump up and take it from her. "Let me do that, missus. No use both of us getting our hands dirty."

And those long hours in the canoe when the men spoke only in their private language—that was exasperating too. At first she had thought the language melodious, as soothing as the gentle slap of water against the hull. But now she felt isolated by their conversations. She was being treated like a helpless child and she did not like it. She did not like it at all.

Laddie had included her in everything. Each and every one of his plans had been discussed with her. He had sought her advice, had given her his unpublished manuscripts to read. No man had ever treated her with the respect Laddie had. No man had ever loved her as Laddie had.

These were Mina's thoughts as she stood on a large, odd-shaped boulder a quarter-mile above the camp. The boulder was black and slick with spray where it stuck out above the water and the top of it was scooped out like a bowl, which made her footing uneven. Surging beneath and beyond this boulder was the first set of rapids she and her crew would encounter on the Naskapi. The water was fast and loud and frothing white. It banged into rock and sluiced around depressions and tossed geysers of spray into the air—all of which generated so much noise that a single shot from George's rifle registered on her ears only as a distant pop.

She inched her way out to the very edge of the slick rock. Heavy drops of cold water splashed onto her skirt. We will have to portage around this, she thought. But despite the river's constant boom and splash she did not feel any malice in it. The violence was not evil but a natural thing. Even playful. She was not the least bit frightened by it. In fact she found the noise and rush of the water quite soothing. The churn beneath her feet was nothing if not hypnotic, and she wondered what it would be like to be immersed in that water, to be a part of it, all darkness and wild thrashing on the surface, all deep serenity at the river's smooth-washed bottom.

George's voice was just a whisper at first, just another murmuring of water. "Missus Hubbard. Missus Hubbard, please."

She became aware of him only after he had crept to within three feet of her, had leaned forward and pulled lightly on the hem of her sweater. "Missus Hubbard, please."

She turned abruptly. How had he got so close? Where had he come from?

"What are you doing sneaking up on me?" she asked.

"Come on back a bit, missus. Will you do that for me?"

It did not make any sense to her. He was standing there with his rifle in one hand, his free hand reaching out to her. A dead porcupine lay at his feet. "What?" she asked.

"Just come back toward me a step or two. Will you do that for me?"

"For goodness' sake, George! Do you think I intend to jump in?"

"You don't intend to, I know. Nobody ever does. But you wouldn't be the first person to get dizzy and fall in by accident. I know you don't intend to."

"Of course I don't intend to!" Why did he look so pale all of a sudden? Why was there a tremble in his voice?

"All I want is for you to come toward me a step or two."

"You are being very silly," she told him. But she said this without looking directly into his eyes. Because now, as she did as he asked and moved gingerly away from the water, she felt how shaky her legs had become, felt the bubble of nausea in her stomach as she wondered, as if waking from a dream, just what she had been thinking about all those minutes on the slippery lip of the boulder, all those minutes while George, unnoticed and no doubt terrified, had crept up close to her, petitioning softly, waiting for that awful moment when she might lean out just a few inches farther ...

She came down off the boulder and stood beside him. "And what is that for?" she asked with a nod toward the porcupine.

"Tonight's supper," he told her. But even as he bent down and picked the porcupine up, holding it by its hind legs, his face remained white, his eyes wide.

Blood dripped from a hole in the animal's side. Mina watched a few drops fall onto the black, wet stones. "I'm sure it will be delicious," she said.

After lunch, as Job scoured the frying pan and Gilbert rinsed the plates, George pointed to a stream that entered the Naskapi just downriver of them. "Me and the boys is pretty sure that's the Red Wine," he told Mina.

All through lunch she had been quiet, even sullen, stinging from something she could not put into words. She felt as if George had scolded her back there at the rapids. Though his tone had been gentle, he had scolded her with his eyes and his fear. Moreover, she had deserved it.

But now, at the mention of the Red Wine, her spirits lifted. "Did you find the Indian trail?"

He nodded and smiled. "Let's go have a look at it."

At the French trading post, Mina had obtained a crude map of the trail from one of the local Indians, and had been told by him that it was possible to reach Seal Lake by this route in two weeks. The trip from Seal Lake to Lake Michikamau would take twenty-two days. A trapper at the post had opined that she would need at least a month to reach Seal Lake if she held to the river. If these two observations were true, the Indian trail might save her party as much as two weeks of travel.

She and George walked downstream to the Red Wine. He had already built a bridge of stepping stones so that she would not have to wade up to her shins to get to the other side. She did not know whether to be angry or amused.

"Take hold of my hand," he told her, and held it out to her, so callused and brown.

But it was not the hand that offended her. "I can make it across on my own, thank you. Besides, what do you plan to do—wade across through the water while I prance over the stones?"

"My boots won't take on water the way your moccasins will."

"My moccasins are well oiled."

"Even so. . . ."

She disregarded his hand. She disregarded the stepping stones as well, and plunged forward into the stream, splashing across. George stood there for a moment watching, shaking his head. Then he stepped across using the stones.

Approximately fifty yards beyond the Red Wine, George pointed to a slender path snaking into the alders. "Here it is," he told her. The trail looked little wider than a deer path. Sparse grass and thorny vines grew ankle-high from the trail's floor.

"Are you certain this is it?"

"It hasn't been used in quite a while, so it's getting all grown over again. But this is it all right."

She stepped to the head of the trail and peered into the dimness. "So what do you think?" she asked.

"I think it might be pretty rough going. We might lose a good bit of time just hunting for the trail. On the other hand, we might go in there a ways and be able to stick to it as easy as a country lane."

She looked back toward the river. "Plus," George said, "there's no telling what it will be like from here to Seal Lake. Could be mossy most of the way, which makes for nice spongy walking. Or it could be mostly boggy. Fact is, we're likely to find a fair amount of each."

She stared down the trail a while longer, then turned to face the river.

George said, "Maybe I'll take Job and go scout ahead a mile or so. See how this trail looks farther on."

Mina studied the river upstream and down. She gazed not only at the water but at the shoreline.

"I walked all along here looking for footprints and drag marks," George told her. "If anybody's been here, they was walking on air."

"And what does that suggest to you?" she asked.

He chewed on the corner of his lip for a moment before he spoke. "Either they went right on by here without stopping . . . or else they haven't got here yet."

"Might we have passed them somewhere on Grand Lake?"

"We didn't lay up long that second night. On the other hand, maybe they didn't either."

She wished he would do more than simply report the view from both sides. "What is your *opinion* on the matter, George?"

Again he paused before speaking. "My opinion, missus, is that you'd of kept your moccasins a lot drier if you'd of used that little bridge I built."

She spun to look at him but found him smiling. He possessed such an innocent countenance, all good nature and noble intentions. And with that smile he made his point about the stepping stones. She had been obstinate and ungrateful. He had only meant to help.

As for the question of whether to take the river or the Indian trail, the first choice appealed to her; the unpredictability and dimness of the second did not. She might not always appreciate the confines of the canoe but she liked the sound and smell of the water and she liked the way the river felt beneath her.

"Why would the trail be any easier to follow farther in than it is right here?" she asked.

"It's not likely it is. Not all grown over like it is."

"So we might in fact lose more time by going that way."

He nodded. "The only thing we know for sure is that the river's going to get rougher from here on up. It won't all be smooth paddling. We'll be fighting the current all the way to the Height of Land."

Mina could see Job and Joe and Gilbert standing near the canoes, no doubt wondering if they should pack up the teakettle or start unloading everything for a long portage up the trail. Finally she said, "I should like to stick to the river, George. If it's all right with you."

He grinned at her. Then he turned upstream and cupped his hands to his mouth. "Load 'er up, boys!"

This time when Mina and George crossed the Red Wine, she tiptoed nimbly over the stepping stones. On the other side, she turned to him and curtsied. He smiled to himself all the rest of the day.

The river turned north and grew swifter. At a place called Point Lucie, still some forty miles from Seal Lake, Mina's party encountered another set of rapids, a torrent of noise and water that made Mina tremble. The crash and boom and angry spray both terrified and attracted her. According to George, this was the place where trappers would leave their boats and make no attempt to take the canoes farther up, portaging their gear the rest of the way to Seal Lake.

Both banks of the river here were lined with last winter's ice, great layered blocks and sheets of ice stacked eight feet high in places. Scattered along the half-mile width of the river beyond the rapids were sand islands and gravel-covered hummocks of ice. When the wind gusted across all this ice it chilled her to the bone, and a part of her felt helpless in the face of it all, the leaping, foaming river and the frozen sentinels that guarded it.

But the men knew what to do. The canoes were pulled to shore just below the rapids. Then George, Joe, and Gilbert, again speaking only in Cree, set about building a fire. Job disappeared into the woods alone. Once the fire was blazing, Mina huddled close to it, trying to stay warm. She did not wish to have to say anything to George about the isolation she felt at being left out of their conversation, for she was reluctant to pull rank on them—especially in the face of the icy obstacles ahead. She was the expedition leader, yes, but, as she knew better with each passing day, in title only. George was the real leader. The best Mina could do was to trust in his plans.

Within a half-hour Job returned from the woods carrying four stout poles, two balanced on each shoulder, his strong arms wrapped around them. The poles had been cut to the same length, about nine feet long, and each was approximately two and a half inches in circumference. These were laid by the fire while Job rummaged through the packs until he found four metal cones. These shods had been brought by George, made in the factory at Missanabie. Quietly and with deft strokes of the axe Job shaved one end of each pole until it was a snug fit for the metal shod. With the shods nailed in place and the teakettle drained, the party was ready for the water again.

"Let's you and me get on up around the point," George told Mina. Without waiting for her acquiescence he set off along the shore, picking his way past the rapids. She had no sooner caught up with him, where the rapids were strongest, the river deep and dark and loud, than she asked, shouting above the roar, "What about the others?"

He grinned and pointed downstream. To Mina's amazement Job was coming up the middle of the river, right through the rapids, standing in the canoe as he poled against the current, the canoe bucking and turning as it rode the wild water. Before long the second canoe, with Gilbert and Joe doing the poling, also came into view. Mina thought she had never before seen such a wondrous sight, three men standing in the midst of the waves, climbing and falling, climbing and falling, working hard as they shoved their poles into the water and pulled themselves and their loads along, all the while laughing like daredevil boys, utterly fearless.

Fifteen minutes later, with Mina and George again in the canoes—Mina seated, the four men poling—she fought the urge to cling to the gunwales and hugged her knees instead. Even with the rapids behind them the current remained swift and filled with dangerous eddies, the water so deep that the men's hands sometimes dipped below the icy water as they worked the poles. Occasionally one of the canoes would scrape across a chunk of ice, and when this happened to Mina's canoe she gritted her teeth and held fast to her knees. Each time a pole was lifted from the water to be repositioned, the canoe stopped moving momentarily, and if the shod was not quickly plunged back into the river bottom the craft would slip backward with the current.

It was gruelling work, but Mina alone did not appear to be enjoying it. She could only sit rigidly in place, wondering when a shod would slip and allow the canoe to spin sideways and be swamped.

In time the water grew even rougher. George looked to Joe in the bow of the other canoe and gave a nod, and both canoes turned toward shore. Now, Mina thought, the first of the heavy portaging will begin, over and around the ice banks, the rough and slippery shore. She climbed eagerly out of the canoe, grateful for the chance to stand on solid ground again and to warm her fear-numbed limbs with movement.

She and George set off in advance of the others. Mina carried her rifle and cameras, George a light pack. She assumed that Job and Joe and Gilbert would soon follow, each laden with as much as he could carry. When the entire outfit had been moved ahead to calmer water, the canoes would be repacked and set afloat once more.

Along the way Mina spotted a pair of tiny blue violets growing amidst the gravel and ice. She picked these and held them to her nose and inhaled the subtlest of scents, but enough to gladden her heart. Laddie, upon making a discovery like this, these violets in the snow, would have placed them in her hair and recited a couplet or two, his hand to her cheek, his eyes gazing into hers, and she would have fallen in love with him all over again.

George gave her a nudge, bringing her back to the present. She looked at him, then followed his gaze downstream. There came Job again, poling a fully loaded canoe up the dangerous rapid.

Later that night she was still reeling from the wonder of it, and she made this entry in her journal:

> The wilder the rapid the more he seemed to enjoy it. He would stand in the stern of the canoe, right foot back, left forward with leg against the thwart, with the pole set and holding it steady in the rushing, roaring water while he looked the way over, choosing out his course. Then he would move the canoe forward again, twisting its nose now this way, now that, in the most marvelous fashion, and when he drove it into the rush of water pouring round a big rock the pole would bend and tremble with the weight and strain he put upon it. Sometimes I could hardly breathe while watching him. After taking one canoe some distance above the bend he went back for the second, and all the remainder of the afternoon Job climbed hills of water in the canoes.

That night she went to bed contentedly, her tent pitched on a bank high above the river, where the ubiquitous mosquitoes were not so abundant. She lay there listening to the music of the water. Such men these were in whose hands she had placed her trust and her life! She knew that night that she could not have chosen better. And Labrador, for all its chill and danger, now seemed a wonderful place. Two violets in the snow . . . a marvel.

At that moment, she could think of only one thing missing from her life.

————

*Dillon Wallace's expedition, June 29, 1905*

"HERE'S THE INDIAN TRAIL," Wallace said. His voice was flat with weariness, heavy with resentment. They had been searching for it a long time and now would have to make camp for the night. Worse yet, the shoreline was veritably trampled with footprints made by moccasins and boots not their own, and in one place they found the skid marks where two canoes had been dragged ashore.

"How in the world did they pass us?" Stanton asked.

Easton said, "We spent a lot of time back at Grand Lake. On shore, I mean. Collecting data."

Wallace tried not to sound as irritated as he felt. "This is a scientific expedition. Not a canoe race."

He had a lot more to say, too—about how a couple of the men had handled, or rather, mishandled, their canoes; about all the time Richards and Stanton had wasted on an earlier scouting mission to locate this trail, only to report back on the presence of three trails, each of which then had to be explored. Yes, they had brought back a caribou for dinner, but was fresh meat, this early in the venture, worth the loss of time?

And then there were these damnable mosquitoes and blackflies! Never had Wallace encountered such a plague of biting and stinging insects. Even the smoke from his pipe failed to discourage their attacks on his face, neck and hands. His hair was matted with their carcasses, his flesh dotted with their blood mixed with his.

And now, most discouraging of all, the Indian trail, discovered at last, bore evidence of recent visitation. "Do you think they took it?" Stanton asked.

Wallace bit down on his tongue. It would do no good to snap at the men. A foolish question was best left ignored. Instead he told them, "We might as well make camp here for the night. Pete and I will see what we can learn from the trail; you other men get busy setting up camp."

What Wallace and Pete found was that the trampled grass and broken twigs ended only thirty yards beyond the trailhead. Apparently the Hubbard party, daunted by the heavy underbrush, had returned to the river. Too rough for a woman, Wallace told himself, his first happy thought of the day.

Back at camp, where the fire was blazing, he announced that his party would here abandon the river in favour of the Indian trail. "It will provide us with better opportunity to conduct our studies of the area."

"Plus it's faster," Easton said with a grin.

Wallace responded with a smile.

"Though pretty rough in there," Pete Stevens said. "Might get better, might not."

"No matter," said Wallace. "What does matter is the contribution we can make to the scientific knowledge of the area."

Besides, in his heart he knew that the Indian trail was his best hope for catching and passing the Hubbard party. And that, he knew as well, was the way it was meant to be.

"This hill is nothing but damn clay!" Easton complained the next day.

They had already climbed the hill once in this drizzling rain, each man with a heavy pack on his back, and that trip up and down to the shoreline had turned the wet ground into a slippery ooze. Every man in the party had stumbled two or three times, crashing to his knees or, in Stanton's case, slipping onto his backside on the descent. Their clothes and boots and hands were heavy with mud.

Wallace had daubed some of the mud on his face as a deterrent to the blackflies, but the mud proved no more effective than the grease and commercial "bug dope" the men smeared over every inch of exposed skin. Even Duncan McLean, a native of this country, was made miserable by the pests.

"Damn these flies!" he said, and slapped first at the back of his neck, then at a cheek. "Goddamn little sonsabitches eat a man alive!"

On this second trip up the hill Stevens carried the front end of a canoe, with Richards bringing up the rear. In front of them, Stanton and Easton hauled the other canoe. Wallace and McLean, at the rear of the pack, shouldered the final loads of gear.

"Where did you learn to swear like that?" Wallace asked.

"Lumber camps," said McLean.

"What else did the white man teach you? Anything useful?"

"Swearing is sometimes useful, sir."

"How so?"

"Keeps me from screaming." He stuck a finger in his ear and dug out a fly.

"They call them the devil's angels," Stanton said over his shoulder.

"Hmpf. More like the devil hisself."

A minute or two later Richards called out, "How much farther to the top?"

Stanton lifted his head from under the bow of the canoe. "Another sixty, seventy yards."

"It must be ninety degrees already. And not even noon."

"At four this morning the thermometer read thirty."

"Freezing at night and hot as Hades during the day. Lovely place you brought us to, Wallace. Remind me to build a summer home here."

The pack straps pulled hard on Wallace's shoulders, cutting his skin. "One step at a time, gentlemen."

He had barely gotten the words out when he heard a loud grunt followed instantly by a thud. Then came more grunts and exclamations and, before he knew it, Stevens and Richards came sliding toward him. They had been bowled over by Stanton and Easton after Stanton slipped and dropped the stern end of his canoe, pulling Easton down as well. Duncan flattened himself against the side of the hill, then Wallace lurched into the brush just as the canoe came shooting toward him, sliding on its side. He watched it go scraping and bumping toward the bottom like an unmanned toboggan on an icy hill. It banged to a halt in an alder bush some two hundred feet below.

Wallace looked uphill at the men sprawled across the trail, the remaining canoe lodged between them. "Everybody all right?" he asked.

"Damn sonsabitching clay," McLean said.

*Mina Hubbard's expedition, July 1905*

SUNDAY, JULY 2, A DAY OF REST. It had been more than two years since Mina had awakened to such an idyllic day. By way of the Naskapi they had passed through a body of water the trappers called Mountain Cat Lake, a small, clear lake surrounded by spruce-covered hills, and their camp not far above this lake was their finest yet, high on a sandy point well away from the rapids, where the only watery sound in the night was a pleasing susurrus of current.

Now, at dawn, Mina hunkered near the water's edge, rubbing her dirty clothes against a large, smooth stone. Across the shore the land rose in a gentle slope to a long wooded hill; at its base were gravel flats blanketed in the fresh green grasses of spring. The flats were criss-crossed by little waterways of burbling crystal water. Now and then, as the sun shone over the hilltops, those streams sparkled red or orange, and the dew on the grass glinted like a scattering of diamonds.

She was amazed by the contentment she felt. Her feet were swollen from long hours of hiking along the rocky shore, now and then turning an ankle, and her face and hands were red and bumpy with the bites of blackflies and mosquitoes, which even now droned and swooped around her. But somehow she felt above all the torment. The men had risen early to bathe in the misty river and all were now clean-shaven and dressed in clean clothes. Gilbert, up by the campfire, was cutting Joe's hair. Job, scouring the skillet, sang softly to himself. George sat in the sun just outside his tent and read his Bible.

They had come together, Mina thought, to a soothing place, this sandy point, this place of wondrous calm.

The sense of peace stayed with her throughout the day. She smelled spruce trees in the air, heard birdsong in the trees. When she went to her tent in the afternoon for a nap before supper, she felt no need to wear herself out first with fervent prayer. Her mind today was not a roil of dark thoughts. She could only wonder if, the day before, they had passed some magic meridian and crossed over into an enchanted land.

A thunderstorm burst upon them in the evening, brief and refreshing, driving the flies away just before dark. Afterward the air was redolent with the fragrance of pine and river and rain-washed stones. And that night, after writing in her journal, Mina crawled between her blankets and listened for a while to a loon calling in the distance, serenading its mate, and Mina knew that she had been given this day as a blessing, a calm that could not last, and she said only "Thank you" before closing her eyes to the soft midnight light.

They slept late Monday and lingered in camp until eight-thirty. Mina sensed that all were reluctant to leave this place. But there was work to be done and there were miles to be covered, and too few days for it all.

After a breakfast of tea and bacon they moved ahead a short way to the next stretch of rapids. There a portage was necessary. The entire outfit was broken down and hauled two miles upriver. Here the water was still too violent for canoeing but calm enough in the shallows close to shore that Job thought the canoes could be loaded again and, if steadied by a tracking line pulled by two men while being poled by two others, taken safely through the rough water. Mina would walk, away from the danger, along the shore.

She carried only her cameras and the revolver and knife she wore on her hip. "If I climb higher up," she told George, "above that line of willows, I can get some fine pictures of the men as you take the canoes forward."

George cast a critical look at the top of the hill. "I think you'd better stick to the shore."

"I'll only be thirty or forty feet away. And it's easier walking up there. Besides," she teased, "this close to shore I might get dizzy and fall in the rapids."

George found no humour in the situation. "What if you come across a bear up there?"

She patted the revolver in its holster. "Then we'll be having bear for supper."

Now George gave her a smile, but a worried one. "All you'll accomplish with that revolver, missus, is to make him peeved at you."

"Then we'll just have to see who can get the most peeved."

George looked back at the men. Mina could have sworn he rolled his eyes. Then he turned to her again. "All right. I'll go with you."

"Oh then just never mind. I'll stay along the shore."

"I think it's better that you do."

"I said I would, didn't I?"

What she longed for most was an hour or so alone. The only time George took his eyes off her was when she was in her tent or attending to the call of nature. Ever since the incident at the first rapid, George—and, to a lesser extent, the other men too—had acted as if she might go plunging into the river at any moment. She knew they would have tied a tether to her ankle if they could have. They were responsible for her, and that, not the success of the expedition itself, they saw as their primary duty. What mattered most was that they bring her out alive. George, particularly George, was determined not to let another Hubbard die in Labrador.

He told her, "You can get started if you want to. We'll be along right behind you."

So that you can keep an eye on me, she thought. But she said nothing, only started picking her way over the rocks. Didn't he realize that his overprotectiveness made her feel small? Didn't he know that his suffocating kindness rankled?

Now and then she glanced back to watch the men at work. The tracking line was slipped through the eye-hook mounted on the bow of the canoe, one end of the line held by George, the other by Gilbert. Both men then waded ahead, pulling the line taut. With Job standing in the bow and Joe in the stern, they pushed off, easing the canoe forward. The water was swift and drove hard against George and Gilbert, splashing onto their chests and soaking their faces. Job and Joe drove their poles against the river bottom and pushed with all their strength.

They moved so slowly that Mina, walking at a snail's pace, frequently had to stop to let the canoes catch up. Once, when she had moved too far ahead, George called out, "Slow down, please, missus!" She would have barked a retort had he not looked so miserable out there in the water, cold and tired, as drenched as a muskrat.

When she came to a slender opening in the heavy brush that lined the shore, she paused for a minute, pretending to fiddle with a camera. Not far ahead in the river, directly in the canoe's path, lay a large black boulder. George and Gilbert, as they waded forward, were discussing how best to circumnavigate this obstacle, whether to turn closer to shore, where the canoe would likely scrape bottom, or into the deeper water farther out.

With encouragement shouted from Job they decided on the latter course. Now their progress became painfully slow. Every footstep had to be tested.

Mina noticed that George, so intent on not losing his footing, had not glanced her way in a while. "Now's the time," she told herself, and quickly slipped into the willows, ducking branches as she plunged ahead for higher ground.

She emerged on the other side of the willows with her face scratched, but she was grinning nonetheless. A short climb would take her to the top of the hill. She looked back to see if her escape had been noticed yet. And at that moment she saw both George and Gilbert suddenly disappear from sight as if they had stepped off a ledge on the river bottom.

Instantly the tracking line went slack, and before Mina even had time to raise a hand to her mouth in surprise the canoe turned sideways, rolled bottom up and pitched Job and Joe into the river.

First George and then Gilbert reappeared, each breaking to the surface and standing upright after being driven several yards downstream. Both still held to the tracking line, but the overturned canoe, as heavy now as a drifting anchor, was carried past them and threatened to drag them away.

Joe came up a moment later, minus his pole. He splashed his way to the tracking line and grabbed hold. Job, who had been tossed farthest out in the river, emerged for just a moment, barely long enough to suck in a breath. Then the current seized him and dragged him under again.

In a flash Joe let go of the tracking line and dove headlong downstream. Mina stood trembling halfway up the hill, scarcely breathing, unable to move.

It seemed to her an eternity before anything happened, anything other than the swift, loud drone of surging water. Then both Job and Joe appeared some twenty yards downstream, close enough to shore that they could stand upright, with Joe holding fast to Job's arm.

Mina sucked in a breath. It was cold and serrated in the back of her throat but she did not care. Job and Joe were alive and well. Everybody was all right. George and Gilbert soon pulled their way back to the side of the canoe, where, with one expert heave, they rolled it right side up. Most of the gear still appeared to be strapped in place.

Suddenly Mina's legs gave out. Her knees buckled and she sat down hard on the side of the hill. She could not stop trembling. What if one of the men had drowned? What if all of them had drowned, and the canoe had drifted away, and she had been left to stand there alone in the wilds of Labrador, a small woman with her cameras and revolver?

"Missus Hubbard!" came Joe's frantic voice. "Missus Hubbard! Where is Missus Hubbard?"

She sprang to her feet and waved her arms back and forth. "I'm here, Joe! Up here! I'm all right!"

The men had nearly drowned and Joe's first thought had been of her. She felt more childish than ever then, awash in guilt for trying to slip away. And at that moment what she felt for the men was unlike any emotion she had ever felt before. She loved those four dripping men down there on the shore, those four men laughing now, slapping each other on the back, all of them soaked to the skin and numb with cold. Those four men were her brothers.

And now she felt responsible for them. She also felt as if she, in trying to slip their protective embrace, had nearly precipitated their deaths. She knew that this was an irrational guilt, that her actions had in no way caused the canoe to capsize or made George and Gilbert step into a hole in the river bottom, yet she could not shake the nagging sting of culpability.

The men were all okay—wet and chilled but otherwise okay—but some of their gear had been lost. Just how much was missing became clear after the canoe was dragged ashore and an inventory was taken. All of the axes were gone, as were all the frying pans, and the extra pole shods George had brought from Missanabie. Plus one pole, one paddle, and the long crooked knife that was so handy for whacking through brush. Two pack straps, one sponge, one tarpaulin and Mina's camp stove. And finally, Job's hat and pipe.

For a few minutes after the inventory was confirmed, everyone stood motionless, staring at the gear spread over the rocks. Then George said, "It's my fault for putting all the axes and pans in the same canoe."

"It's as much my fault as yours," Joe told him.

"We all do the packing," Gilbert said. "We shoulda knowed better."

The men continued to upbraid themselves. Only Job said nothing. His face was pale, eyes vacuous. Mina wanted to go to him, wanted to wrap her arms around his wet shoulders and hold him tight, tell him how sorry she was. She wished George would admonish her for sneaking off as she had, for those few moments of panic she had caused. But he never mentioned it.

George said, "I don't see how we can get by without those axes. We got to have at least one of them."

Nobody refuted him.

"We can't chop wood," he continued. "Which means having to make do with windfalls for our firewood. Plus we couldn't build a shelter now, if it came to that. Can't cut trails through any kind of heavy brush." He shook his head, disgusted with himself. "Without them axes we're just about jiggered."

Again Mina's legs felt wobbly. She would have liked nothing better than to find some shade and lie down a while, talk this situation over with Laddie. But Laddie wasn't there, she could not feel his presence. All she could feel was the fear and weakness in her legs, the throb in her swollen feet, the sting and itch of every single insect bite on her face and neck and hands.

She said, "I can't have us risking our lives unnecessarily."

The men turned their eyes to her.

"As you yourself said, George, it's impossible to go on."

"I didn't say impossible, missus."

"You said we can't get by without the axes."

"What I meant was, we're gonna have to think of some way to make do without them. Mainly I'm just mad at myself."

"You did nothing wrong. None of you did. This is simply the kind of thing that happens out here, isn't it? Wouldn't you say that, Joe?"

"I'm sure we ain't the first ones to upset a canoe. Won't be the last either."

"It's an inherently dangerous place," she said.

With that she gazed down at Job, who had such a look of dejection about him as he sat there on the ground, shivering, hugging his knees.

"I simply won't have it," she said. "I won't put you fine men in danger any longer. Not on my account."

She saw the men exchanging glances. None of them knew what to say to her.

"Why don't you all change into dry clothes," she told them. "We'll build a fire and get you warm, then we can start making our plans for heading back."

She stood very still for a moment, unsure of the response she wanted to hear from them. They said nothing. She decided then that they would not want her with them now in their moment of defeat. She should go off and sit by herself.

It was Gilbert, the boy, whose words brought her retreat to a halt. "I sure hope we don't have to pass them other fellas on the way back out."

The statement was like a hand to the nape of her neck, cold and sharp, pinching.

Then Job said, "Not so bad down there with them fishes, you know. You boys oughta see. They got the prettiest little houses down there. All made outta stone."

Joe chuckled. "You seen them up close, did you?"

"Had my eye right up against one of them's windas. Seen inside real good."

"What was it like in there?" Gilbert asked.

"Oh, they was havin' a tea party, I think. Some such thing. Musta been a dozen of them settin' around a little table and drinkin' from little white cups."

"Did they have their pinkies bent up like this?" Gilbert asked, and raised his right pinkie in the air.

"Fish don't have no pinkies," Job told him.

All the men were laughing now. Each in turn asked Job some question about the fishes' lifestyles, how they kept their tea from mixing with river water, what kinds of chairs they sat in, did they serve biscuits with their tea? And Job had an answer for all of them, even claimed to have been pointed toward the surface by a trout in a railroader's cap.

Mina kept her tremulous smile hidden, her back to the men. The pinch on her neck was fading away. She started walking again.

"We can make do without them axes, missus." It was George who spoke. She turned to face him.

Joe said, "If them fishes can build chairs without axes, we can cut firewood, can't we?"

Gilbert told her, "They don't even have hands or arms. How hard can it be?"

She let her eyes drift from one man's face to the next. Such strong, handsome smiles those men wore. How loyal and brave.

Job told her, "We oughta at least give a try, missus. Only way to know we can do it or not."

It sounded so much like something her husband would have said.

The men's faces began to blur. "All right, Job. We'll give it a try."

And she turned away quickly again. This time, however, there was no ache of sadness in her heart.

"Beyond this point," Mina would later write in her typical understated fashion, "our progress was slow and difficult. There were days when we made less than two miles, and these were the discouraging days for me, because there was ever hanging over me the thought of the necessity of reaching Ungava by the last week in August. . . . However, by poling and tracking, by lifting and dragging the canoe through the shallow waters near the shore, or again by carrying the entire outfit over the sandhills or across boulder-strewn valleys, we won gradually forward."

Frequently they climbed a nearby hill to reconnoitre and choose the most advantageous route. Always their method of travel was dictated by the terrain. The same day might find them slogging through a marsh, then trudging over sandhills, then taking to the canoes for a short paddle to the next set of rapids, then marching through acres of burned-over spruce forest, and finally hiking over a carpet of spongy reindeer moss they were too exhausted to enjoy.

The blue-green moss grew everywhere, on bare boulders and rich soil alike, sometimes to a depth of six inches. When dry and deep it made for cushiony walking, which at first seemed exquisitely soothing but soon tired legs and ankles. When wet the moss was the consistency of jelly, and every bit as easy to tread upon.

Every step was an adventure, every misstep a potential tragedy. Sometimes their path led through forests whose floors were choked with a tangle of rotting limbs, while on every side great dark holes and crevices yawned, some partially or wholly concealed beneath a layer of matted leaves.

All along the way, whether by water or land, mosquitoes and blackflies accompanied them. The flies were tiny things, small enough to crawl through the mesh of the black silk veil Mina wore. Other flies, called bulldogs, were as big as bumblebees and twice as aggressive. On warm nights the interior walls of the tents were black with mosquitoes.

The weather was no more predictable than the terrain. The ground at dawn might be white with frost, yet the noon temperature might soar into the eighties beneath a flawless blue sky, with a shower of icy rain at suppertime.

On the morning of July 6, Mina's party reached a place where the river expanded around a cluster of islands. She described the scene in her book: "Around these islands the river flows with such force and swiftness that the water can be seen to pile up in ridges in the channel." Not only was this an important milestone on their march to Michikamau and the Height of Land, it was also the site of a trapper's tilt owned by Gilbert's older brother, Donald. Each winter the brothers trapped together up the Naskapi Valley, their trapline extending as far as Seal Lake, one hundred miles from the North West River Post.

Tilts like this one, minimalist in construction, were used by trappers as they moved, day by day throughout the season, along their traplines and home again. The door to Donald's tilt was low and narrow and through it came the cabin's only sunlight. There were no windows in the tilt, no floor other than the earth itself. But dangling from the crossbeams were pails filled with rice, beans, flour, lard, and candles.

"Thrown across a beam," Mina wrote, "was a piece of deerskin dressed for making or mending snow-shoes; and on a nail at the farther end was a little seal-skin pouch in which were found needle, thread, and a few buttons. A bunk was built into the side of the room a few feet above the ground, and lying in it an old tent. Beside a medley heap of other things piled there, we found a little Testament and a book of Gospel Songs. The latter the men seemed greatly pleased to find, and carried it away with them. We took the candles also, and filled one pail with lard, leaving one of the pieces of bacon in its place. Already we were regretting that we had no lard or candles with us. They had been cut out of the list when we feared the canoes would not hold all the outfit, and later I had forgotten to add them. The men were hungry for fried cakes, and the lard meant a few of these as a treat now and then."

Gilbert had led the party here with the promise of an axe. But no axe was to be found. He did, however, appropriate a small frying pan and a pail.

Newly provisioned, the party was soon on the move again. They portaged all afternoon over rough ground paralleling the river. Rain fell off and on. Then, toward evening, the rain fell steady and hard, with no indication that it would let up soon. Hurriedly George located a likely spot for their camp.

He called a halt, then instructed Mina to sit on a gear bag so that he could spread the men's tent over her as protection from the rain while her own tent was being set up.

"George's tone of authority was sometimes amusing," Mina wrote. "Sometimes I did as I was told, and then again I did not."

This time she did, though inwardly she chafed at George's protectiveness. Still, she was wet and cold already and therefore inclined to follow his instructions without protest. She only wished the mosquitoes and flies could be so obedient. Or maybe they thought George had invited them under the tent as well, for no sooner had he laid the silk fabric over her head than a few battalions of biting, stinging, buzzing, and droning insects joined her there.

Once her tent was in place, she quickly ducked inside. George knelt at the flap for a moment, watching as she shook the rain from her hair, then ran her fingers over the myriad of throbbing wounds on her face and neck. By touch she scarcely recognized her face; it felt swollen to twice its normal size, every inch home to an itchy welt.

"I wish I had a mirror to see myself right now," she said.

George, bent low while the rain cascaded off his back, said, "Maybe it's a good thing you don't."

She could not help but laugh. Always before, when she had made some disparaging reference to the way she looked, George had assured her that she looked "just right." That he, this time, felt comfortable enough to tell her the truth made Mina blush with pleasure.

In the past she had been a woman prone to blushing, shy and self-effacing, easily embarrassed. But that seemed a long time ago now. When was the last time she had blushed so warmly? Aboard the *Harlow*, the night she encountered Wallace on the deck. But the

heat of that blush, the glow of cold anger, had been far less warming than this latest one.

"I'm pretty frightening, am I?" she said.

George shrugged. "You always look just right to me." And then,
perhaps realizing the implications of his statement, George
blushed too.

With each day Mina's respect and admiration for the men in her
party increased. They were, she wrote:

> gentle and considerate, not only of me but of each other as well. They
> had jolly good times together, and withal were most efficient. Gilbert
> was proving a great worker, and enjoyed himself much with the men.
> He was just a merry, happy-hearted boy. Joe was quiet and thought-
> ful, with a low, rather musical voice, in a pretty, soft Scotch accent, for
> all his Russian name. He spoke English quite easily and well. Job did
> not say much in English. He was very reserved where I was concerned.
> I wanted to ask him a thousand questions, but I did not dare. George
> was always the gentle, fun-loving, sunny-tempered man my husband
> admired.

Mina was finding it increasingly difficult to think of George
without, a moment later, thinking of her husband. The two men
had become linked somehow. And not only because George had
accompanied Laddie on the first trip. Not only because George's
loyalty to Laddie and his sense of guilt over Laddie's death had not
permitted him to refuse to accompany Mina on this trip. George
was every bit as kind to her as Laddie had been, and even more
solicitous of her comfort.

One evening, while the other men prepared dinner, George sat
by the campfire in a light rain and mended Mina's moccasin where
a mouse had eaten through it the previous night. She had not
asked him to do this, had not even pointed out the hole to any-

body. She had removed her moccasins and was sitting there warming her stocking feet near the fire when George pointed to one of the moccasins and asked if he could have a look at it. After she handed it to him he pulled a needle and thread from his pocket and set to work. Later, wanting to do more, he offered to sew her moleskin pouch to her leather belt for safekeeping. Mina protested, but only weakly. Sometimes, as on this night, she enjoyed being tended to. George wanted to take care of her, and she had to admit that sometimes, when troubling thoughts did not intrude, she basked in his attention.

Later she described the incident in her book:

*He finished putting the pouch on, and handed the belt back to me with a satisfied smile. Instead of taking it I only laughed at him, when he discovered he had put the pistol-holster and knife sheath on wrong-side first. There was no help for it, it had to come off again, for the sheaths would not fit over either buckle or pouch. I comforted him with the assurance that it was good he should have something to do to keep him out of mischief. When the mistake was remedied he showed me how to make a rabbit-snare. Then the rain drove me to my tent again.*

The passage ends with the tantalizingly oblique observation, "It was horrid to eat in the tent alone."

But the time alone gave her time to think, time to contemplate why she had come to Labrador in the first place, what she should and should not be doing. And the next day, as the party portaged through especially heavy brush, with the men hurrying ahead to reach calmer water, Mina felt herself weighted down by her thoughts, and could not keep up with the others. Again and again George asked her to hand him her rifle—the only thing other than her cameras that she was ever permitted to carry.

"Thank you, no," she said.

"You will be able to walk faster without it."

"If I am moving too slowly for you, George, go on ahead with the others."

"Just let me carry your rifle for you."

"No thank you!"

Finally, in frustration, he simply reached for it, moved to lift it off her shoulder. She spun toward him, eyes alight with defiance. He lifted his hand away, then backed away from her and looked at the ground until she turned and strode forward again.

In the next moment her anger vanished. How could she treat him so harshly? It wasn't George who made her angry, not really. It was her own confused emotions.

Her diary entry for July 16 illuminates her emotional turmoil:

*Oh, what this trip would be if he were here. I have to keep reminding myself that the hills he is climbing now must be so much grander and more beautiful to escape an ever-recurring feeling that it is wicked for me to be here when he is not and Oh how desperately hungry and desolate and sad. . . . I never dreamed it could be so splendid. And the grander and more beautiful it grows, the more I hunger for the one who made all things beautiful. . . .*

*Dillon Wallace's expedition, July 17, 1905*

AT THE HOUR OF DUSK, after an arduous day of tracking their canoes through icy rapids, then portaging over slippery boulders, sometimes climbing hills to scout ahead, Wallace and his crew were portaging their outfit through a strength-sucking marsh, sunk to their knees in muck, every footstep a Herculean effort. A wind out of the west drove pricking sheets of rain into their faces.

The men had been grumbling for days, complaining about the incessant hordes of insects, the weather, the insufficient rations, the lack of fresh meat. Only Duncan McLean, who had initially agreed to accompany the party as far as Seal Lake, had grown silent, even withdrawn. Wallace, struggling with a heavy load of gear on his back, fell behind the others so as to walk beside Duncan.

"I'm willing to bet the Indians don't take this route," Wallace said with a sheepish grin. It had been he, after all, who, after scouting the rapids, had laid out their present, unfortunate course.

"Not after they'd been here once or twice."

"I imagine you're looking forward to getting home soon."

"It's been on my mind. Yes sir, it has."

Wallace nodded. "Can you stick with us as far as Lake Nipishish? We'll hit it for sure tomorrow or the next day."

"I can do that," Duncan answered.

"We'll have more water after that. Plus fewer and easier portages. Then on to the Height of Land."

"I reckon that's right."

"The only thing that could slow us down after that is the weather."

"You can never tell about it, that's for sure."

They walked in silence a while. Then Wallace said, "I'd be grateful if you could take some letters back with you. Post them for us at Groswater Bay. I would very much like for my sisters to know that I'm getting along all right."

"I'm sure they'll be happy to hear from you."

"I'll start on those letters as soon as I get the chance. And I'll tell the other men to do the same."

Duncan slapped at a mosquito and bloodied it against his neck, then picked off the little corpse and flicked it away.

"It always makes me feel better to write to my sisters," Wallace said. He had done little complaining of his own on the trip, thought it unwise for the expedition leader to voice the slightest misgiving or reveal any breach in his confidence. But now, knowing that

Duncan would be leaving soon, he felt some of his reserve begin to slip away. He looked out across the wide expanse of marsh. Beyond it stood the black spears of a burned-over forest.

"It really is a godforsaken place up here, isn't it?" he said.

"Some of it is. Yes, sir, for sure some of it is."

"But you like it in Labrador all the same."

"Because it's home to me. It's the place I know. Just gets into your blood, I guess."

Wallace thought about his own home then, thought about warm, dry rooms and dry shoes and dry socks. He thought about his cozy office, where he smoked his pipe and sat at the window and looked out upon the city. He thought about the restaurants he liked and the dishes they served, the great heaping platters of beef and the baskets of rolls and the bowls of sweet butter. And sweets—how he missed his puddings and cakes!

And he thought about Hubbard, that uncomplaining, indomitable man. Two years earlier on this same date, Wallace and Hubbard and Elson had barely been on their way but had already made two disastrous mistakes. At the North West River Post, where they intended to purchase a gill net, they had been informed, just as they had been in Rigolet, that no nets were available.

And so, with only a worn-out net salvaged from the post, they had begun on that July 15 what Wallace later described as their "plunge into the wild." Shortly after one o'clock that day they had reached the upper end of Grand Lake and entered what they thought was the Naskapi River. They had a mile of easy paddling; then, soon after,

> the water was so swift and shoal that we could take only a part of the outfit in the canoe, which meant that we had to return at intervals for the rest and track all the way, Hubbard pulling on the line while George and I waded and pushed. Sometimes we were scarcely knee deep in the water, and at other times we would sink up to our armpits.

*Frequently we were swept off our feet.... The work was awful, it was heartrending.*

Even more onerous, though, were the hordes of blackflies that attacked them. "They got into our nostrils, into our ears, into our mouths, into our eyes even, and our faces and hands were streaked with blood from their bites. They were villainous, hellish."

The river, of course, was not the Naskapi but the Susan, a fact Hubbard would never learn. And with that sudden, enervating remembrance, the grief hit Wallace again, coming out of nowhere like a great black-winged bird swooping down: Hubbard is gone. Hubbard was gone, and Jennie was gone, and there was nobody waiting for him back in the city. Here he was, knee-deep in a marsh on his second plunge into the wild, again being eaten alive by insects, and he was unremittingly alone. Yes, Labrador truly was a godforsaken place. But was New York City any better?

His next footstep was the hardest of the trip. He could not extricate his boot from the muck, could not lift it clear. And finally, with a soft moan, a sound he had not meant to make, he came to a halt.

Duncan McLean looked back. "You all right, Mr. Wallace?"

Wallace blinked. Perspiration dripped from his forehead. His feet were numb with cold. "Sometimes," he said, "I . . ." But he would not allow himself to finish. What good would it do?

"I just need a moment to get my breath."

Duncan waited beside him. "We'll likely be out of here soon."

But on this point, Wallace knew, Duncan was wrong. Wallace would never be out of Labrador, no matter where he lived. Labrador would hold him its prisoner forever.

———

*Mina Hubbard's expedition, third week of July 1905*

IN A SMALL CLEARING a few hundred yards from the river, Joe and Job and Gilbert dropped their loads on a bed of moss. They waited several minutes for George and Mina to catch up. After they had, Joe asked, "How's this for tonight's camp?"

"Suits me," George said, and he slipped off the heavy pack.

"We'll bring the rest of the outfit forward," Joe said. He and Gilbert and Job retraced their steps to where they had left the canoes and the remaining gear.

George studied the surroundings. A sparse line of trees ran across the centre of a hill approximately a quarter-mile away. He told Mina, "I bet if we climb that rise there we can look back and see how far we've come."

A half-hour later she and George stood together atop the hill. The sun was slowly sinking toward the western horizon, a magnificent orange glow spreading out from it—reaching toward us, she thought. In the opposite direction lay Seal Lake, winding like a broad river between the hills. Its calm surface caught and held the orange of the sun, glimmered and sparkled. In every direction there were blue hills and, between them, more lakes. From the distance it seemed a fairyland, impossibly beautiful.

"It's been three weeks less a day since we left the North West River Post," George told her. "We've come a hundred and fifteen miles, more or less. It won't be long before we get to Michikamau."

Something welled up in Mina's chest then, a mixture of pride and something else, so heavy in her chest she could not speak.

George pointed to a low ridge of mountains to the southwest. "Over there is where I crossed with Mr. Hubbard. You see that little opening? I think that's where we crossed over from the head of Beaver Brook."

Her voice was hoarse and throaty. "What are those mountains called, George?"

"I don't know that they have a name."

"Then I shall call them the Lion Heart Mountains."

He nodded. It was a good name.

She gazed at the mountains, blue and snow-capped, awhile longer. Finally she turned slowly to take in the entire panorama, where she had been, where Laddie had gone, and where she was headed. "It's almost all too beautiful," she said.

He understood, and said nothing.

"Do you think there will ever be a time," she asked, "when the beauty will cease to bring pain?"

He would have liked to tell her yes, and to mean it. But there was nothing he could say.

Monday morning began with an early breakfast. Then, as always during a portage, the men allowed Mina her privacy in camp while they carried the first loads forward. By the time they returned for the final load, she was ready to join them.

Mina thought this a glorious morning, awash with full, unbroken sunlight, the sky clear and the wind still—a combination of elements not often enjoyed in those latitudes. Their trail led down into a valley enclosed on three sides by steep hills. The hills were covered with the sombre green of spruce trees, but here and there the white bark of a birch glimmered. Above the treeline the hills were bare and windblown, their faces sometimes sheared down to nothing but stone walls and cliffs.

The valley opened before them in a widening corridor toward Seal Lake, their destination, a point of golden light in the far distance. For the most part the party hiked without speaking. The morning itself was hushed and wordless, so that the only sounds were of the singing rapids and the trill, now and then, of a small bird.

Finally they reached a place where the rapids were not so fierce. "The boys can take the canoes through these," George told her. "You and me will walk on ahead some."

But Mina had had enough of walking for a while. She studied the rapids. "If the boys can ride through them safely, why shouldn't I?"

"Nobody said they was perfectly safe."

"Then perhaps we should all continue to portage."

"It's safe enough for the boys, is what I meant."

"And why not safe enough for me as well?"

"They have experience with rapids."

"And how am I to gain experience if you won't let me near one?"

George turned to the other men for help. But all three just stood there grinning at him.

He turned his back to them and stepped closer to Mina. Softly he told her, "I could never forgive myself if anything was to happen to you."

"Well, then," she said with a smile, and briefly touched a fingertip to his cheek, "allow me to absolve you in advance."

With that she strode toward the shoreline and the waiting canoes. "Where shall I ride?"

Joe cut a quick look at George, read the expression of surrender on George's face and told her, "You can ride with me and Job if you like, missus." With a challenging grin cast in George's direction, he added, "We're the ones know the most about handling the rapids."

George came forward. "Let Job go with Gilbert this time. I'll ride with you and Missus Hubbard."

Within minutes the canoe was launched. Immediately a wave broke against the bow and splashed all the way back to George in the stern. Mina, seated in the centre, gasped as the cold slapped her face. Joe turned to look at her, his eyebrows arched.

"Oh, it's fine," she told him. "It's fine! Go on!"

The men dug in hard with their poles, driving the canoe through the waves. Up a wave and down into a trough, then thrust up again, the bow being pushed to the side, corrected by Joe, then tossed up again with a splash, then splashing down. Mina gripped her seat and sat low, huddled tightly, breathing in short gasps and exhalations. The buffeting lasted only a few minutes before the rapids faded, by which time her face was shiny wet. The second canoe pulled alongside and Gilbert called out, "How'd you like the ride, Missus Hubbard?"

"Oh, I liked it fine, Gil! It was exhilarating!"

She turned on her seat to flash a smile at George, but when she saw the strain in his face she lost all desire to tease or gloat. The short ride had obviously been an ordeal for him. He had not only fought the waves and the current, but with every ounce of strength he had been willing the canoe to stay upright, keeping Mina glued to her seat. With every jounce and slip of the canoe he had wanted to reach out and grab her, have her safely in his grasp should the canoe capsize. The effort of not doing so had utterly drained him.

So all she said was, "Thank you for letting me experience that, George."

It took him a while to find enough breath for words. "You're welcome, missus."

Not long after that they came to another set of rapids, these too rough for any of the party to brave. During the portage, which took them along a well-worn bear trail over white moss, George told her, "I've seen men couldn't handle rapids the way you did back there."

"Really, George? Did I do all right?"

"Lots of men would've jumped out of their canoes rather than go through those places."

"They weren't very big rapids, though."

"Nearly as big as we can handle."

"Honestly?"

"I wouldn't want to tackle any much bigger."

"Does that mean I can ride them with you from now on?"

He laughed softly. "I don't suppose I've got much choice, seeing as how I just said what I did."

"You weren't lying, were you?"

"I wouldn't ever tell you a lie, missus. You can count on that."

So many of their moments lately seemed to call for a touch of some kind, her hand on his arm, her fingers squeezing his. But he was two steps behind her, a heavy pack on his back, his rifle in his hands. So she merely kept on walking. Still, the connection felt unfinished.

After a while she spoke again. "You know, George, climbing that hill yesterday and looking back the way we did, and seeing how far we've already come, and then running those rapids with you and the men, all of us in it together for a change . . . I almost feel like an explorer finally."

"It's what you are," he told her.

"Yes, but . . . This is your expedition, really. You've always been the one in charge."

"You're the only one thinks that, missus. This is your trip start to finish. Always has been."

Again she felt the need for contact, and slowed just a bit, hoping he might come up close to her, put out his hand, touch her shoulder, turn her around. But he slowed too and stayed a full pace behind. And she thought, maybe he's leaving me in charge of *that* as well.

Seal Lake was a mile wide where they entered it, but as they moved northward the shorelines drew closer, widened again, then grew closer. On both sides the ground sloped up toward hills of solid rock, some standing monolithic and sharp. One, named Mount Pisa, leaned toward the east. The surrounding countryside had been burned over years earlier, but white birch and alder had regrown from the shorelines to the cliffs. Close to the shores were numerous small islands and sandy hummocks covered with grass.

All along the way they saw geese, ducks, gulls, and muskrats. A family of seals, lounging on the sunny rocks near an island, slipped into the water at the canoes' approach, then watched curiously with only their round dark eyes and black heads visible as the canoes glided past.

Near the northern end of the lake a long arm of water reached some thirty miles to the west. But just ahead to the north lay the opening to the Naskapi River again. Here the hills were low and less rugged, but the river, as it turned southwest toward Lake Michikamau, was fierce and foaming.

By seven P.M., when they pulled ashore, they had made seventeen miles that day. "A good day's travellin'," Gilbert said.

George hopped out of the canoe and held it steady as Mina disembarked. He said, "We've been making good time."

Mina was proud of their accomplishment, but also concerned. "Do you think anyone has done better?"

Gilbert, Joe, and George all spoke at once, a chorus of protests. When they fell silent, she turned to the laconic Job. "Do you agree with the others?" she asked.

"We doin' fine," Job told her. "Wallace nowhere around."

"From your lips to God's ear," she said.

Mina did not sleep much Monday night, tormented by mosquitoes and the drone of troubling thoughts. The walls and ceilings of her tent were thick with insects. Though she huddled inside her blankets and veil, the pests could not be kept at bay. They pricked at her through the veil, crawled into her clothing, slithered under the tops of her stockings. Finally she gave up trying to sleep and, knowing that a candle for reading or writing would only call greater hordes of insects to her tent, embarked upon a systematic extermination of her tormenters, squishing them one by one until her fingers were slippery with blood.

She could smell the smoke from the men's pipes and she hoped they were faring better in the other tent. But if they were sitting up smoking, they too must be unable to sleep.

Around four she heard one of the men moving about outside. She peeked out of her tent and saw Joe building up the fire. By the time she had dressed for the day, the other men were moving about as well, all sleepy and silent and many times bitten.

But before they had finished breakfast the rain came, a hard, unrelenting downpour driven by winds that would have made paddling impossible. They had no choice but to return to their tents and hope the shower would pass quickly.

The rain continued without relief until Wednesday morning, nine A.M. At the first sign of clearing they took to their canoes. Now, finally, the men had something to do, and the effort of paddling up a swift river brought smiles to their faces again. They rode another nineteen miles that day, even with a few pauses for shooting, which added a partridge, two geese, and a muskrat to their larder.

But the good day was not to be soon repeated. Thursday brought another deluge of rain and wind. Despite these conditions, the men could sit still no longer. Around noon Job went off to climb a steep rise they had named Red Rock Hill. Mina, who spent the day reading, writing, and occasionally napping in her tent, heard the other men moving about and talking in low voices outside. When Joe called her to supper she finally saw what they had been up to all day. They had strung up a tarpaulin so that it not only protected the fire but provided ample space for all to sit out of the rain. The ground beneath the tarp was dry and fragrant, covered with a lush blanket of fresh wood shavings.

"What a lovely place you've made!" she said.

"You can't eat fresh goose in a buggy tent," Joe told her.

She was both humbled and flattered by the way the men took care of her. They did so, she knew, not because she was their employer but because they truly cared about her. There was no drama or ulterior motive to their affection; it was quiet and unassuming and real. Each of the men was as tough as a river stone, hardened by his life, but they were some of the kindest and gentlest men she had ever known. There was little anger in any of them and not the slightest trace of malice.

She remembered the way Wallace had described the Labrador natives in his book—as mostly uncouth Indians and half-breeds, incapable of doing much more than following the simplest of directions. Those descriptions were an embarrassment to her. Caspar

Whitney had harboured even harsher sentiments for Indians and had often made his low regard for them known. How was it, she wondered, that her own experience, and Laddie's, had been so different from the others'?

Because kindness begets kindness, she told herself. And contempt begets contempt.

Just in time for goose, Job returned from his long hike up Red Rock Hill. He was soaked to the skin and carrying a pound of mud on each pantleg. Mina asked him, "What was it like up there, Job?"

"Like bein' in the clouds."

Gilbert asked, "Did you see any angels?"

"Seen one. But she just passin' through."

"Can't you at least tell us what she looked like?"

"Looked like girl I knew back home. Only better."

The men laughed and nodded. The goose was too delicious to be shared with conversation, its skin crisp and smoky and dripping with grease, the dark meat buttery in their mouths. They also had flatbread fried in lard, and strong tea sweetened with sugar.

When nothing remained of the goose but a pile of bones to be boiled for broth in the morning, George said, "Did you see anything useful up on that hill, Job?"

"Two rapids up ahead," Job answered. "Then a little lake."

"How far to the rapids?"

"Two mile, maybe."

The rain continued without a break through the next afternoon. After lunch beneath the tarpaulin, George told Mina, "The boys all want to go climb that hill. Get a good look where we're headed."

"That's a fine idea. Just let me change into my boots."

"Oh no, missus," Job said. "Hill too steep for you. Too slippery."

"Nonsense. I'll be fine, won't I, George?"

George looked uneasy. "Job said it wasn't an easy climb, not even for him. There are lots of places where a person could fall off and get hurt."

"A person?" she said. "Or a helpless little woman like me?"

George lowered his eyes. "I'd just rather you didn't try it."

"Well, I am not going to sit here all day with the rain and the mosquitoes while you men have all the fun." Then she had an idea. "You can take me up the rapids, George!"

"That'd be no less dangerous than climbing the hill! With just me paddling we'll turn over for sure."

"I could go with you," Gilbert said.

But Mina had other ideas. "No, you go climb the hill with the men. George will take me up *to* the rapids. We can go at least that far, can't we, without placing my life in jeopardy?"

The way she looked at George when she said this, her eyes sparkling with firelight and the corners of her mouth turned up in challenge, he felt a fluttering in his chest.

"You needn't look so frightened," she teased. "I have no intention of throwing myself into the rapids. But to just sit here and swat mosquitoes all day? How ignominious is that for a famous explorer such as myself?"

She was baiting him, and all the men knew it. George knew it too. And to think that she had turned down Gilbert's offer to accompany them, right in front of everybody! It took George's breath away.

The first set of rapids proved to be nearly three miles above their camp. It swung toward them around a high sandy point that extended a third of the way into the river. South of this point was a little bay, and there George landed the canoe. Afterward he and Mina approached the rapids by foot. The rocks scattered along the shore were in various shades of red and green and blue. Mina stooped to pick up a small green one, a smooth oval speckled with brown. "It looks just like a bird's egg," she said. "See how pretty, George?"

"Put it in your pocket for good luck."

"Can a stone bring good luck?"

"Anything beautiful can. Put it in your pocket and let's find out."

She did so. "We've had good luck so far, haven't we? Do you think it will last?"

"Now that you've got your good luck stone, it will."

A few minutes later they stood together on a flat rock under which the rapids surged and chortled. "They look so wild and fine," Mina said. "I feel almost giddy standing so close to them like this."

"That's what I told you about getting dizzy and falling in."

"I can see how it might happen. It could happen to me now." With that she leaned forward as if losing her balance.

George lunged toward her, but she turned to him, smiling, just before he grabbed her arm, and he stopped himself short.

"Don't you want to save me?" she asked.

"You're only teasing me now."

"But I could tumble in at any moment. Don't you at least want to take hold of my hand, just to be safe?" And she offered her hand to him.

"What if you pull us both in?" he asked.

"Do you think I might?"

Instead of answering immediately he only looked into her eyes. They were wild and fine too, and every bit as dizzying as the rapids. Looking at her like that did something to his balance, made the world seem to tilt beneath him.

"I'd rather we both went in," he told her, "than let you go in alone."

It was late when they returned to camp, past sunset, and the men, having long ago returned from climbing Red Rock Hill, had cleaned up, prepared a supper of four partridges, and begun to worry.

"It was hard paddling against that current," George told them as explanation for his and Mina's late arrival.

But the men noticed how quiet Mina was all through supper, and how George kept his eyes lowered, staring at the fire, so the

men were mostly silent too, and only smiled to one another across
the dance of flames.

The rain continued through Saturday but in the afternoon it
showed signs of coming to an end, and Mina's party, restless to be
on the move, took to their canoes. By evening the rain had ceased
and they enjoyed their first dry camp in several days.

Next morning they agreed that they should take advantage of
the dry weather and forego their Sunday rest. As the canoes were
being reloaded, Gilbert happened to look far ahead where the river
widened into a small lake. He saw a dark shape moving across the
water. "What is that?" he asked.

The others looked up. Before they could follow Gilbert's gaze,
he cried out, "It's a deer!"

In a flash the last of the gear was tossed into the canoes and
tied down. Mina quickly climbed aboard. Too excited to fiddle
with the knot that held the canoe tied to a willow, George
whipped out his knife and slashed through the rope. In seconds
both canoes were plunging toward the lake, the men digging in
hard with their paddles, lifting and driving the slender crafts with
every stroke.

"He seems too far away," Mina said.

But the canoes closed quickly. The caribou, which they could
soon identify as a stag, was swimming toward the north shore, fighting the current just as the canoes were. George reached for his rifle,
slammed a bullet into place, took careful aim, and fired.

Mina saw the bullet's splash a yard or so in front of the caribou,
and she secretly breathed a sigh of relief. Fresh meat would have
been a welcome treat but their provisions were in no danger of running out and she did not share the men's thrill in hunting and
killing. She understood that thrill but she did not share it.

Her relief, however, was short-lived. She soon realized that
George's intention with that first shot had not been to hit the

caribou but to turn it from shore before it could bound away to freedom. And the ploy worked perfectly. The caribou swung east, its thick neck and heavy head ploughing forward with short, plunging movements.

The animal was broadside to the current now, and its pace slowed even more. Soon the canoes were a mere twenty yards from overtaking it. George laid the rifle aside and pulled his revolver from its holster. He stretched out his arm and sighted along the barrel. Mina pulled her hat down over her eyes, leaned forward, doubling over, and clamped her hands over her ears.

She jumped a little in her seat when the revolver barked. She expected to hear the men cheering, but when they did not she looked up. The stag was still ploughing toward shore. Thank goodness! Mina thought. Then she saw the dark stain spreading out alongside the animal, the blood streaming from its neck, the terror in its round, dark eye.

"Oh, George, please," she said. "Use your rifle this time. Please put an end to it."

He did so, and a few seconds later the animal stopped swimming. One last stroke of the paddles and Job had the stag by its antlers. Its legs no longer churned the water.

"Is it dead?" Mina asked.

"It is," George said.

"Please make sure it's dead, Job. It isn't fair that it should suffer."

"No suffer," Job told her. "No feel nothing any more."

A rope was looped and tightened around the stag's head and the animal was towed to shore. Mina spent the next hour sitting alone, well upwind of the men, as they gutted, skinned, and butchered the stag. The meat was cut up and packed in waterproof bags. George washed the hide clean in the river, wrung it dry and folded it as neatly as he could and stowed it in the bow of the canoe. He washed his hands and forearms and then he walked upshore to Mina.

"Two hundred fifty pounds of fresh meat," he told her.

"I suppose it's a good thing," she said. "I just can't stop thinking of how fine he would have looked bounding over the hills."

"We need fresh meat for energy, though."

"I know. I only feel bad for the caribou."

"Life through death," he said quietly. "That's how it works out here."

"I know." She looked up at him and smiled.

She climbed to her feet, brushed the dirt off the back of her skirt. "I know you have to kill animals to keep us fed. I'll try not to mind so much in the future."

"Don't be anything but what you are," George answered. Then he turned away quickly, blushing, and without waiting for her he returned to the canoes.

They made good time all the rest of that day, moving upriver through one small lake expansion after another. The mountains on each side were barren of trees, with sharp, craggy faces of naked rock. From lake to lake there was no telling which way the river might turn next or what lay ahead.

Toward sunset they were moving smoothly across another small lake when George tapped her shoulder. When she turned, he pointed to the northeast. There, approximately eighty yards ahead, the river appeared to be gushing into the lake out of a large hole in the side of the mountain.

"We might as well find a good place to camp," George told her. "We'll be portaging in the morning."

"And now with an extra two hundred fifty pounds of meat to carry," she said.

"Two-forty maybe. I'll make us a nice roast tonight."

And he did just that. The block of meat was seared in the skillet until the outside was crusted black, the centre pink and sweet.

Mina told the men, "I'm almost ashamed to admit how much I'm enjoying this."

"Why ashamed?" Gilbert asked.

"Because I was secretly hoping that George would miss when he was shooting today."

Joe said, "Even George couldn't miss from that distance."

They laughed and chewed and continued shaving away at the roast until the skillet was empty.

That night, before turning in, Mina went to the river to wash her face and hands. George soon left his seat and followed her. He knelt a yard or so from her and splashed water over his face. As always, he kept glancing her way out of the corner of his eye.

But tonight she did not mind his overprotectiveness. Tonight she felt the warmth of it, the depth of his affection. When she had finished washing she sat back against the rocks and gazed into the night sky. Directly overhead, three long fingers of blue-green light were reaching tremulously toward the centre of the sky, fluttering like banners in the wind. All around them was a misty glow of white and pale orange, it too gently undulating, bathing the river and the campsite in soft luminescence.

"The northern lights are so beautiful tonight," she said.

"The Indians claim it's from the glow of lanterns carried by spirits as they lead the new dead into heaven."

"Somewhere in the Bible it's described as 'horsemen charging in mid-air, clad in garments interwoven with gold.'"

"I've not seen them any prettier than they are right now," George said.

After a few minutes he stood and walked toward her and stood there looking at the camp some thirty yards away. He and Mina could see the two tents pitched well behind the fire, could see Joe and Job and Gilbert seated in a half-circle, sucking on their pipes. Neither Mina nor George was in a hurry to join them again.

"Do you know what's strange?" she asked.

"What, missus?"

"I don't feel lonely any more."

"You're getting used to the place."

"I know that everyone at home would expect me to feel lonely out here. And maybe I should still. Maybe it's wrong that I don't."

He lowered himself to his haunches, sat there gently rocking back and forth. He said, "I don't see how it could be wrong. I really don't."

They sat without speaking for a while. She looked over at him once and caught him looking at her. She smiled, then turned away. He imagined then that she would stand and say good night and return to her tent. But she gave no indication of wishing to be anywhere but where she was.

"I think I feel less homeless here than I ever have, ever since Laddie went away."

George felt something thickening in his throat. He tried to swallow it down.

"I never imagined I could really do this. It's only now beginning to seem as if we might."

"He'd be mighty proud of you, that's for sure."

"He'd be proud of you too, George."

"I hope so. I don't always know."

"Oh, I know he would. The way you've taken care of me, and how kind and gentle and brave you always are."

George looked up at the northern lights. He could think of nothing to say, no words to express the confusion he felt.

For just a moment she leaned close to him. "Let's not feel bad, George," she whispered. "Let's not feel bad about anything."

And a moment later she was walking back toward camp. He watched her go into her tent and light her candle and tie shut the flap. He remained on the shore a while longer, alone with the northern lights and the river and the jumble of his thoughts.

———

*Dillon Wallace's expedition, July 20, 1905*

THURSDAY WAS A COLD, WET DAY. Not a pleasant day for travelling, especially over rough, broken ground that showed no sign of the Indian trail. Even so, Wallace decided that his crew should make an early start, considering how slow their progress had been of late. By his reckoning, based on a series of lakes he had spotted the day before from a hilltop, they were not far from Lake Nipishish, which, he had been told back at the North West River Post, was nearly halfway to Seal Lake.

"Stanton and I will go ahead with our packs while the rest of you break camp," he said. "We'll mark our trail for you. If we all move quickly we can make up a bit of lost time."

Stanton gobbled down the last of his breakfast of fried trout, bread, and tea. Seemed like he was always hungry these days and never got the chance to fill his belly. And when he shrugged on his heavy pack the straps bit into his skin as they did every morning, chafing him raw even through his clothing, rubbing new blisters or breaking open old ones.

The first half-hour of these hikes was always the hardest for Stanton. Until the body settled into its rhythm, walking felt awkward and stiff, his body off balance. If the pack rode too high it threatened to topple him forward, splat onto his face. And if it rode too low it put excessive strain on his shoulders, pulling his spine into a concave curve. In either case the mere effort of putting one foot in front of the other felt unnatural—like a vaudevillian striding across the stage in a hurricane-force wind.

Add to this that the mosquitoes and blackflies gave a man no peace. They swarmed to the scent of sweat, which, if you had not bathed in several days, was strong. And in all likelihood your feet were soon wet, soaked through, and the cuffs of your trousers hung heavy with mud.

For the first half-hour or so you fought against all this and in doing so made yourself acutely aware of every discomfort. Only by focusing on other matters—keeping a keen eye on the dim and sinuous trail, for example—could you continue through the day with numbed detachment.

Stanton had not yet reached that state of detachment when he realized that he could no longer hear Wallace's footsteps ahead of him. No snap of branches, no rhythmic squish of boots on wet ground. He looked up from the trail, blinked, cocked his ear. Wallace was nowhere to be seen or heard. Stanton turned this way and that, gradually completing a full circle, taking only a step at a time before pausing to scan for some sign that he was not alone.

Wallace was supposed to be breaking a branch now and then to mark the trail, or, when necessary, using his long knife to hack away at the brush. But Stanton could find no indication that he wasn't the first man to pass through these woods. Worse yet, when he looked down he was not entirely convinced that he had been following the trail at all. There seemed to be a path here, but had it been made by man or animal? Was he lost, or was Wallace?

He considered calling out to Wallace, maybe firing off a shot or two. But the ribbing he would take from the others was sure to be something awful. Just last night he and Richards and McLean had gone fishing only to lose their bearings on their return to camp. The laugh they had got when they finally came straggling in was not something Stanton wished to suffer again.

He felt certain he could find the trail on his own. That done, he would move in double time to catch up with Wallace. And not even Wallace would be the wiser.

Another half-hour came and went. Stanton followed one vague path after another, none more distinct than a slender suggestion of trampled moss or grass. He finally had no choice but to admit defeat and fire his rifle in the air.

Immediately there came back a shout, which he answered. The voice boomed again—"Halloooo!" It was Easton's voice. Back and forth the men called, with Stanton zeroing in on the sound like a hound on a rabbit. It wasn't long before he heard the rumble of rushing water. Then he stepped into a clearing. He was back at camp. The men had extinguished the fire and repacked the gear and had been just about to set off on the trail when Stanton's rifle shots had halted them. Now they were all standing there looking in his direction, each of them grinning like a Cheshire cat.

Stanton, blushing fiercely, walked back into camp. "Don't even say it," he told them.

And the men broke into a chorus of howls.

What worried Stanton most, however, was what Wallace might say. It had become obvious to the entire party that Wallace was increasingly irritated by their lack of progress. Thus far they had spent more time looking for the trail than following it. Hard rains had kept them huddled in camp for days at a time. Ravenous insects were turning their bodies into masses of swollen, pulsing sores. And provisions were running low despite the bushels of fish they routinely caught.

The men were eating like horses, no question about it. Yet they were constantly hungry. They expended more energy in a single muddy mile than would have been required for an all-day hike over solid ground.

As it turned out, Stanton need not have feared Wallace's reaction. Early that afternoon, when they finally caught up with him, he was coming back in their direction. "Did you find the rifle?" was the first thing he said.

Easton asked, "What rifle?"

Wallace admitted, with apologies, that at some time that day Richards' rifle, which Wallace had been carrying, had fallen from his pack. "It must have slipped out onto soft ground. Or else I would have heard it."

"We didn't know to be looking for it," Richards said. "We'll just double back. It's got to be along the trail somewhere."

Wallace was then forced to admit that he had found and lost the trail on several occasions, and had wandered about, zigzagging through the brush, trying to locate it again. So there was no telling where the rifle lay. To make matters worse, the rifle wasn't even Richards' personal property; it had been borrowed from one of Wallace's friends. And it was a brand new rifle to boot.

They searched for two hours, creeping along, spread out in a line. Finally, exhausted, Wallace called a halt. "We might as well camp right here, fellas. The light's no good any more. We'll look again tomorrow."

To Stanton's mind the day could not have gone any worse. But at least, he thought, the comedy of errors was over until tomorrow. Now they could sit down to supper and then relax with their pipes for a while.

Unfortunately, supper brought more unhappy news. Duncan McLean, they were reminded, would be leaving the party soon, returning home to his family. So they should have their letters ready for him to take back to civilization. He planned to hike straight across country to the junction of the Red and Naskapi Rivers, where he had left his boat.

Stanton asked, "How long do you figure it will take you?"

"I'll keep to the high ridges," Duncan said. "Walking's easier there. About two days' walk, I figure."

Two days! Stanton could not believe his ears, nor could he shake the sensation those words evoked in him, the utter heaviness that flooded through him, the wash of something very close to defeat. Two days to the junction of the Red and Naskapi. Two days of easy walking.

He knew what Wallace would say if he expressed his dismay. That their objective was not to win a foot race but to follow the Indian trail and to map the river valley. Besides, Wallace would say, with fifteen hundred pounds of gear and canoes to carry, how could they move as quickly as Duncan would alone, even if they wanted to? Still, the knowledge of how few miles they had covered nagged at Stanton. Their own expedition, bogged down by mud and plagued by mosquitoes and icy rains and trails that were impossible to find, had used up two full weeks in covering the same distance.

*Mina Hubbard's expedition, fourth week of July 1905*

IT HAD CROSSED MINA'S MIND more than once that maybe the mosquitoes and blackflies were God's way of keeping her from enjoying herself too much, a constantly buzzing, biting, stinging, maddening reminder that this was not a pleasure trip.

The insects on the night of July 27 were the worst ever. Her party had camped for the evening on the shore of a small lake after a paddle of only three and a half miles. From noon on the twenty-fifth until mid-afternoon of the twenty-seventh they had been waylaid by illness, with all the men except Job too sick to travel, all suffering from the change of diet—too much caribou meat. Finally they had moved ahead a short distance to this last lake in a group of four, but no sooner had they gathered for supper than a dense cloud of insects descended on them.

To settle the men's stomachs Job made a venison broth thickened with a little flour. It smelled delicious, but every time Mina raised her silk veil to put the spoon to her lips, a dozen insects swarmed into her mouth. Hundreds more crawled atop her veil and stung her through the mesh. In desperation she rummaged through a pack until she found an empty waterproof bag made of rubberized canvas. With her knife she cut eyeholes in the bag, and another hole through which she could breathe. Over it all she sewed three layers of black veiling. But even with ventilation holes cut behind her ears, the waterproof bag, when tied together around her neck, was devastatingly hot. Her face was protected from stings but she could barely see because of the perspiration that ran into her eyes, and she could not lift the bag to eat without inviting a mouthful of insects under her mask. And the way the mosquitoes tapped and poked at her mask, their every sound amplified inside the rubberized shell, made her want to scream in frustration.

She had no choice but to retreat to her tent. There, with a couple of candles giving off a sooty smoke, she found a semblance of relief.

About an hour later a silhouette appeared outside her tent, and she knew by its shape that it was George. He scratched at her tent flap.

"Yes, George?"

"I thought you might like to try to eat something now," he said.

She untied the flaps and pulled them apart. Hunkered down low, George held a bowl of broth in one hand, a cup of tea in the other. She told him, "It's hardly any better in here. If I take this mask off they will eat me alive."

"All right," he said, but he did not turn away.

"I don't know how you men stand it. You don't even wear your veils."

"Our skin is tougher. And the pipe smoke helps a little."

She nodded. "How's your stomach?"

"Job's soup helped, I think. We're all feeling some better. We'll be ready to put in a full day tomorrow."

"I only hope it takes us away from these pests."

"I hope so too." He looked at her a moment, then smiled. "If we come across any Naskapi with you wearing that bag on your head, they'll shoot you for sure."

His remark had the desired effect; she could not help but return his smile, even though he could not see it beneath her suffocating mask. "Oh, George, I'm sorry to be such a complainer. I will be better tomorrow too, I promise."

"You've got no need to apologize, missus. I've seen some men couldn't handle it as good as you do."

"Some men?" she asked.

"Not Mr. Hubbard, I didn't mean that."

"Did he never get dispirited, George?"

"Not that I saw, he didn't. Now Mr. Wallace, that was another matter. He needed a bit of shoring up from time to time."

"And how did you accomplish that?"

"Wasn't me. It was Mr. Hubbard was always the strong one. I can see him sitting there at the campfire right now. Sitting there with his pipe going and him looking up into the sky. And then pretty soon he'd recite us something from that Kipling fella."

Mina could see him too, could see him as clearly as if he were there in the flickering light and shadows behind the campfire. The northern lights were fluttering overhead and the smoke from Laddie's pipe slowly swirled in the subtle hues of reflected firelight, orange and red, and the smoke wreathed his handsome, sculpted face as he sat there thinking, smiling, and as he then drew the pipe from between his lips and declaimed, as movingly as the finest actor might,

> When first under fire, if you're wishful to duck,
> Don't look or take heed of the man that is struck;
> Be thankful you're living and trust to your luck,
> And march to your front like a soldier.

Mina's eyes filled with tears, and when she blinked them away Laddie was no longer at the fire, no longer in the smoke. She could see past George to Job and Joe and Gilbert seated there, the two older men on a piece of log and Gilbert seated on a rock. But Laddie was gone.

She was glad then for the bag over her head and for the layers of veil over her eyes. The tears stung her cheeks, making the insect bites burn even more. Yet somehow she felt better. "And that's what I will do as well," she told George. "Just what Laddie always said. I will march to the front like a soldier."

"You always have, missus."

"Not always. But I will not complain again. I promise."

"Far as I recall, you didn't complain this time."

"Maybe not aloud, but inside my head I certainly did."

"You oughta hear inside of mine sometime." He smiled again. "You want I should leave the tea and soup?"

"No, but thank you. I think I will try to get some sleep now. Will we be getting an early start in the morning?"

"As early as we can manage. Good night then, missus."

"Good night, George. And thank you."

He widened his smile and gave her a wink before letting the tent flaps fall shut. The wink took her by surprise. In her entire life only two men had ever winked at her—her father and, years later, Laddie. And now George Elson could be added to that very short list. It was just a tiny gesture, yet so uplifting that for a while it made even the mosquitoes seem less troublesome.

She awoke at two-thirty on Friday morning, July 28. The first thing she noticed was that the mosquitoes were gone, chased into hiding by the coolness of the air. Immediately she untied the bag from around her neck and lifted it off. How delicious and refreshing was the morning air. She crawled to the tent flaps and untied them and laid them back, then pulled her blankets around her again and lay on her side looking out at the eastern sky, a clear and cloudless firmament, pale blue and softly lit as if by distant lanterns.

Bit by bit the sky brightened, its blue colour deepening until, after an hour, the sun showed itself between the hills. Now the peak of her tent took on a golden glow and she felt the warmth of the sun settling into the tent. She rose to her knees and crept forward until she was half outside. A mist was rising off the little lake in front of their camp, a gossamer mist near the shore, no heavier than the vapour of her breath in the chilly air, but looking so much thicker farther out, a solid white wall of mist down the length of the river.

Gilbert was the only one moving about outside. When he had a good fire going he set the teakettle on a flat stone on the edge of the fire. He filled a frying pan with thick strips of bacon and set it over the fire. He then went to the men's tent and scratched on the canopy. "All aboard!" he called.

When he came back to the fire to turn the meat, Mina asked, "Any mosquitoes out there this morning?"

"Not a one, missus. Too cold for them. I went down to the lake and tried to wash, but I had to leave off, it was so cold."

She moved back inside the tent and closed the flaps. As she pulled on her clothes for the day she could hear the men gathering around the fire, speaking in their sleepy, hoarse voices. It was always astounding to her how smoothly the men worked and took care of each other. There were no assigned duties and no need for them because every man simply assumed whatever task was required at the moment. Gilbert had awakened before the others so he had gotten the fire going and started breakfast. On other mornings it had been George or Joe or Job. When breakfast was over, one of the men would gather up the plates and cups and carry them to the water's edge to be scoured clean. The others would go about the business of breaking camp. All without a single word of instruction to each other.

This time the men had a quick cup of tea while Mina was still in her tent. Then Gilbert moved the frying pan away from the fire and the men each shrugged on a heavy pack and marched forward for a half-mile portage. By the time they returned, Mina was seated by the fire with her own cup of tea. "The bacon's ready," she told them.

By seven A.M. breakfast was long over and the canoes and other gear had been moved forward past the rapids at the head of the lake. Mina's party took to the canoes again, had smooth paddling for over an hour, then portaged around more rapids, then paddled a while longer. Around noon they glided onto another lake expansion, but here the lake appeared to curve to the east. At George's suggestion the canoes were beached and the entire party disembarked to climb a low, moss-covered ridge. From the ridge George hoped to see the river flowing out of this maze of lakes, their path clearly demarcated.

Job and Gilbert set off at a much faster pace than the others. By the time Mina reached the top of the rise, she could only just make out the figures of the two men as they crossed a valley to her left, heading, she assumed, toward a higher hill to the northwest.

Every way Mina turned revealed nothing but lakes and more lakes, the water the colour of tea and often surrounded by a soup-green bog. There was no sign of the river. "Have we made a wrong turn?" she asked. Neither Joe nor George ventured an answer.

As they set off down into the valley, following Job and Gilbert, Mina's heart was in her throat. Again she felt that familiar nausea of fear. What if they had indeed made a wrong turn somewhere and paddled up the wrong channel? This land was a labyrinth of streams and trickles and swamps and lakes. Had she allowed her party to become nonchalant in the relative ease of their progress? If they were lost they would probably have to backtrack, and that would mean the loss of precious time. If they lost too much time they would fail to reach Ungava before the last ship departed in advance of winter. And perhaps, if they lost too much time, they might never reach Ungava at all. All of a sudden the precarious nature of their situation hit her with full force.

She was out of breath and leg-weary when they crested the next ridge. There they found Job and Gilbert sitting near the edge of the ridge on the bare knob of a smooth grey boulder, their backs to the others. But when Gilbert heard them coming he turned to look at them. His wide grin made Mina's stomach flutter, but this time it was a good feeling, and suddenly the strength returned to her legs and she had no trouble keeping up with George's long strides as he hurried to where Gilbert sat.

Ahead of them lay the river—their beautiful river, dark and deep and inviting, a wide, clear path to Michikamau. There would be more lake expansions along the way, more waterfalls and rapids to bypass, more portages, but Mina did not care. They were not lost. They had now travelled some fifty miles beyond Seal Lake and, best of all, there was the river, the wonderful Naskapi, precisely where it should have been. Just to see it again felt like a kind of homecoming.

To the north the hills were low and wooded, the trees thick with green. Some thirty miles away the highest of the hills were capped in glowing white. "I wish I had brought my cameras," Mina said.

George said, "It's good to look at, isn't it?"

After a while Joe mentioned that his stomach was in fine shape again. He thought he could tackle another pound or so of fried venison. In fact, all the men were ravenously hungry. And so they turned away from the magnificent view, Mina most reluctantly, for the long march back down.

As they walked, Mina turned to George. "Why shouldn't I come back up here after dinner with my Kodaks? The walking is tiresome but it isn't rough at all."

George pursed his lips but said nothing. Obviously, he was not comfortable with the idea.

"You men could go ahead up the lake," she suggested. "I'll take my pictures and then catch up with you."

Still he said nothing.

"George, really. There's not a thing to worry about. I couldn't possibly lose my way even if I tried."

He came to a halt and stood awhile looking down their path, checking from side to side for rough places where, on her own, Mina might slip and fall. He turned to look back to the top of the hill. And finally he told her, "Well, since you want to so bad, I guess you might."

The prospect of being on her own for a couple of hours, of moving about wherever she wished and not merely following somebody else, of doing something self-chosen and purposeful, thrilled her more than she could say.

"If you go back down this way," George told her, and pointed out the path she should take, "you'll be able to meet us at the end of the lake. You'll be able to see from the hilltop when we come along in the canoes, and that will give you time to walk down to meet us."

"Oh, thank you, George! Thank you for trusting me!"

She was so eager to be on the hilltop again that the two-mile hike back to the canoes, most of it through low sandhills where the heat of the day seemed to pool, felt like six miles to Mina. Back in camp at last, she rushed through lunch and, only because George begged her to do so, she lay down for a while to rest her legs.

When she came out of her tent thirty minutes later she was ready to go. In addition to the two cameras and the notebooks she carried, she wore her revolver and Bowie knife and had stuffed her leather pouch with cartridges, a barometer and a compass.

George said, "I think you'd better take your rubber shirt too. It's going to rain some this afternoon."

Mina studied the sky. A few silvery clouds drifted above the hills. "Oh, I don't think I will. I have enough to carry already. Besides, I don't think it's going to rain at all."

George wanted to say more but he held his tongue. This was, after all, her expedition. He wished he could tie a rope around her waist and pay it out as she worked her way up the hill. She was just too darn eager to make this hike alone. The prospect of having her out of his sight for two hours or more made him sick with worry. On the other hand, he could not bring himself to disappoint her.

After lunch the party travelled by canoe to a little cove at the base of the hill Mina would climb. She all but leapt out of the canoe. "Goodbye!" she said with a quick wave, and then she was on her way, striding briskly into the trees.

"It seemed beautiful to be going off without a guard," she later wrote, "and to think of spending an hour or two on the hill top, quite alone, with a glorious sky above, and the beautiful hills and lakes and streams in all directions."

Below her, the canoes shoved off again, but George could not force himself to look away from the trees. "I hope I don't live to regret this," he said.

Joe told him, "That goes for all of us."

Mina thought it a perfect afternoon. To be alone like this, cameras slung around her neck, revolver on her hip, made her feel like one of the early explorers, like Meriwether Lewis trekking into the rugged unknown, or Champlain ridge-walking above the St. Lawrence. She was standing atop a hill where, quite probably, no white person had ever stood. Certainly no white woman. No shy little nurse from Bewdley, Ontario.

A beautiful sky that seemed to go on forever, pale blue, a few slow-scudding clouds. Rock-studded hills and calm lakes and glittering streams as far as the eye could see. From Mina's perspective it hardly seemed "the land God gave to Cain."

"Fit only for wild beasts," Jacques Cartier had said. Well, maybe so, Mina told herself. Yet I feel quite at home here.

She took as many photographs as she thought necessary, a few in every direction. Then she wrote awhile in her notebook, describing what she saw. Every fifteen seconds or so she scanned the lake for a sign of the canoes. But two hours passed and her party did not come into view. Who would have thought the men would take so much time to make the portage? Maybe in her absence they had dallied awhile before getting started, had smoked an extra pipeful of tobacco. But a proclivity for dalliance hardly seemed in their nature.

She decided to walk down to the lake anyway and wait for them there, because, just as George had predicted, the sky was beginning to darken. A thunderstorm was on the way. How had he known? It must be a kind of instinct, she thought, such as birds and animals have. Like having a barometer in your blood.

No, it would not be a good idea to be caught in the open on a barren hill when the lightning and rain began. She might find a bit of protection down by the lake, though. And there too she would be able to see the men coming in their canoes. Even if the rain came hard and fast and cold, they would not leave her stranded there. But it would be nice to have her rubber shirt now. Why must George be right all the time? It was infuriating.

She had no more than begun her descent, however, coming down off the ridge along the route George had pointed out earlier, when something appeared below her, something anomalous in her intended path. It was too far away to distinguish clearly, but by size and shape and colour it looked for all the world like a huge brown bear. She stared and stared, heart pounding, breath coming in quick, shallow gasps. Maybe it was just a log. But no, it was much too wide for a log, wide in the middle but thinner at both ends. A moss-covered boulder? Maybe, but . . . had it moved? Just a little, a shift at one end, maybe? Yes, she was sure of it, almost sure—the thing had moved!

Well, what now? she asked herself. Think, Mina. Think! Should she fire a shot from her revolver and hope to frighten the bear away? Or would the noise merely wake him from his torpor, provoke him into looking up the hill, sniffing her out? If she veered away from her intended route to find another one and had to go crashing through the brush, surely the bear would come to investigate. She could never outrun him, that was for certain. And there wasn't a tree sturdy enough to support her out of his reach for miles around. If she backtracked to the top of the hill, hoping to wait him out, what if he too decided to investigate the view from on high, and found her cowering there like a mouse? The only thing she knew for sure was that she had no desire to be anybody's supper.

But what if that thing below wasn't a bear at all? Once before, during the early days of the trip, she had cried out that there was a bear on a distant lakeshore. The men had merely smiled to one another but paddled closer so that she could see. A flock of ducks. And what a ribbing she had taken for that mistake! Could that large brown object below her be a flock of ducks? But what would ducks be doing sitting in a small opening surrounded by alders? Having a picnic?

It must surely be a bear. What else could it be?

There was only one way to find out for sure. She drew the revolver from its holster and, hand sweaty on the grip, index finger nestled close to the trigger, inched forward. Her heart was beating like a hummingbird's. She walked as tall as she could make herself, even held her left hand up beside her head for a moment, thinking it might make her appear larger. Then she realized that a bear might see her hand and outstretched fingers as an antler. So she quickly brought her hand down again, held the palm flat against her hip.

With every cautious step she strove to keep an eye on the bear lest it hear the slow crunch of a footstep and lift itself up and turn toward her. But more than once as she picked her way around obstacles, her path dropped or twisted through the lower brush and she lost sight of the creature. When that happened she would freeze in position, holding her breath, and attempt to hear through the thunder of her pulse whether she was being pursued. When she heard no such sound she would reclaim a tiny bit of aplomb and move on.

She made less than thirty yards in the first ten minutes. And that was when the rain began, a sky-emptying downpour that came without warning to steal away what was left of her breath. It came as abruptly as if she had stepped into a hitherto invisible and sound-less waterfall. It nearly knocked her to her knees.

She stood there trembling, afraid to move. The rain was so heavy that she could see no more than a few feet ahead. Every drop felt like a bumblebee trying to drive itself into her skull. Maybe this *is* the land God gave to Cain, she thought.

She had no choice but to keep moving. One step at a time, heel to toe, calf muscles aching. The good thing about the rain was that it muted the sounds of her movement. The bad thing was that it muted and concealed the bear's movements too, if indeed the thing was a bear and if indeed it was moving. To make matters worse, the rain brought the blackflies out in droves, and they clung to her by the hundreds, sticking in her hair like nettles and crawling over her rain-slicked cheeks.

Another twenty minutes or so and she came at last to the place where she had thought the bear must be. But the little clearing was empty, with no tracks or trampled grass to indicate that a large animal had been there. Had she been fooled by her eyes again? A trick of the light? She was relieved to find the clearing empty but she was utterly drained by the experience of getting down to it, each step an ordeal that strained every muscle. She told herself, I think I won't bother to mention this to the men.

But where were the men? By the time she reached the bottom of the valley, the rain had lessened from a deluge to a steady downpour. From the shoreline she could see the entire length of the lake, and the canoes were nowhere to be seen. What was keeping them? Was George perhaps trying to teach her a lesson about not going off without him and not paying heed to his weather prognostications?

She stood there awhile longer, alternately worrying and fuming. Meanwhile the rain drummed down and the blackflies chewed away at her. Not long ago, upon spotting the thing she had thought was a bear, she had speculated that she would not care to be anybody's supper. Well, the bear was gone, poof, just like that, but thanks to the flies she was the *plat du jour* anyway.

The flies had not bothered her up on the rocky hilltop, she remembered. Not a single one had buzzed her there. And besides, she would be able to see farther from on top. But this time she would climb to a different ridge, the one to the east, because from there she would be able to look back to the falls, around which the men should have portaged by now.

From the top, another twenty minutes later, she could see the mist rising from the falls, could see the rock outcroppings and the path the men would have had to take up and over the ridgeline, but the land all around was unpeopled, no sign of her party. The rain continued to fall but not so hard as to obscure her view. So if the men had been back there anywhere, she would have seen them. It was as if they had vanished from the face of the earth.

And now she truly did feel alone—not so much an intrepid explorer as a stranded one. For just a moment a bubble of panic rose in her chest. But it was nonsense to imagine that the men had disappeared. They were down there somewhere, she simply needed to locate them. And when she did, was she ever going to give them a piece of her mind!

She hiked north along the ridges, which here were nothing but long, crooked lengths of naked rock, weathered to a smooth surface on top but sheared off sharply on both sides. She walked to the very end of the ridgeline, a full mile. From there she could see down to the little bay where, before lunch, the canoes and other gear had been deposited. And where, to her amazement, the men remained.

They had not yet even started across the lake. The canoes had been turned upside down over the packs so as to keep the gear dry. And the men were seated snugly under a tarpaulin stretched over the campfire—smoking their pipes and drinking tea!

Her pulse hammered again, but this time with a flush of anger. What did they think they were doing down there, enjoying themselves, while she was up here getting soaked to the skin and nearly drowned and—

"Take your rubber shirt," George had told her. "It's going to rain." And now she thought she understood; the men were teaching her a lesson in the advisability of taking good advice when it was offered. She imagined that she could see George sitting down there right now, chuckling to himself, all the men joking about the good drenching she was getting, speculating as to how she would never again disregard their advice, never again entertain thoughts of going off like that on her own.

They were teaching her a lesson, that was what it amounted

to. And the more she thought about it, the less angry she felt. The men, in choosing to stay put, hadn't placed her in any danger—not really. She would have encountered the bear, if it was a bear, whether they had moved forward or not. So where was the harm in their little joke? Besides, George had been right about the rain. She *would* trust him from now on, at least in regard to his weather forecasts.

The men were safe and she was safe, so why be angry? In fact, she felt a rekindling of her fondness for the men. Brothers teased sisters, didn't they? And that was what the men were to her. It was only natural that they should have a little fun at her expense.

In her book she described her reaction to the situation this way: "I laughed a little and thought: 'Oh! I know something better than that. This afternoon I shall go where I like and do what I please, like the little fly, and have one good time.'"

To let them know she was safe and sound, no harm done, she fired off two shots from her revolver. As long as the men knew where she was, why not let them enjoy their snuggery and tea while she continued her explorations? She couldn't get any wetter, could she? So off she went to climb the next ridge—the highest one yet, promising an even more impressive view.

Along the way, she stopped to admire a great grey boulder balanced precariously atop a pile of smaller rocks. What an artist is Nature! she thought. The sculpture was as impressive as any by Rodin. She walked around it for several minutes, studying it from every angle. Then came the pop of two rifle shots. She walked fifty yards to where she could peer down at the cove, and there were the men standing outside the tarpaulin, Joe with a rifle in his hands, all four of them peering up in her direction.

Mina fired her revolver once in reply. She waved, a wide wet smile on her face. "I'm fine!" she shouted, though she knew they would not hear her small voice so far below. "I'm having a grand time!" Then she thought, And now let's see who has the last laugh.

Moving as briskly as was safe, she hurried ahead toward the next ridge, meaning to get there before the men could round her up and corral her again.

To obtain the next ridge she would first have to descend the current one, and the only way down was very steep. Moss, rock, and dirt were all slick with rain. She slid and scraped along a wide crevice in the rock, but finally made her way to the bottom. Here lay a bog that had to be crossed. She intended to race across it, but by the third step she was sunk halfway up to her shins in the muck. Only by holding onto the tops of her high moccasins as she retreated could she prevent them from being sucked off with every step.

Back on solid ground, she considered her options. If the bog could not be crossed she would have to go around it. Again she hurried on her way, and laughed to herself to think how terrified the men would be if they could see her heedless pace. They had meant to teach her a lesson but she was having none of that. Despite the rain and the ravenous flies and the squish of her moccasins she was having a wonderful time on her own. A bully time, as Laddie would have said. Maybe there was more than a little of his frontier spirit inside her after all.

She had only begun her ascent of the second ridge when two more rifle shots echoed up from the lake. She grinned and moved even faster. Who's getting the lesson now? she thought. The flies had once again become desperately thick, so she broke a bough from a spruce tree and waved it back and forth in front of her face as she walked. Her ears and neck were sticky with blood from the insects' bites, but she asked herself, What do flies matter when you are free? She resolved to go just as far as she could that afternoon, and not to return until somebody caught up with her or darkness fell, whichever came first. She felt confident that at least two of the men would take the gear forward to make camp along the lake at the point where she had originally been directed to meet them. So she had no fear of getting lost. Even in complete darkness she could follow the shoreline back to a campfire. In the meantime she would show George once and for all who was an explorer and who wasn't. More important, she would prove it to herself.

To her disappointment, she was unable to see the full course of the river from the top of the next ridge unless she crept dangerously close to the precipitous edge, which looked as if it might crumble beneath her weight. So she decided to continue along the ridge as far as she could. There she would surely find a way down to the river and eventually back to camp.

In mid-afternoon, after walking two miles along the ridgetop, she paused to rest. She sat on a rounded boulder and, now that the rain had dwindled to a drizzle, considered the panorama spread out below. I didn't let a bear stop me, she told herself, whether it was a real bear or not. And I didn't let the rain stop me, nor the flies nor the bog nor the cliffs. I got here all by myself and I didn't let anything or anybody stop me from doing it.

She had had many good days in Labrador so far, but this, she decided, was the best of them all. She was tired, but it was the sweetest fatigue she had known in a long time. The only thing she could compare it to was the lovely exhaustion she had felt lying naked and sweaty in a tent with Laddie after a long day of hiking and fishing and frying trout and eating it and sopping up the butter with chunks of bread, and then crawling under a blanket with the man she adored, smelling smoky sweet and loving her so completely. And afterward there had been only the two of them in the whole world and they had had the stars and the loons calling and that was the happiest she had ever felt in her life. And the happiest, she now knew, she would ever feel. They had had dozens of nights like that together, but she would give up all of Labrador and all of America and all of existence just to have one more of those nights with him.

But she never would. Never again. And with this thought the old familiar ache swooped over her, heavy and chilling. She sat there on the rock and all the happiness went out of her. She was cold and tired and hungry and nothing mattered or would ever matter again.

Her reverie was broken by the pop of several gunshots. "The sounds were very faint," she later wrote,

> but followed each other in quick succession. I laughed, and thought I knew what was happening where they came from. The shots seemed to come from the ridge I was on; but for some time I could not see any one. Finally, I caught sight of one of the men. He was waving his arms about wildly, and I could hear very faintly the sound of shooting. Then another figure appeared, and they started running towards me.
>
> Suddenly I became frightened. Perhaps all the excitement was not on my account after all, and I began to wonder if something dreadful had happened. Had any one been hurt, or drowned? I started quickly toward them, but as soon as they were near enough for me to see their faces plainly, I knew that I had been the sole cause of the trouble. It was George and Job. The perspiration was dripping from their faces, which were pale and filled with an expression, the funniest mixture of indignant resentment, anxiety, and relief that could possibly be imagined.
>
> When they came up I smiled at them, but there was not any answering smile.

George stood for a few moments before her, catching his breath. Then he folded his arms across his chest. "Well," he finally said, and looked at her directly. "I guess you very near done it this time, didn't you?"

"What did I do?" she asked.

"Why you just about had us crazy!"

Job halted a step behind George. Mina looked to him for a reaction but he was bent double, trying to catch his breath. She faced George again. "Had you crazy? About what?"

"Why, we thought you were lost!"

It made no sense to her. "Didn't you see me over on that ridge when I fired those shots?"

"Yes we did. And when we got up to the end of the lake *we* fired two shots, and we thought you would come back then. I went up to the ridge to meet you. And when I saw you weren't there I was sure you must have went down to the rapids. So I ran down there. And when I didn't find you there I thought you either fell in the rapids or you got lost somewhere."

He was so breathless when he spoke, his voice so tight and shaky with fear, that for his sake she tried to soften her tone. But his assumption that she must have done something stupid or careless was annoying. "Didn't I promise not to go to those rapids?" she asked.

"I know you did. But I thought, when you went up there on that mountain all alone, maybe you would think different and go down to the rapids anyway."

She kept her voice even and low. "When I got to the end of the lake and I saw you weren't coming, and the thunderstorm was on its way and the flies were as bad as I've ever seen them, I thought I might as well be doing something interesting while I was getting soaked and eaten alive. I wasn't going to just sit there for who knows how long and be miserable while I waited for you men to show up."

He nodded, his face still grim. "That's just what we said to each other. Who would ever think of climbing that hill in a thunderstorm?"

She understood that he did not mean the statement to be derisive, but a strange kind of compliment. She laughed softly.

George's scowl deepened. "Look at us," he said, and waved a hand toward Job. "Just look at what you done to us."

"What have I done?" she asked.

"When I went to meet you and then couldn't see you on the ridge, and then went to the rapids and couldn't find you there, we begun to walk faster and faster, and then to run like crazy people. Poor Job, he could hardly speak, he was so worried about you. And neither could I. So there was both of us out of breath and half-crying all the time and not knowing where to look. And now we can never trust you to go off on your own again. We just can't."

His last statement was uttered so despairingly, empty of accusation or anger but heavy with disappointment, that it nearly broke her heart. She had no desire to be the cause of such turmoil. On the other hand, she had had a taste of freedom and it had thrilled her. She was not willing to give it all back to the men and resign herself to being mere baggage again.

"I'll make a bargain with you," she said. "If I can have someone to go with me whenever I want to climb a hill or do anything else I think is necessary for my work, I promise not to go away alone again. But my escort has to go with me wherever I want to go. He will have to follow wherever I say. Agreed?"

George said, "What if you say you want to go into a rapid?"

"George! For goodness' sake!"

"All right," he said. "I suppose you wouldn't ever say that, would you?"

"You know I wouldn't. You have to learn to put some trust in me."

"It's not that I don't trust you, missus."

"You know what can happen out here, I understand. And so do I." She thought of the bear that had blocked her trail, of the creature that might have been a bear and might have been a shadow, and of how all this trouble had probably started with it. She had been distracted by the bear and lost a lot of time in trying to avoid it, then trying to sneak up on it, only to find that it hadn't been there at all, a probable phantom, a thing like fear itself, which, when confronted, evaporates into the mist. Before embarking on this trip she had been afraid of so many things. Now here she was telling George he had nothing to worry about, when in her own heart she understood that this very expedition was the result of a fear that would never leave her.

Her smile was small but sincere, a reconciliation. She held out her hand. "Do you accept my proposition?"

Wearily, George smiled too. He placed his hand atop hers. "I accept."

Job, without so much as a grunt, turned and headed back toward camp. Mina and George followed a minute later.

"And the thing is," George said, after a while, "you did it all so quick. Why, I was watching you go up on that mountain where you first went, and you were so busy and running about up there, just as busy as a Labrador fly. You looked just like a little girl that was play-ing at building something. And I thought how nice that you were enjoying yourself. Then the first thing I knew I heard the shots on the other side of the lake. We looked across the lake and couldn't see anything, and we wondered about those shots and who could be there. Then it wasn't long at all before Joe said, 'Look there! Up on the mountain!'"

He shook his head, still shaken. "Then we saw you, but I never thought it was you. I didn't see how it could be, that you could have gotten there so fast. Then Joe said, 'Why, it's a woman!' And we knew it had to be you. But even then we couldn't believe it. Who would ever think to look at you and the little short steps you take that you could move so quick? Why, we just couldn't believe it. And the men got on me for it too. They said they had been on lots of trips before where there were women along, but they never were on a trip where the women didn't do what they were told."

She could not help but laugh at the incredulity in his voice, the tone of awe and confusion.

"Oh yes," he said, as sombre as ever, "you go ahead and laugh if you like. It just shows me that you don't care a bit about my feelings. Not a bit, do you?"

He had never before expressed his feelings to her so nakedly, and now here he was sounding forlorn and pathetic. Mina knew she shouldn't laugh, but she couldn't stop herself. So as not to give him the wrong impression, though, she leaned closer and laid a hand on George's arm.

At first he looked wounded by her laughter, as if she were mock-ing him, but with her hand on his arm the hurt soon passed and he laughed too, if only a little. "I just thought I was never going to see you again," he admitted. And now his pace slowed a bit, and they fell even farther behind Job. "I'm never going to forget about that and how bad it felt. I kept thinking about how frightened you would feel when you realized you were lost. It's an awful thing to know you're lost, and I just never wanted you to feel that. If I hadn't ever been lost myself I wouldn't know how bad it is."

She rubbed her fingers over his forearm. "Thank you for worrying about me, George. But I was never really in any trouble."

"But how could we know that? Don't you see? And what would we do if you had got lost or fell in those rapids? Why, I could never go back again. None of us could. How could any of us ever go back without you?"

"But why not?" she said.

"Don't you know what everybody would think if we came back without you? A white woman alone out here with four Indian men? Don't you know what they would do to us if we was foolish enough to come back without you?"

The full force of their fear and their dilemma struck her like a blow. Of course they were protective of her. Of course they wanted to shield her from all harm. They cared about her, yes, and that was a large part of their concern. But she had never stopped to think of the other aspect of their fear. If any accident befell her on this trip, if she drowned in the rapids or was attacked by a bear or got lost and could not be found, the men would be blamed for it. White society would not ask if Mina had behaved foolishly or if she had ignored their advice; judgment would be swift and harsh. She was a white woman, inexperienced in the wilderness, and they had been hired as her guides. They would be held responsible.

Mina understood then that the men had risked their lives in more ways than one by agreeing to accompany her on this expedition. And this afternoon she had abused their courage and loyalty by playing a trick on them, a silly game meant to teach them a silly lesson. She felt small and childish and stupid with regret.

"Plus I just kept thinking," George said—his voice was husky now and he would not look at her, he kept his eyes on the ground— "I just kept thinking I might never see you again. And that was the worst feeling of them all."

She let her hand slip down his arm and brush across his fingers. Then, side by side and without speaking, they walked back toward camp.

Joe and Gilbert had just finished setting up her tent when she arrived. They too had been searching for her earlier and now they did not know whether to smile. It was as if they had all agreed to scold her with their expressions but no one was terribly interested in doing so now. She did not say anything at first but went inside her tent and changed into dry clothing. When she came out again, all four men were seated around the fire underneath the tarpaulin and there was meat frying in the skillet and a pot of rice nearby.

Mina walked over to the fire quickly in an attempt to stay dry. The rain continued to fall, though in a light drizzle now. It made a soft pattering sound on the tarpaulin and dripped steadily over one edge, which had been pitched lowest for good drainage. The men had scattered pine boughs under the tarp and the air smelled of woodsmoke and frying meat and of pine resin and rain.

She took off her hat and shook the rain from it and laid it aside. "Oh, isn't it nice and warm and fragrant in here," she said. She sat on the ground next to Gilbert and looked at each of the men in turn. Only George would meet her gaze, his own soft and forgiving. The other men seemed to be waiting to be told how to react to her.

She said, "I want you all to know how sorry I am for what I did today. I don't mean for going off alone, which I enjoyed very much, but for making you worry about me."

She waited and said nothing more. Gilbert was the first to look in her direction, just a quick glance and a small quick smile. Then Job did the same. Joe poked at the fire with a stick. A few moments later he lifted his eyes enough to look in George's direction, and when he saw that George was smiling, Joe too gave Mina a smile and a nod.

"I think I should get my brandy bottle out now, don't you?" she said. "I want us all to have a good bracer together, all right? Then we can all forgive each other and have a nice supper."

The men understood that she was making a concession to them, an act of contrition. The brandy bottle had been passed around on only one other occasion, the first day of the trip, a toast to their success. Joe said, "You're not going to get an argument out of any of us when it comes to the brandy, missus."

She put her wet hat back on and hurried through the rain again and into her tent. A few moments later she returned and handed the bottle to George, then went back to her seat at the other end of the line.

George uncapped the bottle and took a long swallow. Then he had another short one before passing the bottle to Job. Job drank from it and passed the bottle to Joe. The men were all being very solemn now, she thought, all but Gilbert, who sat with his head bowed. When the bottle was passed to him he took only a short gulp before lowering it. But Joe gave him a nudge with an elbow and Gilbert raised the bottle again and had another drink. He could not even look at Mina when he held the bottle toward her, but sat there with his head averted and his shoulders shaking.

Mina took the bottle and held it out toward the men as if to toast them. Then she raised the bottle to her lips and tilted it up. Only then did she realize that the day's games were not yet over. The men had drained the brandy bottle completely. They had left not a drop for her.

———

*Dillon Wallace's expedition, last week of July 1905*

A RESPITE FROM DRUDGERY finally came to Wallace's party on the twenty-sixth. The previous Sunday, Duncan McLean, anxious for home, had bid the party goodbye and set off alone. The men missed him sorely. "As he disappeared down the trail," Wallace would write, "a strange sense of loneliness came upon us, for it seemed to us that his going broke the last link that connected us with the outside world."

They spent the next three days moving through a series of lakes, alternately paddling and portaging. Then, on the twenty-sixth, they happened upon a flock of five geese floating along on the water. Pete downed three of the geese with his shotgun. Wallace later described their special dinner that night: "This was Easton's twenty-second birthday and it occurred to me that it would be a pleasant variation to give a birthday dinner in his honor and to have a sort of feast to relieve the monotony of our daily life, and give the men something to think about and revive their spirits." He instructed that two of the geese be prepared for the feast. They would also have plenty of hot bread and a pudding concocted from the few remaining prunes. Their supply of coffee was running so low that it had now been restricted to Sundays only, but for this occasion he eased the restriction.

"How we enjoyed it!" he wrote.

*"No hotel ever served such a banquet," one of the boys remarked as we filled our pipes and lighted them with brands from the fire. Then with that blissful feeling that nothing but a good dinner can give, we lay at length on the deep white moss, peacefully puffing smoke at the stars as they blinked sleepily one by one out of the blue of the great arch above us until the whole firmament was glittering with a mass of sparkling heaven gems . . . the vast silence of the wilderness possessed the world and, wrapped in his own thoughts, no man spoke to break the spell.*

But the spell would be broken. On the morning of Saturday, July 29, Stanton crawled out of his bedroll at five-thirty, utterly depleted after a torturous night. Never had the flies been so insistent, so insatiable. His skin was black with their corpses and blood, stinging as if from several loads of birdshot. His only comfort, and it was cold comfort indeed, was that the insects had not singled him out in their carnage. Every face in camp was swollen and blood-speckled, as red as raw sausage.

There was no denying that Wallace's crew were a miserable bunch, and not solely because of the insects. Morale had been fading day by day ever since the birthday banquet. How could they possibly hope to be on the George River and gliding toward Ungava by the last of August when now, with but three days left in July, they hadn't even found Seal Lake yet? By Stanton's calculations, which he kept to himself or grumbled out *sotto voce* when only Pete Stevens could hear, they spent more time searching for the damn Indian trail than actually walking on it. And those searches invariably carried them through hostile, if not downright malevolent, terrain. In the morning a mosquito-infested bog might threaten to suck them under; in the afternoon a lifeless sand desert would blast them with radiated heat; and in the evening they would struggle through a field of ankle-twisting rocks, or across a barren ridge scoured by an icy wind, or over a hundred acres of willow brush so thick they had to crawl on their hands and knees. And because every man was responsible for two loads during these portages, every mile of advance meant having to walk three miles, two of them while hauling a back-breaking load every inch of the way.

By now Pete Stevens' khaki trousers were ripped in a dozen places. Even so, they were in better shape than the Mackinaw trousers worn by Richards and Easton, which had been shredded to rags. Wallace's moleskin trousers had fared the best of any, sustaining but one small tear so far. But even with fresh clothing the men would have been footsore and heart-heavy. What they craved most of all was not comfort but progress, and that commodity was in very short supply.

As was fresh meat. They had been catching as much fish as they could eat, but even with a bellyful of trout the men felt unsatisfied. Days earlier they had spotted three caribou swimming across a lake, and every man had scampered to get into position. But the animals made the shore and bounded into the brush before a single shot could be fired. The next day the party came upon another caribou swimming, but their three desperate shots fell far short of it.

So it was hardly surprising that Stanton should doubt his eyesight when, a few minutes after climbing out of bed that Saturday morning—still picking the sticky corpses off his neck while he sat by the fire and watched Pete Stevens boiling fish for their breakfast—he saw a large buck walking toward him down the shore.

Stanton blinked several times, shook his head, and waited for the taunting apparition to disappear. Instead it grew more substantial. A big, thick-necked stag, too intent on the moss to notice the men.

Stanton hissed to get Stevens' attention. Then he nodded toward Wallace's rifle, propped against a rock. In a whisper Stanton said, "Hand me the rifle, Pete. But move real slow. And look up there."

Stevens looked first, then he made a grab for the rifle. He would have liked to take the shot himself, had been hungering for a kill since the trip began. But Stanton had spotted the buck first so it was rightly his shot. Stevens passed the rifle over to Stanton, who slid a bullet into place. The buck, as if asking to be brought down, strode onto a narrow neck of sand protruding into the water and obligingly turned broadside to the men.

"Should I take him now?" Stanton whispered.

Stevens gauged the distance. "Hundred-forty, fifty yards. Maybe wait. He maybe come closer."

Stanton went down on one knee and took aim. "He'll be hard to miss from here."

"Maybe wait. See what he does."

What the buck did was lift his head suddenly, sniff the air and, having caught the scent of smoke, wheel around in an instant and bound away. Stanton fired off several shots. Their only effect was to bring the remaining men running out of the tent. That morning's boiled fish was seasoned with a fair measure of resentment.

After breakfast, Wallace, Easton, and Stevens climbed to a snow-covered summit, hoping to see Seal Lake. Instead they saw another fifty or so lakes of varying sizes, none of them large enough to be Seal Lake. Yet another long maze of water and land and bog to be navigated. The sight was as disconcerting as it was dismaying. For the most part they were travelling by hearsay, what they had been told by trappers and Indians. The information had sounded reliable enough in the comfort of the North West River Post, but out in the wild, with the vast and trackless panorama laid before them, it seemed anything but precise.

They marched and waded and trudged all day, their only reward another disappointing supper of fishcakes, bread, and boiled rice. Near the end of their meal Wallace made a sombre announcement. "I think we'd be wise to cut back on our bread, fellas. We've got a long way to go yet and there's a real danger we'll run out of flour before the end."

Easton said, "It's the bread that keeps us going."

Stanton agreed. "Rice and fish don't stick with a man long enough."

"I don't see as how we have a choice," Wallace told them. "We cut down now or we run out before the end. And in the end we might need it more."

"Cut down how far?" Richards asked.

"Down to a quarter-loaf per meal for each man."

Easton groaned. Even with a full loaf at each meal, he was always hungry.

Pete Stevens said, "Indian need more bread than white man."

"We all need more bread," said Richards.

"We need to get used to having less."

"Indian need more bread. Always have."

"I know you think you do, Pete. But that's only because you're used to it. I've studied this long and hard and I have come to the conclusion that a bit of rationing is absolutely necessary. So from now on it will be one-quarter loaf per meal for each of us. Instead of baking four loafs for each meal, Pete, you'll make just one. And when we have cornmeal or pea meal or lentils, we must do without bread altogether."

Every man but Richards groaned aloud.

"Once we get to Seal Lake we can get some flour from Duncan's tilt," Wallace said. "Until then we have to be careful."

Stanton muttered, "If we ever get to Seal Lake."

Wallace chose not to acknowledge that remark.

Richards then said, "Maybe it's time to start thinking about giving up on the Indian trail and taking to the water again. We could be to Seal Lake already if we had travelled by the route Duncan and the trappers use."

"I have been thinking about that," Wallace said. "The river would no doubt be quicker and easier."

"Here here!"

"But it was Hubbard's intention to locate the old trail if he could, as we have done, and to follow it whenever possible. To abandon that intention now, after all we've been through, just to make things easier on ourselves . . . well, it would feel like a surrender."

Even as he said this, Wallace was wondering how many of the men were thinking, Better to surrender than to end up like Hubbard. Try as he might, he could not help thinking it himself. Was this trip doomed to play out as Hubbard's had?

Damn it all, Wallace thought. In *The Lure of the Labrador Wild* he had plainly laid out Hubbard's original intentions—to follow the old Indian trail to Lake Michikamau, then locate the headwaters of the George River and pass down that river to the Naskapi Indian

camps, there to witness the annual eastward migration of the caribou. Moreover, Wallace had stated to more than one newspaper
reporter his own intention of fulfilling Hubbard's dream, his belief
that he was compelled to do so by his friend's dying exhortation.
How could he renege on that commitment now?

A cold, drenching rain fell that night, and the men lay silent in
their bedrolls, already hungry for more bread. More bread, more
meat, more of all the things they did not have. They had each signed
on for this trip hoping for a fine adventure, a chance to prove their
mettle and maybe share in a bit of the glory. None, but for Wallace,
perhaps, had expected to have to endure such hardship and depri-
vation. And even Wallace had been confident that he could somehow circumvent the trials that had plagued Hubbard's expedition.
But this morning he had been forced for their own good to subject
his crew to another hardship. The portages were an ordeal, yes, but
until today the men had been able to propel themselves forward
with the prospect of a hearty meal at the end of each march. Now
that incentive had been whisked away. No meat and less bread.

Stanton lay awake a long time, remembering what Duncan
McLean had once said: "If there aren't any flies in hell, it can't be as
bad as this." And if there is bread and meat in hell, Stanton thought,
I hope we find our way there soon.

*Mina Hubbard's expedition, final days of July 1905*

THE END OF THE MONTH brought melancholy times to Mina. A
listlessness descended out of nowhere and infected her party, a kind
of Sunday laziness stretched through the entire weekend. A heavy
rain on Saturday morning kept the party in camp until noon. Then
came several hours of portaging, a late supper, and a long, still night

through which Mina lay awake thinking of her husband. It bothered her more than a little that she was finding so much pleasure on this trip. She had expected to suffer but, except for the insect bites, her suffering thus far had been insignificant in comparison to Laddie's. It hardly seemed fair or right to Mina that she should be treated so generously to the wonders of this experience, free from sickness and hunger and debilitating fatigue, when her Laddie, who had loved the wilderness more than she did, had been denied this.

Rain fell again on Sunday morning, and again the sky cleared by noon. To Mina's eye they were now on the most picturesque part of the river, a series of waterfalls and rapids that took her breath away, each more spectacular than the previous one. To each she gave a name. First came Maid Marion Falls, a fifty-foot plummet into a narrow gorge carved through the gneiss and schist of Laurentian rock. Then Gertrude Falls, ten feet higher than Maid Marion, a gushing, roaring cataract. And finally Isabella Falls, a mile-long series of falls and rapids and chutes. Here, she would write, "the water poured over ledges, flowed in a foaming, roaring torrent round little rocky islands, or rushed madly down a chute."

Even the rocks were beautiful, varying in colour from a rich umber to a subtle purple. The rock walls rising up on each side of the river had been sheared off nearly perpendicular, and moss grew in most of the cracks, adding lines of grey, green, and vermilion to the palette. The surrounding countryside had not been burned over but was blanketed everywhere by luxuriant reindeer moss, above which grew tall spruces and balsam trees.

But every time Mina caught herself smiling at the beauty of the landscape, marvelling at the quiet, harmonious air of the place, a troubling thought intruded: Do I deserve all this?

A laborious portage around the falls brought them to a succession of small lakes. Here, in the green woods along the shore, they spotted several wigwam poles left behind by Montagnais Indians. Mina was thrilled by this discovery. The men remained strangely silent.

After Mina and her crew had paddled over the fourth of the small lakes, they came to a place where the river turned south through three sets of heavy rapids. Joe and Job scouted for a portage route around these and returned with the happy news that they had come upon the old Indian trail to Michikamau. The blazes were old and faded but the path was clear. It promised easy portaging to the next calm water.

After a portage of a quarter-mile or so, Mina's party took to the canoes and passed through another lake. There George pointed to a high hill on the opposite shore, perhaps three miles away. "We should be able to see Lake Michikamau from that hill," he announced.

This time it was the men's turn to be delighted. Mina, however, felt a peculiar heaviness in her stomach, a dread. Michikamau had been such an important landmark for her husband, that point in the journey where all the hard passage would lie behind them; the point from which success would be virtually guaranteed. But Laddie had never reached Michikamau.

"For all I know we might be on the lake already," George told her. "This might be a part of it. In any case, we'll be able to tell for sure from up on that hill."

Mina's legs felt suddenly tired, her back weak, and as the men paddled toward shore she searched her mind for some excuse that might keep her from having to climb that hill with the others; might keep her from having ever to lay eyes on Lake Michikamau. But in the end she said nothing. And march to the front like a soldier, she kept telling herself. And so she climbed.

It was just as George had said, a panorama of mountains, lakes and islands. And there, to the west, the great glittering expanse of Lake Michikamau, that ninety-mile spread of smooth water. She looked at it with tears in her eyes.

"Over there," George told her, and pointed east, "that's where we came through from Seal Lake."

"And over there," he said a moment later, pointing to a lonely-looking grey mountain a few miles to the southwest, "that's Mount Hubbard. That's where Mr. Hubbard and me stood when we first saw Michikamau."

Mina could only nod, she could not speak.

"That dark line running across the brow of that hill, that's the line of bushes where we shot all the ptarmigan." He paused for a moment, then added softly, his voice hoarse, "We had us a fine supper that night."

The view all around was a beautiful one, but Mina felt only agony. She could almost see George and her Laddie standing over there atop Mount Hubbard, hugging each other and jumping up and down with joy, haggard and weak but hopeful at last. It had been, perhaps, her husband's last happy moment. "BIG DAY," he had written in his journal.

On that afternoon—September 9, 1903, a Wednesday—with their spirits buoyed by the imminence of Michikamau and the nine ptarmigan and one rabbit they had shot, Laddie and George had hiked the four miles downhill to where Wallace was picking blueberries. "It's there! It's there!" Hubbard had shouted when he first spotted Wallace. "Michikamau is there, just behind the ridge. We saw the big water. We saw it!" Then all three men had hugged and danced a happy jig.

Ravenous, they quickly built a fire on the rocks. By then it was early evening. They had eaten nothing that day but for a watery soup made from a portion of their emergency rations—three slices of bacon and three spoonfuls of flour. They were so hungry that, while waiting for the birds to cook, they wrapped the entrails around sticks and roasted them over the flames and devoured them half-raw.

They ate several of the ptarmigan that night and considered it a feast and thought that finally their luck had changed for the better. Michikamau, their salvation, was at hand.

But all through the next day and the next, and the day after that, Laddie and George and Wallace had searched in vain for a route to Michikamau. On the mountain their path had seemed so obvious. Now, in the valley, it eluded them. Then came a sleet storm that lasted for several days and kept them windbound in camp, again with almost nothing to eat.

Wallace wrote of those hard days in his first book:

> *I observed now a great change in Hubbard. Heretofore the work he had to do had seemed almost wholly to occupy him. Now he craved companionship, and he loved to sit with me and dwell on his home and his wife, his mother and sister, and rehearse his early struggles in the university and in New York City. Undoubtedly the boy was beginning to suffer severely from homesickness—he was only a young fellow, you know, with a gentle, affectionate nature that gripped him tight to the persons and objects he loved. Our little confidential talks grew to be quite the order of things, and often as the days went by we confessed to each other that we looked forward to them during all the weary work hours; they were the bright spots in our dreary life.*

On the morning of September 15, a Tuesday, with a high west wind squealing around them and needles of sleet pricking their faces, the three men took stock of their emergency rations. They had about two pounds of flour left, a pint of rice, and three pounds of bacon. Plus eighteen pounds of pea meal—"to be held for emergency," Hubbard wrote in his diary. They had travelled less than half the total distance to Ungava, had not yet reached Michikamau, and the weather showed no signs of improving. A Labrador winter was nipping at their heels.

In his diary Hubbard chronicled his thoughts. "To go on is certain failure to reach the caribou killing, and probable starvation. If we turn back we must stop and get grub, then cross our long portage, then hunt more grub and finally freeze up preparatory to a sled dash to Northwest River. . . . I don't see anything better to do."

The men sat huddled around their fire. The wind howled and blew the fire's heat away and drove the sleet into their faces. After a few minutes Laddie shoved a couple of sticks into the fire. Then he climbed to his feet and, with a wet blanket wrapped around his reed-thin shoulders, he looked out across the water some twenty yards away. After a while he walked down through the brush and stood alone on the sandy shore. No matter which way he looked, he could see no opening to Michikamau.

Finally he turned and pushed back through the brush to stand again at the fire. His face was gaunt, his clothes ragged. He ached in every joint. For days now he and Wallace and George had been able to think of nothing but food and home. All were walking skeletons.

"Boys," Laddie said—and Mina could imagine the way he must have smiled at them then, that wry turn of his beautiful mouth— "what do you say to turning back?"

*Mina Hubbard's expedition, August 1905*

THE FIRST WEEK OF AUGUST brought good hunting to Mina's party. All week long the weather on Lake Michikamau and then the smaller Lake Michikamats was squally and kept the crew in camp. But it did not keep them from hauling in one trout after another on their troll lines, including a fifteen-pounder caught by Joe and a whopping twenty-pounder hooked on Mina's line. Later, while windbound on Michikamats, the party took four red-throated loons and a spruce partridge. On that same day, the seventh, while the loons were being prepared for lunch, Job caught sight of a caribou stag swimming across the lake to their south.

Within seconds he and Gilbert had a canoe in the water. A half-hour later the men returned to their island camp with a load of fresh venison.

That same day held yet one more surprise. While the men cut up the caribou and arranged the pieces of meat on a drying rack, the sound of wild geese calling to one another echoed across the water. Goose was a delicacy that had thus far eluded the party. George and Gilbert immediately dropped their hunting knives and, with their hands and forearms still bloody from the caribou, grabbed their rifles and raced on foot across the island. They returned an hour later with two young geese in hand.

A cold rain had been falling all day and the men had been out in it the whole time, fishing and hunting. But not one complaint was heard. They had laid in enough fresh meat to keep the party provisioned for quite a while, and they were exultant.

Only Mina harboured mixed feelings about the bounty. At supper she sat under the tarp with the others until Gilbert brought her a plate piled high with slices of venison. "Thank you, Gil," she told him, and managed a smile, though her stomach was in knots. "But if you gentlemen don't mind, I think I will dine in my tent tonight."

Alone in her tent she sat cross-legged facing the open flap, the plate balanced on her knees. She appeared to be gazing out at the blazing fire and her happy, well-fed party, but in fact she was thinking about a previous caribou hunt, two years past. She had read the passage in Laddie's journal so many times by now that she could envision clearly every moment described. She could see Laddie and George and Wallace creeping along the edge of a marsh, staying as low as possible. Sixty yards ahead, a lone caribou wanders along with its backside to them as it grazes on tender moss. This caribou isn't a large animal, only an immature buck, but it could well be their salvation. All three men are thin and wasted from weeks of near-starvation and illness, their clothes in tatters, moccasins split.

Back in camp they have only a bit of pea meal left and a handful of charred goose bones, nothing more. Laddie is faring worst of all, weakened by a long bout with diarrhea. Still he pushes himself forward. His rifle is as heavy as an anchor. He can barely keep it from scraping the wet ground as he drags himself along in pursuit of the caribou.

George, carrying the second rifle, touches Laddie on the shoulder, a signal to stop. Wallace, armed with only a pistol, sinks to one knee beside them. George whispers, "We're not getting any closer. Better take our shot while we can."

Laddie nods. With a slow deliberation that makes his muscles ache he raises the rifle to his shoulder. He sights down the barrel. But the rifle is so heavy and he is so weak that the weapon wobbles in his hand, he cannot draw a steady bead. Meanwhile the caribou is moving farther away. Laddie lets out a breath, lowers the rifle, takes the strain off his arms for a moment. He blinks and shakes his head, tries to clear his vision, tries to find the strength to accomplish this feat which, not so long ago, he could have pulled off with ease. Then he lifts the rifle up again, quicker this time, resolute. Shoot now or die, he tells himself.

His bullet goes wide. The caribou flicks its head to the side, stretches its neck, sniffs the air. Its ears twitch. Now George takes aim but he is too quick, too desperate, and his shot splashes into the sodden ground at the caribou's feet, sends a geyser of spray into the air. In an instant the caribou leaps away and, before the men can get off another shot, is gone.

They are too weak to follow. Too weak to even drag themselves back to camp, back to another bowl of watery pea meal soup, another nibble of charred bones. They remain with their faces pressed to the wet ground.

This was the image Mina was seeing from her tent that night. It was why every bite of food she forced down lay in her stomach like a cold weight. It was why her every accomplishment not only pleased but stung. She was grateful, yes, and made sure to offer up a prayer of thanks for the food. Still, she could not help but think that her party's good luck, in fact her party's very presence on the beneficent lakes, had been bought at a cost that could never be recovered.

*Dillon Wallace's expedition, early August 1905*

WALLACE'S PARTY SPENT the first few days of the month as they had spent most of the previous days, battling chilling rain, pestilential insects, torturous terrain and their own gnawing hunger. But they were on a river now that Wallace had named the Babewendigash. It flowed to the northwest, and to Wallace that was an encouraging sign, for it could mean only that the river had as its outlet the Naskapi River. Even so, August 4 was to prove a particularly challenging day.

After an early and unsatisfying breakfast of lentils and tea, the men searched for a portage route around dangerous rapids. Finding none, they were forced to run the rapids. To do so with fully loaded canoes would be not merely dangerous but foolhardy, so Stanton volunteered to carry as much as he could up a steep rise of 250 feet, then down the other side to the riverbank. He soon had reason to regret his choice. The hillside was so precipitously pitched that with a heavy pack strapped to his back he could not stand upright but had to crawl on his hands and knees, grabbing hold of bushes when he could, and at other times digging his nails into the earth to keep from sliding backward all the way to the bottom.

He had never worked so hard to advance such a short distance. Many times he paused, feet braced against a root or stone, certain he could go no farther, on the verge of surrender, nearly ready to shrug off the heavy pack and let it go cascading down the gelatinous slope. After what seemed half a day but could not have been much more than an hour, he reached the summit, mud-blackened from head to toe, exhausted and sore to the very tips of his fingers. There he found the other four men waiting for him. They had successfully navigated the rapids, then climbed the far side of the hill so as to assume some of his load. But the ensuing descent from the ridge was no easier. One by one the men slid, rolled, stumbled, and pitched headlong into the bushes as they made their way down to the river again.

The next day, finally, brought a change of fortune. After another meatless and breadless breakfast, this time consisting of cornmeal mush and tea, the party progressed less than a mile before Pete Stevens lifted his paddle from the water and pointed it at a sandy beach a hundred or so yards ahead. On the sand, sleeping, lay a caribou buck.

Breathlessly the men landed their canoes. Pete, rifle in hand, crept toward a bank from which he could look down on the buck. Easton moved upshore to take a stand opposite the caribou, while Wallace remained below it. Inch by inch they closed in.

Awakened by the men's scent, the buck sprang to its feet and raced into the willows. Wallace and Easton lost sight of it almost immediately and lowered their rifles. But Stevens could hear the animal crashing through the brush. The noise it made seemed to be getting louder. He stood frozen in his spot, rifle butt tight against his shoulder.

Stevens' pulse was hammering in his head, drowning out all other sounds now. And finally the animal emerged onto a burned-over plateau above the beach. It stood two hundred yards away from Stevens. He steadied his hand, aimed and fired. The buck twitched but otherwise did not move. Stevens raised his aim just a fraction and fired again, and the caribou dropped where it stood.

Pete Stevens let out a whoop that could have been heard a mile away. This was the moment he had been waiting for ever since the trip had begun, his chance to be more than a mere cook and camp servant. A marksman, a hunter. The provider of life-saving meat.

The men wasted no time in building a fire on the shore. A thick tenderloin steak was cut for each of them even before the animal was fully dressed, then set to roasting over the flames. They had had no fresh meat for nearly a month now and all were determined to enjoy every bite of it. The brisket was served for supper that night, the liver fried for breakfast the next morning, the heart and tongue boiled for lunch. Their bellies full for a change, they found the long portages and relentless onslaught of insects more tolerable, if only because, at the end of each march, another serving of fresh meat awaited them, tender and black-crusted and sweet.

But five ravenous men can make short work of a caribou. In no time at all the best cuts of meat had been devoured. Then came several meals of caribou stew, breakfast, lunch, and dinner. The stew was hearty and filling at first, then dished out in smaller and smaller portions. The portages grew long again. The hours and miles dragged. Hunger returned and loads grew heavier. Weariness never abated.

Then one evening, after a supper of rice and fishcakes and a last dollop of stew, after the men had gathered in the candlelit tent and all the pipes were going, Wallace startled them by asking, "Who wants to go home?"

They all wanted to go home. On the other hand, none was willing to do so.

"We'll get another caribou soon," Richards said.

Stevens nodded enthusiastically. "More deer up ahead."

But Wallace reminded them of how far they had yet to go. He pointed out that their flour and pork were getting low, the lentils and cornmeal were nearly gone. How many caribou would they have to kill in order to sustain themselves along the way? And, considering the number of caribou they had seen so far, what were the chances of coming upon more game with any regularity? The odds were against them. Their luck, of which they had had damn little thus far, had all but run out.

"Winter is just around the corner," he reminded them. "Three of you men should turn back before we get snowed in. I'll go ahead with one other man and try to finish this thing."

"What other man?" Stanton asked.

Wallace considered each of their faces, the sunken eyes and hollow cheeks. "Who wants to try to see it through with me?"

Four voices sang out in unison. "I do!"

He could not bring himself to point out their individual shortcomings and failures, though he had already essayed each man's abilities many times. And he could not bring himself to send a man back if he did not wish to go. He had hoped for volunteers, in fact had expected a couple of the men to jump at his offer. Later, Wallace would write:

> The loyalty and grit of the men touched my heart. Not one of them would think of leaving me. Nothing but a positive order would have turned them back, and I decided to postpone our parting until we reached Michikamau at least, if it could be postponed so long consistently with safety.

He studied their faces. Finally Richards asked, "Do you think there's a quitter here?"

The question made Wallace regret that he had even broached the subject of splitting up the outfit. "All right," he conceded. "We'll stick together awhile longer."

But every man went to bed that night knowing his reprieve could not last forever. Wallace had raised the spectre of failure, had given voice to it, and now it would haunt them every step of the way.

———

*Mina Hubbard's expedition, August 8, 1905*

YOUNG GILBERT BLAKE must have sensed good fortune in the air that morning, for in the clear dawn calm he awoke Mina with an exuberant rendition of "Glory, glory, hallelujah! as we go marching along!" When she emerged from her tent a short time later she found the other men in an expectant mood too. They had already packed away most of the gear and were ready to join her in a light breakfast.

A half-hour later Mina's tent was taken down and packed with the rest of the outfit, and soon the canoes were launched once again. As they now neared the head of Lake Michikamats, all talk turned to speculation as to how easy or difficult it would be to locate the George River. Like Lake Michikamau, the George was an important milestone, the attainment of which would inspire and embolden. For it was the George they would ride down the northern slope of the Height of Land, no longer fighting the current but moving with it all the way to Ungava Bay.

Paramount in Mina's mind was the knowledge that if they did not reach Ungava by the last week in August they would miss the *Pelican's* departure from the post and would be stranded in that northern realm through a long, harsh winter, month after month of being locked in a prison of ice and snow. All that time Mina would be financially responsible for her four guides until she could get them home again—conceivably a full year from when she had first hired them. And five extra people would put quite a strain on the post's stores; what would they do when supplies ran out?

But merely getting to Ungava was not her only objective. She also hoped, just as her husband had hoped, to meet the Barren Ground Indians, otherwise known as the Naskapi, whose inland camps, as far as anyone knew, had never been seen by a white person. Old wigwam poles and other signs of Montagnais habitation had been spotted several times so far by Mina's party, but as yet no physical contact had been made. Mina wanted desperately to add to mankind's meagre knowledge of how the natives survived in such an unpredictable and frequently inhospitable land.

Additionally, she wished to witness the migration of the barren ground caribou herds as they moved eastward toward the highlands between the George River and the Atlantic Ocean. Although massive herds were often observed west of Hudson Bay, there was no record of the animals' movements through the interior being witnessed by a white person. And a great deal of luck would be needed to make Mina the first such witness, for the caribou's movements were known to be erratic and, as with all life at those latitudes, influenced by the vagaries of weather.

And always, always, Mina wondered about "the others." One night she wrote in her diary, "Always there is much talk of the other party and their probable doings, esp. the probability of their getting lost. All are familiar with the story of W.'s prowess in wilderness travel. Geo. and Gil both know Stanton. Gil says: 'If Stanton falls off his seat in the canoe, he'll get lost.' . . . Then his boy's merry laughter in which everybody joins."

Despite their derision of Wallace's outfit, Mina could not help worrying. Was Wallace ahead of her or behind? Would it really matter whether she saw the Indians and the caribou if she arrived at Ungava Bay to find Wallace and his crew waiting there already, with Wallace smiling his smug, imperious smile as he sucked on his pipe?

She needed speed of movement if she hoped to be first to Ungava, but she also needed the opportunity to conduct the research that would validate her expedition in the eyes of the scientific world. Her goal, after all, was to fulfill her husband's dream of charting the river valley and learning as much as possible about the way the Indians lived. Could she possibly succeed at both? Could she conduct the research *and* reach Ungava first? Day after day, hour after hour, she wrestled with the question of which objective should predominate.

What bothered her most were the delays forced upon them by the weather. That Tuesday morning, not long after they had started out, a fierce wind blew up from the southwest, raising waves that threatened to swamp the canoes.

"We're too heavy for this wind!" George shouted over the howl. He pointed his paddle at a little cove scooped out along the sandy shore. "Over there!" he called to the others, and all four men paddled hard for safe harbour.

Mina did not accept the detour with equanimity. Now out of the howling wind, she looked back across the whitecapped lake. "Can't we just keep moving, George? Even if we move slowly, it's better than not moving at all!"

George's ambition was simpler than hers. He only wanted to get Mina Hubbard to Ungava Bay in one piece and in time to catch the *Pelican*. But it was an ambition that made him, too, resentful of delay. "The problem is," he explained, "we're riding too low in the water. But how about this? If we leave some of the load here, I can take you on forward some." He scanned for a likely spot, and soon found it far ahead on the western shore.

"There, that sandy point. That point will make a nice break-water. Should be a lot calmer up there. We'll take both canoes forward to it, then Job and Joe can come back here with one canoe and pick up the rest of the stuff."

"And in the meantime," Mina asked, "I will have to sit and wait up there?"

"We'll find some exploring to keep us busy," he promised.

What they found at the sandy point was a beautiful little bay. There, while Job and Joe returned down the lake, Gilbert waited with the remaining canoe as George and Mina climbed the high banks to a plateau covered in luxuriant reindeer moss. Not far away the ground sloped upward to moss-covered hills standing against a backdrop of spruce forest. But most thrilling of all to Mina was the sand mound overlooking the bay. The mound was blue-green with its blanket of moss, and standing out sharply atop the mound were four wooden crosses.

All of the graves—one large grave with three smaller ones below it—were enclosed by a simple fence of wooden pickets. Each cross bore an inscription in Montagnais, which George read to Mina. All of the inscriptions, but for one marking a smaller grave, were darkened by weathering.

Out on the sandy point stood the skeleton of a wigwam. Inside this framework the ground had been covered with spruce boughs that were still green, and all around the wigwam fresh shavings lay scattered. Mina scooped up a handful of shavings, inhaled their still sweet fragrance and let them tumble from one hand to the other. "This is where he made the cross," she said. "He sat here outside his wigwam and made a cross for the newest grave."

George nodded, his lips pursed solemnly.

Mina said, "He keeps coming back here to bury his family. His babies."

George stared out at the water. There's reminders everywhere, he thought. Even in a beautiful place like this. Death everywhere we go.

But Mina surprised him. "It's a good place," she said. Her eyes were sparkling and wet but she was smiling. The realization came to George then that she was no longer the shy little woman he had first met down in New York, that quiet, deferential woman who with her eyes had followed her husband's every move, as if to lose sight of him would have been to lose sight of herself.

Mina turned and saw George looking at her. Her smile broadened. "Let's keep exploring," she said.

Everywhere they walked they found slender paths cutting across the reindeer moss. "A lot of caribou have been through here," George told her. "And not so long ago."

They found several old Indian camps as well, each marked by a fire ring made of rounded rocks. And in the shelter of a spruce thicket they were delighted to find a deep bed of fresh green boughs where an Indian had recently passed the night. Just outside the thicket he had set up three poles pointing north.

"He's probably following the caribou," George explained. "The poles are meant to show which way he went."

"He certainly had a comfortable little bed in there," Mina said.

George said nothing. It seemed he was unable to stop looking at her, admiring her, thinking thoughts he usually confined to his journal. Not long ago he had written, "She is more than good to me. My sister could not be any kinder to me than she is . . . what a good friend I have."

He forced himself to turn away, and the first thing he saw was a patch of tiny blue flowers growing out of the moss. He went straight for them without thinking, bent down and plucked three of the flowers and, holding them by their fragile stems, returned to hand them to Mina. "I know how much you like flowers," he said.

She took them from his roughened hand and held them close to her nose. "They're just like little bluebonnets," she said. "And they smell wonderful! So fragrant. Did you smell them?"

He nodded that he had, thought he must have, though in truth it was something other than the flowers' delicate perfume that made him light-headed.

Still holding the flowers to her nose she turned and looked out across the shining waters of the lake, saw the blue rounded hills in the distance and the blue and silver sky above them. "I almost wish we never had to leave here," she told him. "Don't you, George?"

Yes, he surely did, though he answered with only a nod.


Mina's party made their lunch that day on the sandy beach below the Indian graves. Afterward, with the canoes fully loaded again, they pushed northward. The wind was not as treacherous now, though it continued to gust and to drive a fine, pricking rain into their faces, so they held close to the relative shelter of the western shore. All along the way Mina did as she had always done while the men paddled; she made observations and notes in her journal, wrote about the Indian graves while they were still fresh in her mind, described the abandoned camps they had seen, "one a large oblong, sixteen feet in length, with two fireplaces in it . . . and a doorway at either end."

They had progressed little more than a mile when Job suddenly sat up very straight in the bow of the canoe. Gilbert, in the stern, was the first to notice the change of posture, and he reacted instantly by half-standing so as to follow Job's gaze. Both men stopped paddling, seemingly frozen in position. The second canoe drew closer, and its passengers too now looked to the east. And there, on the crest of a ridge not far off the water's edge, silhouetted against the ashen sky, was a patch of dark colour—a group of four caribou grazing.

Without a word the canoes were turned and steered across the lake to land at the base of a rock wall directly beneath the ridge. Job, Joe, and Gilbert each took up a rifle. Using only hand gestures, they picked out a path that, winding up through the rocks, would bring them onto the ridge just below the caribou. George was anxious to join them but he held his excitement in check as he and Mina followed twenty yards behind the others.

The three men were lying flat on their bellies when George and Mina caught up with them on the summit. The four caribou they had first seen had now merged with a herd of fifteen, all of them nuzzling at the sweet grass in a swampy area a hundred and fifty yards to the north. Mina's heart thudded in her chest at the sight of them. Gilbert slowly drew the rifle up to his shoulder, raised himself onto his elbows and squinted along the barrel.

"Oh, please, please don't shoot them," she whispered. "They're much too beautiful to shoot. Please don't."

Gilbert turned to smile at her, then faced the herd again. His finger slid inside the trigger housing. One, two, three, four times his finger twitched, and each time the rifle barrel swung an inch or so to the side as he took dead aim on another animal. But he only pantomimed shooting the caribou, and with each twitch of his fin-ger he made a soft whistling noise as of a bullet flying. All four cari-bou mock-shot, he turned to Mina and flashed an even broader grin.

George whispered to her, "We only kill when we need the meat. So you don't need to worry. Those animals out there might save somebody's life someday. It would be a sin to kill them just for fun."

Every man in the group wanted to raise his weapon, ached to raise his weapon and fire—she could tell this by the brightness of their eyes, the eager way they watched the caribou feeding. But they held those desires in check, and Mina loved the men all the better for it.

They watched the caribou for a quarter-hour or so, until some small noise or faint scent caused a quiver of alarm to ripple through the herd. Then off the animals trotted into the nearby brush.

"How about if the rest of you go back to the canoes," George sug-gested, "while Job and me go investigate? Maybe there's a bigger herd up ahead somewhere."

It was one of the few times George had opted to go off without Mina, and she felt the separation immediately and viscerally. But she knew how loyal a companion he had been all this time, even though she had never been able to match his natural pace and had forced him to walk at hers, so she said nothing to deter him. A bit sullenly despite her efforts not to show her emotions, she watched as George and Job headed off.

Gilbert became her escort on the trip back to the canoes, and all along the way he entertained her with his speculations about the size and age and sex of each of the animals he had felled with his imaginary bullets.

Mina and the others did not have to wait long with the canoes before George and Job came trotting down the rocky path, grinning from ear to ear. "What did you see?" Mina called out. But neither man would say a word until they were ten yards from the others. Then George told them in a half-whisper, "Get in the canoes!"

Mina Hubbard gets ready for another day on the water, 1905.

Mina resting on
the trail, 1905.

Mina tends to
breakfast, 1905.

Mina does some mending in camp, 1905.

Three of Mina's crew members manoeuvre
through shallow water, 1905.

Mina attempts to
communicate with the
Naskapi women, 1905.

A Montagnais boy offers
Mina a shy smile, 1905.

Some of the native
women and children
Mina met, 1905.

Some Montagnais Indians
pose for Mina, 1905.

George and the other men skin a caribou, 1905.

One of the men looks back on Gertrude Falls, 1905.

Mina and her crew are welcomed to Ungava Bay, 1905.

One of Mina's last visits to Laddie's grave in
Haverstraw, New York, date unknown.

Mina scampered into her seat. "What did you see?"

George shoved the canoe into deeper water and hopped aboard. "Tell me!" she begged.

But all he would say was "You better get your camera out. And let's try not to make any more noise."

The men dipped their paddles with a delicacy that barely made a hiss. The canoes glided forward another half-mile. "Here," George finally said, and pointed to his right, and both canoes were turned ashore.

If Mina's pulse had raced earlier, it was hammering now at double speed. She could feel it in her temples and even in her fingertips as she clutched the Kodak close to her chest. Then, disembarked, the party again made its way up a rocky slope, wincing with each noisy tumble of a loose stone. This time George took the lead and placed Mina directly behind him.

Not quite at the top, George paused, stood on his toes and peeked over the ridge. Grinning more broadly than ever, he turned and held out a hand to Mina. "Ladies first," he said.

She took his hand and moved past him and climbed onto the ridgetop. What she saw there took her breath away. The next hillside from top to bottom was literally covered with caribou, a solid mass of brown and grey white-breasted animals feeding on luxuriant moss, bucks and does and fawns intermingled.

She did not hear the men coming up beside her, wasn't aware, as she and somebody else started inching forward, who was at her side, didn't want to look away from the magnificent herd for even an instant. She walked forward, the ground sloping away toward the hill where the caribou grazed. She snapped a couple of pictures but wanted desperately to be closer, closer yet, and she kept walking forward, one cautious step at a time, almost dizzy with excitement.

She and George—for it was he, of course, who accompanied her—had closed to just over two hundred yards when one of the stags near the bottom of the herd quivered, tossed its head, then looked directly at Mina. Neck stiffened, splendid antlers held high, the animal turned from broadside to face her head-on. Within seconds the entire herd was alert and turned. Several more stags came forward to form a wall of imposing antlers.

Mina and George stopped in their tracks. She could hear nothing but the thunder of her heart. Slowly she raised the camera as high as her chest, held it steady. Took another step forward.

And with that movement the entire herd, thousands of animals, came stepping toward her, their massive antlers lowered. The horns were in velvet but looked nonetheless deadly. She shot a glance at George and he nodded to the rear, and it was all the encouragement she needed to retreat.

Job and Joe and Gilbert kept grinning even as Mina hurried past them. She was about to start back down the rocky slope to the canoes when she realized that she was alone and turned to look back. Now she saw why the men had not followed. The herd was not in pursuit of them after all. It had come only a few yards down the hillside, a bluff charge. The caribou were happily grazing again.

Sheepishly Mina returned to stand beside George. Then, as if to shame her further, Job and Joe and Gilbert all strode boldly toward the herd.

A large buck snorted and pawed the ground. A second later the caribou's front line surged forward again, and now it was Mina's turn to smile when the men wheeled around and raced back past her. She laughed all the way down to the canoes.

Later, pushing northward again, as the canoes came around a point, Mina's party spotted an island in the middle of the lake, three-quarters of a mile ahead. Stretched between the island and both shores of the mainland, moving from west to east, was a solid, seething line of swimming caribou, a bridge of animals two or three abreast. Several hundred stood bunched up on the island as if waiting their turn to wade into the water again and swim to the eastern shore, where, one by one, the caribou came streaming up onto the shoreline, dripping water and flicking their tails, only to trot briskly across the rocks and over the hilltop.

Mina's crew approached this spectacle slowly, watching from a distance until the entire herd had crossed onto dry land. Then the men paddled hard to land the canoes just above the point where the caribou had crossed. Mina and the others disembarked and followed on foot as the herd, now broken into companies of ten to twenty animals each, sauntered up and over the next hill, down its slope and up and over the next one. There they seemed to find a hillside to their liking and they spread out with a few sentinel stags at the bottom and started grazing again.

Mina had been enjoying this promenade for quite a while before she realized that she had no pictures of the animals at close range. Those on the far hill, spread out as they were, seemed much less dangerous than the ones that had chased her earlier, so she decided to venture nearer. The ground at the foot of the caribou's hill was boggy beneath the moss, however, and Mina soon found herself sinking in up to her ankles. The squishing, sucking sound as she tried to move forward alerted the herd to her presence; they trotted farther up the hillside. For the next twenty minutes or so the herd moved ahead at a leisurely pace and only occasionally looked back to check on the progress of the lone woman and the four men who followed behind her.

By the time Mina's party crested the next summit, the caribou were several hundred yards away. She knew then that she would be unable to get any closer. But instead of feeling disappointment Mina experienced a deep, quiet contentment. At one point, when she realized how silent her party had been all this time, how respectful and reverent, she looked from George to Joe to Job to Gilbert. "The enjoyment of them," she later wrote, "showed itself in the kindling eyes and faces luminous with pleasure. All his long wilderness experience had never afforded Job anything to compare with that which this day had brought him." She and her crew had been witness to what relatively few individuals ever saw, the spectacle of migration, of thousands of caribou moving in one breathtaking mass.

From the hill where Mina's party now stood they could see Lake Michikamats from end to end. To the north, where the hills on either side of the lake grew gradually smaller and smaller, falling away toward the Atlantic Ocean and Ungava Bay, was a series of lakes dotted by islands.

George came to stand close behind Mina. He laid his arm across her shoulder and pointed, his finger tracing a line in the air, drawing a squiggly path from lake to lake. "That's our route," he told her. "That's where we'll find your river."

*Her* river! She could not stop blushing, could not quiet the tremble of excitement. Was she really going to do it? Would they find the George River as easily as that? Was she really going to succeed? She dared not contemplate the possibility.

She pivoted slowly, taking in the panorama. "Oh, look!" she said. A brilliant rainbow was arcing out of the sky and seemed to come to rest on a boulder at the foot of the hill. It wasn't the first rainbow they had seen in Labrador, but it was surely the most vivid and the nearest.

"Who wants the pot of gold?" she asked.

The men turned to her with puzzled looks.

"Don't you know about the gold at the end of the rainbow?"

No, they had never heard of such a thing.

"There's supposed to be a pot of gold buried at the foot of every rainbow, right where it touches the ground."

George narrowed his eyes a bit and considered her with a wry smile. But Gilbert had heard all he needed to hear. In a flash he was racing wildly down the hill, arms flying.

But when Gilbert reached the boulder at the bottom of the hill, the rainbow had moved. It had slid away from him, out into the middle of a lake. He turned and looked back up the hill and held out his arms in a gesture of confusion. The men howled with laughter and slapped their thighs. Mina did not even mind the drizzle of rain when it started anew, would not mind anything at all if only this moment would never end, this joy.

*Dillon Wallace's expedition, mid-August 1905*

WITH NO MAN YET WILLING to give up, Wallace decided to let the entire party continue on together at least as far as Lake Michikamau. The problem was, he had no idea how far ahead the great lake lay. So on Sunday, the thirteenth, he provided for an eventual retreat by having some of their scant provisions cached. Buried in a hole they dug in the ground, then covered with stones to protect them from scavengers, were thirty pounds of pemmican in tin cans, forty-five pounds of flour, some tea, and ammunition. The men were happy to have their loads lightened but none rejoiced at leaving behind so much precious food. On one hand, they might never see it again. On the other hand, retreat for at least some of the men seemed inevitable, and without these emergency rations those men would in all likelihood starve.

Stanton was particularly aggrieved to see the pemmican go into the ground. Only that morning had they sampled the first tin of it— a combination of ground meat, tallow, and currants hermetically sealed in six-pound cans by Armor and Company of Chicago, and sold at the staggering cost of sixty cents per pound—and he had found the concoction much tastier and satisfying than expected. Finally, a flavourful and belly-filling breakfast again. But now, as he laid stones atop the cache, he felt an emotion very near to despair. There was no guarantee, when some of the men eventually turned back, that they would return by this same route or be able to locate the cache again, so he was not convinced of the wisdom of leaving the food behind. Days later he was still secretly mourning the loss of the pemmican. In his journal, his only confidante, he wrote, "I almost felt as though I had buried my best friend . . . as indeed it was in this country, for without it we would die."

Despite the burial of a hundred pounds of supplies, the load did not feel lighter for long. After lunch the next day, during an eleven-mile portage to the shore of another lake, Stanton staggered under his burden and fell. His heavy pack twisted sideways as he tumbled, which caused him to wrench a muscle in his back. For most of that day he straggled along a mile or more behind the others. Finally Easton, with the stern end of a canoe resting on his shoulder, noticed that Stanton was nowhere to be seen. Nor did Stanton respond to the men's calls. Easton backtracked, found him sprawled and breathless on the trail, and relieved him of half his load. Stanton was in too much agony to manage more than a few words of gratitude.

Even with the weight of his pack cut in half, Stanton was unable to keep up with the others. Only after long hours of trudging on alone, wondering at times if he would ever see home or even his crewmates again, the whomp of an axe came echoing toward him, and he followed that inspiriting sound as if it were a lifeline until he eventually came to where Easton was chopping wood for a fire.

Stanton arrived in camp just in time to hear Easton cry out in pain. The axe blade, after a particularly weary strike, had caromed off the log to strike his leg on the shin bone. Stanton, who was near-est, immediately shrugged off his load and hobbled to the scene of the accident. The other men came running. Easton lay grimacing on the ground, rolling back and forth as he clutched at the wound. Blood seeped through his trousers and between his fingers. Richards knelt beside him and gingerly pushed up the pantleg to expose the wound. There was so much blood that the men feared the worst. How could they possibly carry Easton out of this wilderness? Could they manage a litter, along with the canoes and all their provisions, and with one fewer man to share the load?

Water was brought from the lake and the blood was washed away. Stanton—who with shaking hands now found himself in charge of the ministrations, if only by virtue of being the first at the scene—breathed a sigh of relief. "It's not as bad as it looks," he said. "I don't think the bone is injured. Bring me the boracic acid and some plaster and we'll get this cut cleaned and dressed."

Unfortunately the adhesive plaster had gotten wet and was of no use. So after cleaning the wound, Stanton had Wallace hold the edges of split skin together while electrical tape was wrapped around Easton's leg.

Over the next few days the party's progress was even slower than usual, owing more to the weather than to Easton's wound. In two days they covered only eleven miles. A cold, driving rain with gusting winds made it impossible for one man to portage a canoe; the wind would lift it right out of his hands. With two men needed for each canoe, they had to break the outfit into three loads each, which meant that eleven miles of progress required fifty-five miles of actual walking, thirty-three of those miles with loads on their backs.

But if the weather was harsh, the terrain was brutal. They waded through marshes, trudged over rocky hills, crawled through tangled, dripping brush. Each day consisted of one portage after another toward yet another lake that, when seen from a distance, glimmered enticingly, only to prove too shallow to float a canoe in.

It had been awhile too since the men had come across any Indian signs. They had no idea where the trail to Michikamau lay. All they knew for certain was that they were not on it.

Most vexing of all was the sudden disappearance of game. No caribou tracks were to be seen. And not a single fish could be coaxed onto their hooks or into their net.

The men talked incessantly about the foods they missed from home, recalling their favourite bakeries and restaurants, vainly struggling to conjure up spiritual sustenance from remembered smells and textures and tastes.

On August 16, at breakfast, they scraped the last of the caribou stew off their plates. The meat had turned green but they dared not waste it. On the nineteenth they awoke to find the ground stiff with frost, the water glazed with ice.

On the twentieth they finally hit upon a lake deep enough to carry the canoes. The land all around this lake had been burned over in recent years and the reindeer moss was still brittle and black; it sent up little puffs of ash with every footstep. The few remaining trees were dead—black, broken spears. There were no Indian signs and no sign of game and no sign of the trail to Michikamau. The land was dead and the streams feeding into the lake were dead. They christened this long body of water Lake Desolation.

On August 21 they opened their last bag of flour.

The next day they ate the last of their rice.

They were not yet halfway to their destination, unsure of their location, with nothing but a compass to guide them. Wallace considered all this as he raised a spoonful of rice toward his lips. But then he paused, his eyes on the spoon, the swollen kernels of rice a pale yellow streaked with brown. For the past twenty-two months he had not been able to look at rice without remembering a Sunday in October 1903, one week before Hubbard died.

What a beautiful, clear day that had been, but cold. So cold that Wallace and Hubbard had spent the afternoon wrapped in blankets in front of the fire, talking of food, of course, of chocolate and pies and puddings and French toast, of roast turkeys and baked hams, of fresh apples by the bucketful. George had gone off that day to one of their previous camps in search of any scraps of food they might have left behind, and when he returned at dusk with nothing but a few old caribou bones and two hooves he had dug up he apologized for letting the men down. But Hubbard had tried to be cheerful as always, had said they could make a bully soup from the bones. So George pounded up the bones and dropped them in a kettle of boiling water with the hooves. The hooves were filled with maggots but nobody suggested they be thrown away. The maggots floated in the water like great, swollen grains of rice, and the bones gave up their gristle and marrow and the hooves released a lovely, greasy aroma that made the men's mouths water.

"It smells and looks just like rice soup," Hubbard had said. "My mother used to boil off a pile of ham hocks and put rice in with it. I could never get enough of it."

"If we had some milk and flour and a little sugar we could make a rice pudding," George joked.

They drank three cups each of the maggoty broth and then they chewed on the bones until every bit of gristle and hide had been gnawed away. Then George gathered up what was left of the bones and put them back in the pot for the next day's breakfast. He had salvaged a set of antlers too, and these he broke up and added to the kettle. "They're still in velvet and nice and greasy on the inside," he told the others. "I saved the wenastica too"—the digested contents of the caribou's stomach—"but it smells pretty rotten. What do you fellas think?"

"Put it in tomorrow's soup," Hubbard told him, and the next day they ate from the kettle three times, chewed on the same bones again and savoured the strong, rancid taste of the broth. And they joked again about the fat, meaty "rice" they had enjoyed the day before, and all of them wished they could dig up another supply of that rice. Maybe when they got back to New York they would try to get it on the menu at the finer restaurants. "Labrador rice soup with caribou hooves," Hubbard said.

"Followed by a moss salad with wenastica dressing," said Wallace.

"Then boiled caribou head," George said, "with sliced snout."

"Followed by Labrador rice pudding, of course."

"Labrador rice could become as popular as caviar."

"We'll grow it on rotten meat in our backyards and pack it in tins and sell it for ten dollars an ounce."

"We'll be as rich as kings, and all thanks to our Labrador rice."

But on Thursday, October 15, Hubbard could go no farther. "I got shaky and busted," he wrote that night in his journal. Three days later he chewed on his last meal, a caribou moccasin. He was alone by then and planned to boil his belt and a pair of cowhide mittens for his next meal, but before he could do this he went to sleep and did not wake up. And now, two years later, Wallace could not even swallow a spoonful of rice, real rice and his last precious bit of it, without having his throat constrict and fight against it, swollen with memory, with guilt and grief and loss.

*Mina Hubbard's expedition, mid-to late August 1905*

Mina's party continued paddling from one lake to the next, progressing gradually higher up the interior plateau at whose summit they hoped to find the headwaters of the Naskapi River. She fretted constantly and wondered aloud if this climbing would ever come to an end. Then, on the afternoon of August 10, they reached the northern end of their second lake for the day, and here they were stopped. They could locate no way out of the lake, could find nothing but a tiny stream feeding into it from the north. They scoured the lakeshore for some indication of which way to proceed.

Just when their frustration and confusion were at a peak, when it seemed sure that they had searched every inch of shoreline, they found it: the Indian trail. "What a glad and reassuring discovery it was," Mina wrote, "for it meant that we were on the Indian highway from Lake Michikamau to George River."

Shortly after four P.M. they started a portage that, to their delight and surprise, lasted only a hundred yards or so. At the end of the hike they came upon yet another lake, but this one had no stream feeding into it, nothing but a wide bog to the north. The men checked it again and again. Only when they were certain did George make the announcement.

"This is it," he said. "The headwaters of the Naskapi."

"Are you sure?" Mina asked.

Unable to hold his wide grin in check, George said, "All the water so far, everything south of this bog, which way does it drain?"

"Why, southward, of course."

They walked to the northern end of the bog. "Now look," he said.

But she had already looked, had already seen, and Mina's grin was as irrepressible as his. Because here the water from the bog flowed northward—toward Ungava Bay! After three hundred miles of paddling and poling and portaging they had arrived finally at the summit of the interior plateau, the Height of Land, Labrador's Great Divide.

Though she was standing at no great altitude, Mina could not escape the feeling that she stood at the top of the world. The land was flat and sparsely wooded and it fell away from her on all sides, most dramatically to the north and south. Unfortunately, because of her profligate use of the camera during the first week of the expedition, when everything she saw seemed exciting and new, she now had only a few films left. But this moment was an auspicious one—perhaps the most auspicious of the entire trip thus far—and she felt well justified in taking two more photographs. For the first she turned to the south, the way we came, she thought, back toward Lake Melville and the cold Atlantic. For the second picture she pivoted 180 degrees. The way we go, she told herself, and shot a photo of the lake just north of them, the gateway to their next three hundred miles.

In camp that night a strange contentment came over her. Not long ago there had been little room in her heart but for grief and resentment; now a whole other emotion was making room for itself. As always, she attempted to sort out her feelings by writing in her journal.

"How little I had dreamed when setting out on my journey," she wrote, "that it would prove beautiful and of such compelling interest as I had found it. I had not thought of interest—except that of getting the work done—nor of beauty. How could Labrador be beautiful?" It was, after all, a cruel and inhospitable land. Its temperatures seared your skin during the summer day and froze your flesh on summer nights. Labrador teased you with a bounty of fish and game one week, then tormented you with emptiness the next. Its waters tried to drown you, its land tried to suck you under. At every turn Labrador sent clouds of insects to sting and bite and drive you nearly mad. And what of winter? It could descend on them at any moment, could freeze them in their tracks. They might yet find themselves snowbound, might wake up tomorrow morning to water choked with ice, the trail buried beneath a foot of snow.

Worst of all, Labrador had stolen Mina's soulmate, had starved her Laddie into submission, had knocked him flat and frozen him while he slept. How could such a place be beautiful?

Even so,

*how beautiful it had been, with a strange, wild beauty, the remembrance of which buries itself silently in the deep part of one's being. In the beginning there had been no response to it in my heart, but gradually in its silent way it had won, and now was like the strength-giving presence of an understanding friend. The long miles which separated me from the world did not make me feel far away—just far enough to be nice—and many times I found myself wishing I need never have to go back again. But the work could not all be done here.*

The work, the redemption of her husband's reputation, required that she continue on, no matter how strong the urge to remain there at the top of the world. Another long journey lay ahead, but this time they would move with the current rather than against it. The change of flow, however, did not guarantee an easing of their labour. The water would be swifter now, and in many places dangerously fast. Instead of pushing their canoes away from deadly rapids and roaring cataracts, the current would now do its best to draw them to their doom.

The first three hundred miles had been completed by Mina's party in just under two months. They now had little more than two weeks to complete the last three hundred miles. If they failed, the *Pelican* would depart Ungava Bay without them and they would be stranded there until spring—if, indeed, they even made it that far.

And there was another nagging question to consider. Where was Wallace—ahead or behind? Her accomplishments would mean nothing if he bested her. In that case her Laddie would be doomed to ignominy.

Mina prayed that the rest of the journey would be swift, that the weather would hold awhile longer, not grow too cold nor the wind blow too fiercely. And as for fierceness, what of the Indians? She felt in her bones that her party would soon come across the natives, and none of her group knew what kind of welcome to expect.

So she prayed. She prayed for the safety of her guides and that their food would last and that no one would fall sick and no mistakes would be made. She prayed not for herself but for George and Joe and Job and Gilbert. And always, always, she prayed for Laddie.

The next day, around noon, as the group portaged below the lake atop the divide—which Mina had christened Lake Hubbard—dark clouds rolled across the sky and all but obliterated the sun. For nearly a week the sun hid from them. Violent storms of rain and wind and snow assailed the expedition. At the end of that week, six days after their joy at attaining the Height of Land, they found themselves a mere thirty miles from the site of their accomplishment. The men, who heretofore had shown little of Mina's anxiety, grew more and more restless. They attempted to hide their concern from her by speaking in Cree, but she could read the worry on their faces. Their troubled looks had grown increasingly frequent after the fourteenth, the day they came upon an Indian camp recently abandoned—and to which the Indians obviously intended to return soon.

Several uncovered wigwam frames remained erect in this camp, including one large oblong structure with three fireplaces. Lying about in piles were pots and kettles and tubs, plus clothes, piles of fur scraped from deerskins and heaps of broken animal bones. Hanging from a tree were several steel traps and the iron pounders used for breaking bones. On a stage under two deerskins George found a rifle, a shotgun, and a piece of dried meat.

Everything was left undisturbed, and soon the party took to the river again. The volume of water seemed to be increasing now, the current growing swifter. Then the rapids began. Mina later described the experience in her book: " . . . as the little canoe careered wildly down the slope from one lake to the next with, in the beginning, many a scrape on the rocks of the river bed, my nervous system contracted steadily till, at the foot where we slipped out into smooth water again, it felt as if dipped into an astringent."

Evening in their camp brought little relief from her nervousness. After supper that night the men sat around the campfire and exchanged stories they had heard about various groups of Indians. Some of the stories attested to the Indians' hospitality toward strangers. But the men also spoke of the Hannah Bay massacre that had taken place in the middle of the previous century, when a band of Indians from the interior, angered that greedy fur traders were depleting the game, had sneaked into the fort at Rupert House on James Bay and killed all the whites. Then they had slaughtered the half-breeds and coastal Indians too because of their friendship with the whites.

All during the conversation Mina busied herself giving her revolver a good cleaning. Joe tapped the ashes from his pipe and said, "If it were only the Hudson Bay Indians we were coming to, there would be no doubt about the welcome we'd get. But nobody knows about the Naskapi."

The other men nodded soberly. George, a few moments later, turned to Mina. "You're giving that revolver a fine rubbing up tonight."

"Yes," she replied, and laughed a little. "I'm getting ready for the Naskapi."

But none of the men returned her laugh. "They would not shoot you," George told her.

"No?" she said. "Why not?"

"It would be us they would kill if they took the notion. Whatever their conjuror tells them to do, they will do."

Mina thought George's remark just a little too grave, and she laughed softly. Again, she laughed alone. "Well, maybe when their conjuror sees me coming at them with my pistol, he'll tell them to kill me too."

"No," Gilbert said, "they would not kill you, Mrs. Hubbard. It would be to keep you at their camp that they would kill us."

She lay awake through most of that night, a very clean revolver at her side.

Well before dawn Mina climbed out of her blankets. All of the fretting she had done through the long, quiet hours of night had wearied her. Every tiny sound made by wind or animal had seemed the stealthy approach of an intruder. So many times she had wished she could scurry over to the men's tent and find a pair of warm arms to wrap herself inside. Some things about Labrador were elemental and straightforward, but some things were too complicated.

Now and then through the night, turning back had seemed the most prudent choice. But now, with the sky gradually lightening, retreat seemed the least appealing option. She had four good men to accompany her and they had plenty of food and she had been silly to entertain thoughts of giving up. If only the men had not frightened her with their talk about the Indians. Yes, the dangers were real, but every step of the way there had been dangers. There were dangers too in New York City and on her father's farm in Ontario and in every hospital where she might someday work.

She decided that as long as she had her revolver she would be all right. Wasn't that what Laddie would have told her? But what if the Indians somehow disarmed her? What if she emptied her pistol and still they kept coming?

There was no patter of rain on her tent canopy now but the air was cold and she had to rub her feet beneath the blankets to warm her toes. Then she lit a candle and reached for the small book that was always kept close, and as she often did she opened it at random, laid her finger on a page and read the passage beneath her finger. It was her way of waking to Laddie's voice.

This morning she read the entry for Tuesday, September 15, 1903:

*Temperature 31 degrees, 5 AM. West wind, spits of sleet and fair. Wind continued hard all day. Could not leave shore. I lay awake all last night, thinking over the situation. George is worried and talks of Indians who starve. Tries to be cheerful, but finds it hard. Here we are, wind-bound, long way from Michikamau. No hopes of wind abating. The caribou migration is due to begin. Yet we can't start and are at least two weeks from their grounds, with no grub and no prospects of good weather. Our grub is 18 pounds pea-meal—to be held for emergency—and 2 pounds flour, 1 pt rice, 3 pounds bacon. To go on is certain failure to reach the caribou killing, and probable starvation. If we turn back we must stop and get grub, then cross our long portage, then hunt more grub and finally freeze up preparatory to a sled dash for Northwest River. That will make us late for boat. But we can snowshoe to St. Lawrence. All this, with what we have done so far, will make a bully story. I don't see anything better to do. I asked*

*Wallace. He opposed—then said it was best. I said to George—
would you rather go on or turn back? "I came to go with you and I
want to do what you do." When I said we will turn back, he was very
greatly pleased. Now my job is to get the party back to Northwest
River, getting grub as we go. We will take the back track to some good
fishing grounds, catch fish, try to kill a caribou, and wait for freeze.
We can't take the canoe down the Naskapi—hence the need of
freezing.*

*Staid in camp all day. Could not launch canoe. No place to fish or
hunt. Feel better, now that the decision is made. Ate very thin rice and
bacon soup and drank tea. Long chat with Wallace. Feeling good in
spite of short grub. George is telling again how he will visit his sister at
Flying Post and what he will eat. We are talking of plans for our home
going, and are happy despite impending hunger.*

Unfortunately the message failed to direct Mina, as she had
hoped it would, in a specific course of action, a specific approach to
the day. So she flipped ahead several pages and laid her finger down
again.

*Thursday, October 15, 1903:*
   *Dreamed last night came to New York, found M. and had my first
meal with her. How I hated to find it a dream. Lightened packs a good
deal. Left Wallace's rifle, cartridges, rod, my cleaning rod, my sextant
and 15 films and other things, cached in bushes at left side of little
stream between two lakes. Wallace hated to leave rifle, and I hated to
leave other stuff. Spent most of forenoon getting ready. Ate for breakfast bit of skin from old caribou head, boiled with bone broth. At
lunch—on Montagnais Lake—same, but skin was that from old
caribou hide which we had carried to mend moccasins. Were almost
to our second camp—where we ate first goose—when I got shaky and
busted, and had to stop. Wallace came back and got my pack and I
walked to camp unloaded. In PM George shot three partridges which*

*jumped up before us in swamp. Killed them with my pistol. Made us very happy. Ate one for supper, and oh, how good. In spite of my weakness I was happy to-night. I remember a similar happiness once just after I went to New York. I got caught in the rain; had no car fare—got soaked—spent last 10 cents for rolls and crullers—then crawled into bed to get dry and eat, not knowing where next meal would come from. Talk of home. George not thinking now of eating of recent years, but just the things his mother used to make for him as a child. Same way with Wallace and me, save that I think of what M. and I have eaten that she made.*

Was he telling her to give up, to turn around before it was too late? No, it couldn't be. Laddie would never countenance surrender. In fact, the more she thought about it, the more convinced she was that he was advising just the opposite. *I got shaky and busted and had to stop.* And what had been the result of that decision? It was against Laddie's nature to throw in the towel and he had done so only when his body gave out, and what had been the result of it?

Even in that terrible moment he had found some happiness. Just as in New York, with no money and no prospects, homeless and cold and wet, he had been happy. That, if anything, was his message to her.

*I think of what M. and I have eaten that she made.* To the very end he had been thinking of her and taking comfort in the simple moments of their lives. I thought of you, he seemed to be telling her with those words. I thought of you then just as you must now think of me. She could almost hear his voice in her ear, could feel his breath warming the side of her face. *Push on, brave girl. Push on.*

By the time the eastern wall of her tent turned from charcoal to ash grey, she had dried her tears and warmed herself with a new determination. She reached for her woollen stockings and pulled them close. They were frozen stiff. But she was anxious to be out of her tent and moving again, so instead of digging through her pack for dry stockings she pushed the cold ones beneath her blanket and bit by bit worked them on.

When fully dressed she peeled back the tent flap and peeked out. Frost sparkled on the rocks and low bushes, a scattering of diamonds. The men were out and moving about too, though stiffly, sleepily, getting a fire ready for a bracing pot of tea.

By the time they all finished their tea, the wind had picked up again. Row after row of little whitecapped waves raced across the lake. But the wind was blowing the mist off the lake and every now and then Mina could catch a glimpse of the distant shore.

"It isn't too rough, is it?" she asked George. "I really do want us to get moving this morning."

He studied the sky. Eventually a sliver of blue appeared, though just for an instant before the rising fog obscured it. "I think we can try it," he said.

Two hours later the breeze had driven most of the clouds away. For the first time in seven days they saw the sun again. Mina sat in the centre of the canoe with her head laid back and her face raised to the sun, soaking up its warmth. "It's going to be a good day," she announced.

The men said nothing. She knew they were still worried about the Indians.

"Really," she said, "everything is going to be fine today. You wait and see."

Gilbert and Joe's canoe glided along beside hers. Gilbert asked, "How do you know, missus?"

"I just know, that's all. I can smell it in the air."

Gilbert raised his head and sniffed. "All I can smell is Job," he said.

They passed down that lake and along a narrower stretch of the river, then onto a longer lake that Mina named Resolution. The entrance to this lake was crowded with small islands, but beyond the islands Resolution opened up clear and calm and wide. For the first four miles the lake was bordered by low, bushy banks, but then the canoes approached a high sandy point that reached out into the water from the eastern shore, and at the moment Mina first saw that hillside in the distance, and especially the irregular patches of shadow near its top, her pulse began to race.

"It might be caribou," Joe said.

But Mina knew that those shadows were not made by caribou. And as the canoes drew closer, a flash of light flared from the centre of a shadow, the glint of sunlight on metal. "It isn't caribou," George said sombrely.

A minute or so later a short volley of rifle shots rang out from the hillside. The men reached for their own rifles and laid them across their knees. Mina slipped her revolver from its holster, raised it into the air and fired a single shot in reply.

Twice more the Indians on the hillside fired a quick volley, and each time Mina answered with a single shot. She had no way of knowing the intention behind the Indians' shots, nor how they were interpreting hers. But for the moment it was their only form of communication. George directed his canoe farther out into the lake. The other canoe followed.

Eventually the shadows on the hillside took recognizable form—a group of twenty or so women and children. The men paddled very slowly now, ready at any moment to swing their canoes to the far side of the lake. One of the women stepped forward from the group and shouted something. Soon the entire group took up the shout, all the time waving their hands as if to push the canoes away.

George said, "They're telling us, 'Go away, go away. We are afraid of you. Our husbands are away.'" He had learned the language of the Montagnais two years earlier, when, after the first Hubbard expedition, he had been forced to winter over at the North West River Post, where some of the Indians did their trading.

"*Tanto sebo?*" Job shouted into the din—Where is the river? "*Tanto sebo?*" He and the other men had visibly relaxed, even exchanging a few smiles, when they heard that there were no men in camp.

Upon hearing their own language coming back to them, the Indians quieted. In Montagnais George called up to them, "We are strangers and are passing through your country."

Now the shouts of fear from the hillside turned to laughter, and four of the women raced down toward the shore to welcome the strangers. "Is it safe?" Gilbert asked.

Mina said, "Of course it's safe. They want to meet us. And I want to meet them."

George spent a few moments longer studying the hillside for signs of any other Indians. Finally he agreed to turn the canoes toward shore.

By the time everyone in Mina's party had shaken the hands of the first four women, several other women and children had come down off the hill. Mina was more than a little surprised by how open and at ease the Indians were, especially in light of their fear only minutes earlier. They displayed not a trace of shyness or suspicion. She was also impressed by their appearance:

*Their clothing was of a quite civilized fashion, the dresses being of woolen goods of various colors made with plain blouse and skirt, while on their feet they wore moccasins of dressed deerskin. The jet black hair was parted from forehead to neck, and brought round on either side, where it was wound into a hard little roll in front of the ear and bound about with pieces of plain cloth or a pretty beaded band. Each head was adorned with a toque made from black and red broadcloth, with beaded or braided band around the head. Both the manner of wearing the hair and the toque were exceedingly picturesque and becoming, and the types were various as those found in other communities, ranging from the sweet and even beautiful face to the grossly animal-like. They were not scrupulously clean, but were not dirtier than hundreds of thousands to be found well within the borders of civilization, and all, even the little children, wore the crucifix.*

Through a series of exchanges between the Indians and Mina's men, she learned that the Montagnais males had gone to Davis Inlet on the east coast to trade for winter supplies. They had been gone for five days and were expected to return in three or four, bringing with them all the eagerly awaited goods from the trading post, including tea, sugar, tobacco, clothing, and trinkets.

As for the Barren Grounds Indians, the Naskapi, whom Leonidas Hubbard had hoped to meet, they, the Montagnais women said, could be found at their hunting grounds farther north along the river. "You will sleep twice before coming to their camp."

Mina instructed George to ask if the women had had any other visitors recently, particularly four white men and an Indian.

No, said the women. Nobody but you.

"Ask them how far it is to the George River Post at Ungava."

When the answer was received, George's face darkened.

"How far?" Mina asked.

"Two months, they say."

Her stomach fell. *Two months!* In that case they would not reach Ungava until October. Not only would the *Pelican* be long gone, but her party would be caught fast in the grip of winter by then. Would they even be able to reach the post? Laddie had died in a blizzard on October 18. Was that to be their fate as well?

"That can't be right," Mina told him. "Ask again."

But the answer came back the same. "Two months," one of the women repeated, and several others nodded in agreement.

From that moment on Mina wanted only to find a place to sit alone for a while. She needed to decide on a course of action. It had taken two months to get this far. Ungava lay two months ahead. Should they push on toward Ungava, all the while praying against the odds for a late winter? When just this morning her stockings had been frozen stiff? Or should she direct the party to turn east with the intention of wintering over at Davis Inlet? If the Montagnais men could reach it in less than a week, surely her party could too.

Unfortunately she was afforded no time to contemplate the dilemma. The women and children took each member of her party, including herself, by the hands and, laughing and grinning and nodding, pulled them up the path toward their camp. It was all Mina could do to keep a smile on her face.

She had to admit, though, that the panoramic view of Resolution Lake from the top of the hill was breathtaking, and that the camp itself was picturesque. But she was finding it difficult to revel in her latest accomplishment, and felt rather like a child who, shown a bowl full of candy, is warned, "Isn't it pretty? Don't touch!"

She refused to give in to her misery. No white person had ever before seen one of these interior camps, so she knew how important it was to be observant. She later made extensive entries in her notebook, describing the camp as consisting of one oblong wigwam and one round wigwam, each with walls of deerskin stretched over poles. By looking through the doorway of the larger, oblong wigwam she could see that the interior was kept very neat, the dirt floor covered with freshly cut boughs of fragrant balsam. All possessions, such as white enamel tea sets, dishes, pans, and rifles, were clean and well cared for and placed out of the way in an orderly fashion.

Through translated conversations Mina learned how poor the camp was. The women and children, while the men were away, had nothing to live on but the fish they could catch, and their luck with fishing was not great. At the moment there was no tea or sugar or tobacco anywhere in camp.

George said, "They have no idea that the caribou are so near. But even if they did, all the hunters are away at Davis Inlet."

"If only we had known," said Mina. "How easily you and the others could have killed some caribou for them."

Afterward Mina wandered about the camp, followed by several children and dogs. The women seemed more interested in her crew, and openly flirted with the men, running their hands along the men's arms and tugging at the hair at the napes of their necks. Mina found all of this amusing but in a bittersweet way; the camp was so poor, the women's clothing so plain and unadorned, the eyes of the hungry children so haunting.

It was not long before Mina announced that her party must return to their canoes; a long journey lay ahead. When George passed this information on in Montagnais, several women again seized the men by the hands and urged them to stay. After one exchange Job's eyes lit up particularly bright, and a broad smile creased his face.

George interpreted for Mina. "Apparently we can have as many wives as we wish," he said. "Temporarily, of course. If we promise to stay awhile longer."

Mina blushed. "In that case we had better leave right now. Before I lose my crew."

Had she not been faced with the prospect of a long, uncertain journey, Mina would have gladly shared her provisions with the Indians and would have sent her men back to hunt for as much caribou as they could carry. She regretted being unable to do so. But two months' travel to Ungava! Her mind was still reeling with this information, her stomach queasy.

Once again on the shore of Lake Resolution, however, she could not resist sending George back up the hill with a small gift, a bag containing a few ounces of tea. As a result George was literally swarmed by the women, who danced up and down in delight. They offered him a new pair of moccasins in return, but it was too much, he told them, too valuable, and he could not accept.

Before taking to the water again, Job, who rarely spoke in English, stood up tall in the stern of his canoe. He whipped off his hat and made a very elegant bow to the women on the hillside. "Goodbye! Goodbye, my ladies!" he called.

His was the last smile among Mina's party for the next several hours, for without a word they pointed their canoes northward and paddled down the lake. Nobody mentioned the prospect of turning back or turning east toward Davis Inlet, though the information that Ungava lay two months ahead weighed heavily on all their minds. It was with silent and sullen determination that they pushed forward, down through Resolution and ten miles beyond. There, where the river dropped through a series of three rocky gorges, they made their night's camp.

After supper, when the men brought out their pipes—though more sombrely than ever before—Mina knew she could avoid the subject no longer. "Do you think it can possibly take us two more months?" she asked.

Joe said, "I just don't see how that can be right. We made ten miles easy just this afternoon. Down on the lower George we should be able to do fifty miles a day."

Gilbert said, "We should have asked if they've ever been to Ungava. Maybe they've never even been there."

"You know," George said, "I think that's right. Not if they do all their trading at Davis Inlet."

Mina was quick to seize upon the possibility. "I knew two months couldn't be accurate!"

"But even if it's off by half," George pointed out, "we'll still miss the *Pelican*."

Again her spirits fell. "Well," she said, "what shall we do?"

The others all looked to George. "I'm for pushing on," he said.

"Same here," said Gilbert.

Joe said, "Wouldn't make any sense to turn back now."

Only Job remained silent. He sat motionless, his eyes on the fire.

Gilbert said, "Job's still thinking about all those women back there. That's where he wants to go."

Mina offered a smile. "Job?" she asked.

He looked across the fire at her, deadpan. A moment later he returned her smile. "Ungava first," he said. "Make women miss me more."

———

The day after leaving the Montagnais camp, they made another twenty-two miles, and though the men still bent to their paddles with grim determination, Mina felt better about their decision not to turn back. It could not possibly take another two months to reach Ungava—not, she decided, unless they had to walk the entire way.

The portages over the next two days, however, were never longer than a half-mile each, and the swiftness of the river more than compensated for the slowness of those short hikes. And on the morning of August 20, a Sunday, Mina awoke in a high state of expectancy. As she later described the premonition, "It seemed this morning as if something unusual must happen. It was as if we were coming into a hidden country. From where the river turned into the hills it flowed for more than a mile northward through what was like a great magnificent corridor, leading to something larger beyond."

She and her party had slept three times since leaving the Montagnais camp, and the women there had told her that the Naskapi hunting camp was but two sleeps away. So she fully expected to encounter the Naskapi not far ahead. For that reason she decided that her party would forego its Sunday of rest and travel on.

Joe and Gilbert were the first to get their canoe loaded and onto the river. The water that morning appeared dark and still, like shiny black glass. But with only a few strokes the canoe pulled far ahead of the one still on shore, and from this Mina knew how strong the current truly was.

In time George and Job brought the second canoe close to the first, and all four men settled into a steady rhythm of paddling. By now there was a kind of harmony to their dipping and pulling, a music Mina found soothing. She sat with her notebook open on her lap, meaning to write in it, but instead she kept scanning the countryside, alternating between hope and fear.

"In the distance we could see the mountain tops standing far apart," she later wrote, "and knew that there, between them, a lake must lie. Could it be Indian House Lake, the *Mush-au-wau-ni-pi*, or

'Barren Grounds Water,' of the Indians? We were still farther south than it was placed on the map I carried. Yet we had passed the full number of lakes given in the map above the water. Even so I did not believe it could be the big lake I had been looking forward to reaching so eagerly."

To this point they had progressed little more than three miles. Then George sat up very straight and shouted, "There it is!" High on a hill stood a covered wigwam. Within seconds another wigwam came into view. Then the small dark figure of someone walking leisurely between the wigwams.

"He doesn't see us yet," Mina said.

No sooner had she spoken than the person on the hill stopped walking. He cupped a hand over his eyes and stood motionless. Then he turned toward one of the wigwams. Though he could not be heard down on the water, it was obvious that he had called out, for immediately several individuals came racing out of the wigwams to look toward the water.

Cautiously, the canoes drew closer. Now Indians were hurrying back and forth over the hill, running from one wigwam to the other, alerting the camp. It wasn't long before dozens of people stood gathered on the hill. A man holding a rifle came to the foreground, the weapon raised in the air with one hand. Then the crack of two rifle shots echoed down to the water.

Mina answered with a shot from her revolver.

Another shot from the Naskapi. Another shot from Mina.

Ten or so men came trotting down a well-worn path toward the water's edge. But instead of coming all the way to the shore they stopped behind a line of spruce trees just above a sandy landing point. There they launched into an animated discussion.

Mina's party kept their distance too, holding the canoes twenty yards from shore. "Bo jour!" George called. Bonjour!

He was answered by a chorus of a half-dozen voices. "Bo jour! Bo jour!"

George then called out to them in Cree, and with that the Naskapi came striding through the trees and down to the river. Mina asked, "What did you say to them?"

"I said, 'We are strangers and are passing through your country.'"

Mina's canoe was the first to pull ashore. As it did so, one of the Naskapi drew apart from the others. He came forward and caught the bow of the canoe. From his regal bearing Mina knew he was the chief.

"Of course you have some tobacco?" he said.

George told him, "Only a little. We have come far."

With this the chief held out his hand to George in friendship, and George took it gladly.

Mina was nervous, unable to forget Gilbert's speculation earlier about the Indians' possibly hostile intentions, but she was nonetheless observant.

*It was a striking picture they made that quiet Sabbath morning, as they stood there at the shore with the dark green woods behind them and all about them the great wilderness of rock and river and lake. You did not see it all, but you felt it. They had markedly Indian faces and those of the older men showed plainly the battle for life they had been fighting. They were tall, lithe, and active looking, with a certain air of self-possessiveness and dignity which almost all Indians seem to have. They wore dressed deerskin breeches and leggings reaching from the ankle to well above the knee, and held in place by straps fastened about the waist. The shirts, some of which were of cloth and some of dressed deerskin, were worn outside the breeches and over these a white coat bound about the edges with blue or red. Their hair was long and cut straight round below the ears, while tied about the head was a bright colored kerchief. The faces were full of interest. Up on the hill the women and children and old men stood watching, perhaps waiting till it should appear whether the strangers were friendly or hostile.*

The chief asked George, "Where did you come onto the river?"

"We have come the whole length of the river. Up the Naskapi and through Michikamau."

The chief's eyebrows lifted. "It is a long journey."

"Very long," George said.

"I have been to Northwest River, many years ago. But I know the way." The chief then turned to the men gathered behind him and related all this to them. All came forward and gathered close to George, eager to hear more.

"We are going down the river to the post at Ungava," George told them. The chief's reply made George grin from ear to ear. Beaming, he turned to Mina.

"What?" she asked. "What did he say?"

"He said, 'Oh! You are near now.'"

"How near? How near are we?"

George asked the chief, "How near?"

"You will sleep only five times if you travel fast."

When Mina heard the translation, she felt like leaping out of the canoe. Not two months from Ungava, as the Montagnais women had said, but a mere five days! She felt dizzy with relief, giddy with the joy of it. But the discussion was continuing fast and furious now between George and the Naskapi and she did not wish to miss a word of it. She did her best to let George decide when to turn and interpret for her, but it was hard not to blurt out every ten seconds or so, "What did he say?"

"And how is the river from here to Ungava?" George asked.

"Very fast," he was told.

"Many rapids?"

"Rapids all the way. Some this steep," indicated by an arm held out at a slight angle, the fingers pointing down, "and some this steep," with the elbow pointing into the air.

"How many portages?"

"A few. Not too many."

"And not long," another man said. "A short lift over the falls."

The chief then told George, "And when you come to a river coming in on the other side in quite a fall, you are not far from the post."

It was then Mina remembered the warmth, back on the lake she had named Resolution, of Laddie's whispered voice in her ear. *Push on!* he had told her. *Push on!* Her throat tightened and her chest ached with the knowledge of how close she had come to giving up.

"Did you see any Indians?" the chief asked.

"Yes," said George. "We have slept three times since we were in their camp."

"Were they getting any caribou?"

"No. The men were trading at Davis Inlet."

"Had they not seen any signs of the crossing?"

"No. But we have seen the caribou. More than all of us could count."

This news excited the Naskapi enormously. They asked several questions at once as to precisely where the caribou had been seen and how fast they were moving and in which direction. Then they discussed among themselves the likelihood of the herd coming their way.

"Will you go after them?" George asked.

The chief shook his head. He answered in a funereal tone, "Not our country."

Upon further questioning George learned that the Naskapi men had themselves returned only recently from Davis Inlet. Unfortunately, the trading ship had not yet arrived and the post store was empty, so they had been forced to return empty-handed. All summer long they had been able to take only an occasional caribou, just enough to satisfy their present needs. There had been no meat to put aside for winter. They did not know how they might survive.

"You see the way we live," an old man told George, "and the way we dress. It is hard for us to live. Sometimes we do not get many caribou. Perhaps they will not cross our country. We can get nothing from the Englishman, not even ammunition. It is hard for us to live."

George then asked how far it was to Davis Inlet.

"Five days' travel," he was told. "Seven days' coming back. This year an Englishman travelled part of the way with us."

When Mina heard this she asked, "An Englishman? That couldn't be Wallace, could it?"

George explained, "To an Indian any white man is an Englishman. But I don't know why Wallace would have gone to Davis Inlet unless he got lost or gave up."

The chief did not recognize the name of Wallace.

"Was it Mr. Cabot?" George asked. Earlier in the year, William Brooks Cabot had told Mina that he would be visiting the Naskapi along the coast, and that he planned to travel the George River in hopes of being the first white man to visit their home camp.

The chief recognized the name. "Cabot, yes, that is the man. He turned back two days' journey from here. He was going away on a ship."

Mina had only a moment to savour the accomplishment of besting Cabot, of being the one to find the home camp of his beloved Naskapi. By now many more Naskapi had descended to the shore, and all were pressing close to the canoes. Several old women, grinning toothlessly, held out their hands to Mina and begged for "*Tshistemau, tshistemau.*"

"They want tobacco," George told her.

Mina held out her empty hands and smiled apologetically.

"She is not giving us any tobacco! See? She is not giving us any tobacco!"

"She does not smoke," George explained. "She has no tobacco to give you. But she has other gifts."

Now the toothless smiles returned. Quickly George asked Mina if, now that they were so near the post, she would like to share some of their provisions. "Of course!" she said, and in short order an opened bag of flour was lifted from the canoe and laid on the beach.

"Please hand me some tea and rice too," she told Job. "We can wrap it in these silk handkerchiefs."

She saved only enough rice for one more batch of pudding, and just enough tea to provide for five days' journey. She instructed Joe to fill a tin pail with salt and a slab of bacon. In the meantime she found a few trinkets among her things and distributed these as well.

With the Naskapi now grinning ear to ear and nodding their thanks, Mina brought out her camera and motioned to the chief that she would like to take his picture. He understood immediately and, drawing away from the group, stood up very straight, his shoulders back and chest full, chin lifted high, mouth set in an imperious scowl. Afterward the chief smiled again and told her, "You will come up to our camp now."

George was not at all comfortable with this invitation, as his expression conveyed when he relayed the information to Mina. But she said, "Oh, yes indeed!" There would be great interest, she knew, in her observations about how the Naskapi lived. How could she justify being a few minutes from the camp and not investigating it? Besides, just imagine how green Mr. Cabot would be when he read of her success! And if Cabot was green with envy, what colour would Wallace be?

Reluctantly, George acquiesced. He would accompany Mina up the hill. But the rest of the crew must remain at the canoes, not only to protect their remaining provisions and gear but to be ready to depart at a moment's notice.

As Mina walked toward the camp, flanked by the chief on one side and George on the other, a young Naskapi man did everything he could to catch her eye. He preened and strutted, ran ahead, paused, allowed her to catch up, then ran ahead again, all the while putting himself on display for her. His efforts did not go unnoticed. Mina later described the amusing exhibition:

*One of the young men, handsomer than the others, and conscious of the fact, had been watching me throughout with ardent interest. He was not only handsomer than the others, but his leggings were redder. As we walked up towards the camp he went a little ahead, and to one side managing to watch for the impression he evidently expected to make. A little distance from where we landed was a row of bark canoes turned upside down. As we passed them he turned and, to make sure that those red leggings should not fail of their mission, he put his foot up on one of the canoes, pretending, as I passed, to tie his moccasin, the while watching for the effect.*

George noticed the blush of her cheeks and her coquettish smile. "It's probably not a good idea to encourage him," he said. He laid a light hand on her back and nudged her forward.

Mina couldn't resist a bit of teasing. "But he's quite handsome, don't you think? Perhaps you should tell him I said so."

She nearly laughed out loud at the look of alarm in George's eyes. "Don't worry," she told him. "He's not as handsome as you, despite those wonderful red leggings."

What a wonderful time she was having!

At the top of the hill she could see several miles to the north. The river lay "like a great, broad river guarded on either side by the mountains." The camp itself consisted of two large wigwams, the poles covered with deerskins sewn together. But the skins were worn and weathered, much like the faces of the Naskapi who stood around the wigwams, watching her approach:

*Here the younger women and the children were waiting, and some of them had donned their best attire for the occasion of the strangers' visit. Their dresses were of cotton and woolen goods. Few wore skin clothes, and those who did had on a rather long skin shirt with hood attached, but under the shirt were numerous cloth garments. Only the*

*old men and little children were dressed altogether in skins. . . . The*
*faces here were not bright and happy looking as at the Montagnais*
*camp. Nearly all were sad and wistful. . . . Even the little children's*
*faces were sad and old in expression. . . .*

Initially the women hung back from Mina, too shy to speak to
her. She wondered how best to approach them. Then she spotted
a young mother holding a baby bundled in a blanket. "I stepped
towards her," she wrote, "and touching the little bundle I spoke to
her of her child and she held it so that I might see its face. It was
a very young baby, born only the day before, I learned later, and
the mother herself looked little more than a child. Her face was
pale, and she looked weak and sick. Though she held her child
towards me there was no lighting up of the face, no sign of respon-
sive interest."

Mina took a few photographs of the group and did her best to
communicate by gesture with the women who crowded around her.
It wasn't long before George's restlessness got the better of him. He
motioned to her that they should return to the canoes.

"A while longer," she said. "We don't have to hurry now, do we?"

Considering how desperate the Naskapi were, how bereft of winter provisions, George did not trust their geniality to last forever.
But he did not want to frighten Mina unnecessarily, so instead he
told her, "We don't know about the *Pelican*. It might come early. Even
an hour's delay on our part could make us miss it."

The prospect of gliding triumphantly into Ungava only to see
the *Pelican* steaming off, irretrievable, was all the encouragement
Mina needed. Quickly she made her goodbyes. Most of the Indians
walked as far as the edge of the hill with her and George.

"Send us a fair wind," George told them.

"Yes," the chief assured him. "A fair wind all the way."

Minutes later, feeling a bit light-headed from the events of the
past hour, Mina again seated herself in the centre of the canoe.

From there she looked back up the hillside. The Naskapi were standing just as she and George had left them, looking still and sombre. How she regretted that she had not been able to give them more! Wistfully, she took out her handkerchief and waved it back and forth over her head. In an instant the hillside blossomed with colour and movement as the women slipped off their shawls and kerchiefs and waved them in response.

After George shoved the canoe out into the river again and the rhythmic slap and dip of paddles began, Mina felt like crying. She had done so much she had never expected to do. Michikamau. The Height of Land. The Montagnais. The Naskapi. And soon, in just five short days, Ungava. She should have been exultant, but instead she felt overwhelmed with sorrow.

What she had thought unattainable was now close at hand. Why could she not rejoice? Because she was not worthy of the accomplishments. The one who had been worthy had been denied, stymied at every turn, while her way had been easy in comparison. While Laddie had fully expected to succeed, she had fully expected to fail, had even hoped, in her darkest moments, to experience the same hardships, the same fate, as had befallen him.

George kept a close eye on her. He seemed to understand what she was thinking. He too was experiencing the bittersweet taste of their success. He too felt the guilt that was eating away at her.

But young Gilbert Blake's enthusiasm remained untainted. "On to Ungava!" he cried out.

George flinched. To his mind the moment deserved, at the least, humility. Still, he could not chide the boy for brimming with youthful energy. He only said, "We have to make it through the rapids yet."

"Will they be bad?" Mina asked.

"As bad as any we've seen so far."

She did not know if she was more frightened or excited by the prospect.

———

Indian House Lake glittered calm and serene in the morning sun-
shine, and the pull of the current made paddling easy. After lunch a
gentle breeze blew up from the south, so George called for the sails
to be rigged and soon the canoes were speeding along gracefully,
pushed by wind and pulled by current.

In most places the lake appeared to be approximately two miles
wide. Occasionally a wedge of sand stretched into the water from
one shore or another, and frequently a stream came pouring down
from the hills. In the afternoon the eastern and western shores
closed toward one another, and where the lake was only a quarter-
mile wide the party saw their last caribou of the trip, a single animal
walking along the shore on their right.

"It's a female," George said.

Joe agreed. "Maybe three years old or so."

"Let's take the sails down and see if we can get close to it."

The doe stood at the water's edge some fifty yards ahead, alert
and watching as the canoes drew closer. Mina said, "You're not going
to shoot it, are you? Surely we don't need the meat now."

"We just want to play with it," George told her.

The canoes were kept in the shallows as they continued their
approach. Only at the last minute did the caribou show any fear at
all, and even then it seemed not the least bit skittish. Almost dain-
tily it stepped into the water and started to swim toward the opposite shore.

"Now!" George told the others. "Paddle hard!"

They came toward the caribou at an angle, cutting it off. The
moment the doe reversed direction, so did one of the canoes, with
George and Job herding the caribou from the east, Gilbert and Joe
from the west. Laughing and shouting directions at one another, the
men set the doe on a zigzag course northward up the lake.

"Oh, please stop tormenting her!" Mina cried.

George, in the bow, told Job, "Get me up as close as you can." Job
did so. And a minute later George leaned forward as far as he could,

reached into the water and seized the caribou by her tail. Mina felt the canoe being jerked forward. The other men cheered. Job, content to be towed all the way to Ungava, laid his paddle across his lap, leaned back, crossed his arms and grinned like a sultan.

The men thought it a grand thing for them to be towed by a wild animal. Mina did not. And she knew that the doe did not think so either. But she was reluctant to order George to let go. Then the doe turned west, cutting across the bow of the other canoe, refusing to be turned northward again. A couple of minutes later the doe's feet touched bottom and dug in hard, jerking the canoe along, and George was forced to relinquish his prize or be dragged up onto the rocks. The caribou bolted halfway up a steep hillside before pausing to look back.

"It thinks it escaped with its life," Joe said.

In a girlish falsetto Gilbert asked, "Oh, my my! What was that thing had ahold of me? Oh, my, but it was heavy!"

Only Mina did not laugh. "Someday something might grab you by the tail," she told them, "and maybe then you will understand how the poor thing felt."

For a few moments the men were silent. Then an explosion of laughter echoed over the lake.

"Current pull harder and harder," Job told them. His face seemed exceedingly pale that morning, August 22, and he did not attack his breakfast as he usually did but held the tin plate balanced on his knees, his gaze going off over the campfire and into the mist on the river. His eyes, Mina thought, looked like those of the caribou George had caught by the tail—glazed with fear.

"We try slow down but no good," he continued, speaking haltingly now, recounting his dream. "Try get ashore but current too strong."

Only Mina was not troubled by the dream. What troubled her was the deadly seriousness with which the other men sat listening.

"Water get faster and faster. River louder and louder. Then no water up ahead. Only sky up ahead. We paddle like crazy but it no good. Bert go over edge first, canoe tippin' down and him slidin' over with it. Then I go out behind him. Then George and Joe and the missus come too. We all go over and down. Long, long way down. We still fallin' when I wake up."

He had said more in one minute than he normally said in a day. And the impact of his words left all the men with no appetite, only a sick feeling in the pits of their stomachs.

Mina tried to calm their fears. "You only dreamed of the rapids because you could hear them from your tent, Job. And because the Naskapi told us to be careful of them."

Gilbert said, "Dreams tell the future, missus."

She turned to George for some assistance in the matter, but he too looked stricken. "Well," she finally said, "I think a dream like Job's is meant to warn us of a *possibility*, not a certainty. It only means we should be exceedingly careful from now on. As we will be."

As a precaution, that day the men made certain not to re-create the specifics of Job's dream. Instead of riding with Gilbert, as he had in the dream, Job rode in the stern of Mina's canoe, with George in the bow seat. The other canoe, which usually took the lead, followed behind. Each man kept his foot atop an extra paddle, lest one break or be lost in heavy water.

Even so, from their first moments on the river that morning it seemed likely that Job's dream might come true. The river, which had already been dark, now seemed the colour of ink. They could not see the bottom nor pick out boulders submerged only a few inches below the surface. Also, the slope of the river steepened sharply, and the rapids swelled in both quantity and amplitude.

Nor was there any break in the rapids. One chute led to the next one, with at most a few moments of smooth water in between. The men almost never paddled to increase their speed but employed their oars as rudders and as drags to slow them down. The water foamed and churned around standing boulders, heaved and leapt over submerged ones.

After every run the canoes were pulled ashore so that the party could catch their breath and quiet the trembling in their limbs. Mina considered proposing that they spend more time portaging, but she knew how unpredictable were the arrival and departure of any ships to the remote posts, and even more than she feared the rapids she feared missing the *Pelican*.

So they continued on. Job stood in the stern of Mina's canoe, shouting directions over the roar of the river while George struggled with his paddle to turn the canoe aside from a boulder rushing toward them. Hour after hour it continued, day after day. All the while, Mina sat helplessly in the centre seat, hunkered low and gripping her knees so that she would not lurch to the side and throw the entire canoe off balance.

It was stressful work for all of them. So stressful that, though they were making good time and covering more miles per hour than ever before, their muscles ached, especially in the neck and arms and shoulders, and they cut each day short, for a longer night was needed to ease the strain of even a few hours on such demanding water. And from the night of the twenty-fourth on they all had troubling dreams, including Mina—dreams of tumbling over cataracts and plunging into black, frigid pools, of being driven down into an icy, bottomless river. They came to breakfast with blank stares and wan expressions, all wondering to themselves if today would be the day their luck ran out.

Yet disaster, as it often does, seemed to come out of nowhere. The set of rapids they were travelling that morning was no worse than others they had run, but the party was exhausted by now, depleted by the constant strain. Job, standing in the stern, was the first to notice the black boulder coming toward them, charging like a bull submerged under the foam. For a moment he could not make up his mind whether to take the canoe to the right or the left of it, and he shouted his directions to George an instant too late. The right side of the canoe banged against the rock, sending the stern lurching toward the centre of the river. Job caught hold of the gunwale just in time to keep from being ejected, and plunked down heavily on the seat. But the canoe was turned broadside in the current, and a moment later the bow slammed against a rock protruding from shore. The stern turned downriver, but not far—only far enough to wedge itself against another boulder. With the canoe turned nearly perpendicular to the rushing water and locked in place at both ends, the waves banged against the side one after another, violently bucking the craft and its passengers up and down.

Mina, gasping from the cold shock of each surge as it slammed against the canoe and splashed over her, could barely get the words out to shout, "What should I do?"

"Don't move!" George answered.

Gingerly he picked a coil of rope off the bottom of the canoe and looped it around his neck. Then, moving forward an inch at a time, he managed to grab hold of the long, pointed rock protruding into the river and, with fingertips digging in, straining for purchase on the slippery surface, he pulled himself up out of the canoe and onto a precarious ledge. From there he leaned over awkwardly, looking as if he might fall into the water at any moment, and secured the rope to an eye-hook on the bow.

Meanwhile Job was moving too, another rope in hand, crawling bit by bit over the stern, stretching out his body until he could reach an eye-hook mounted at his end. He lay half-turned onto his side so that his back was braced against the boulder, with water pouring over him front and back. After securing his line he crawled back into the canoe, then very delicately crept past Mina to the bow and climbed onto the pointed rock beside George.

With the men's weight out of the boat, the bucking, lurching motion became even more violent. Mina sat huddled tight, every breath a gasp. She prayed that she would not be told to climb out of the canoe too; she doubted that she could make her body move.

But no, she was told to sit tight. Soon George and Job positioned themselves along the edge of the boulder. They pulled the bow and stern lines taut, then lifted the front end of the canoe clear of its impediment. This allowed the current to turn the bow downstream again, and gradually the stern slid free as well. Now Job took hold of both lines and, grimacing with the effort, held the canoe in place while George eased himself onto his seat and took up his paddle. Job held the ropes a moment longer, then suddenly tossed both into the canoe and, with an alacrity Mina could only marvel at, dropped down onto his seat as they shot forward down the river.

The incident had a strangely salubrious effect on all the men, especially Job. He viewed the near disaster as the one predicted by his dream, and now it was behind him, no harm done. At supper that night, despite a freezing blast of wind that had the party huddling close to the whipping flames of their campfire, he laughed and ate heartily and, for the first time all week, played a few songs on his mouth organ.

Mina found herself in a more contemplative mood. Alone in her tent that night, she wrote:

> *Fire in an open place tonight, and I do not like to go out to supper. It is so cold. Thinking now we may possibly get to the Post day after tomorrow. . . . All feel that we may have good hope of catching the steamer. Perhaps we shall get to tide water tomorrow. There have been signs of porcupine along the way today, and one standing wigwam. There is one big bed of moss berries . . . right at my tent door tonight. So strange, almost unbelievable, to think we are coming so near to Ungava. I begin to realize that I have never actually counted on being able to get here.*

———

*Dillon Wallace's expedition, late August through mid-September 1905*

IN THE SECRET DEPTHS OF HIS HEART, Dillon Wallace often despaired of ever finding his way out of this cursed land. The other men in his party made no secret of their disgruntlement, especially Stevens and Richards, who grumbled often and loudly about the rapidly dwindling provisions and the unsatisfying rations. To a man, Wallace's crew were dog-tired and ragged. The spectre of a starved and frozen Leonidas Hubbard was never far from their thoughts.

Then came August 30. In the afternoon Stevens and Easton came trudging back to camp after a scouting mission that had taken several hours. They had climbed a summit named Corncob Hill in hopes of spotting the big waters of Lake Michikamau at last, and as the two men marched wearily into camp their colleagues waited, silent but hopeful. Both Stevens and Easton wore tired smiles, but there was no way to interpret those expressions with certainty. A smile could mean success or it could mean wan resignation to yet another failure.

Wallace, who had been sitting near the tent, putting an edge on his knife, scarcely moved as Easton and Stevens covered the last few yards. What will I do, he wondered, if they didn't see the lake? If they didn't see it . . . I will have no choice. The decision will be made.

Richards said, "Well, boys? Give us the news."

Pete Stevens hunkered down in front of Wallace. "Hill very steep," he said. And then his smile widened. "I not care. I must know soon as I can, and I run to top. There I shut my eyes awhile, afraid to look. Then I open them and look. Very close I see when I open my eyes much water."

For Stanton, Wallace and Richards, those words were like a blast of pure oxygen. Wallace closed his eyes dreamily and felt himself sinking down into sweet relief. When he opened his eyes a moment later he was happy to see Stevens still there, still grinning, still bursting with the news.

"Big water," Stevens said. "So big I see no land when I look one way, just water. Very wide too, that water. I know I see Michikamau. My heart beat crazy and I feel very glad. I almost cry."

Every man in camp felt like crying. Their relief was too great, their gratitude too huge. They had no words for it, no response but for an ache in the chest, a constriction in the throat. Stanton thought, Easy sailing from here on in, and considered saying it aloud, but the moment was too special—it felt sacred somehow, and even he held his tongue in reverence of their discovery.

The next morning, Pete Stevens had occasion to cry again. After breakfast, just as the men prepared to clean up and break camp, Wallace asked them to sit by the fire awhile longer. When they had settled into their seats again, he told them, "The time has come for three of you to turn back."

The notion of sending part of the crew back was not new to them; it had been proposed by Wallace on an earlier occasion, with the rationale that two men could move faster than five and that it would be preferable to have the mission completed with a partial crew rather than not at all. But Wallace's pronouncement now, with Lake Michikamau glittering like an Eden so near at hand, struck the men like a blow. Wallace gave them no time to protest.

"Richards is the natural choice to continue on with me," he said. "He's the most experienced man in the rapids, as well as best suited to the scientific work that remains. But he needs to be back in New York by winter for his university duties. And I made a solemn promise to his people that I would have him back to them by autumn."

He paused for a moment to swallow. His throat had grown husky. "Pete, too, would be a logical choice. But if he comes with me, how can the others be assured of getting back to civilization? Pete has to go along as their guide."

Wallace dragged his heel across the Labrador earth. This morning's chore was his hardest task of the expedition. It was like deciding which of his arms and legs to cut away and which one to keep.

"Easton and Stanton have both spoken with me about their desire to continue to Ungava. Both know what a dangerous undertaking it is, another four hundred miles to traverse . . . the heaviest rapids yet ahead . . . the near certainty of disaster if any one of us has another accident or becomes unable to travel. And I would like to keep them both. I would like to keep all of you with me. But winter is coming on fast and the food is running out and . . . well, you know this already. Success now depends on being able to move quickly. And so . . ."

He was silent for a few seconds, then looked over at Stanton and offered a soft smile. Stanton knew what was coming, but he shook his head. "I won't go back without you. I won't."

Wallace could only nod and smile, not an acceptance of Stanton's refusal, but a recognition of his loyalty. Then Wallace said, "Easton was the first to ask. In New York, in fact. He as much as told me, before we even started, that unless he could see this through to the end, he saw no reason to sign on for it at all. So for that reason, Easton is my choice. He and I will continue on alone."

Both Richards and Stevens had tears in their eyes. Only Stevens, whose English was limited, could fit his feelings into words. "Wish you let me go with you. Shoot grub, maybe. I hunt. Don't care what danger. Don't care if grub short. Maybe you don't find portage— what then? Maybe not find river. I find him for you. I take you through. I bring you back safe to your sisters. Then I speak to them and they say I do right."

"I'm sorry, Pete, but no, I can't. I'd like to take you through, but I've got to send you back to see the others safely out."

"I never think you do me this way. I don't think you leave me this way."

Then, in an instant, his self-pity turned to concern for Wallace and Easton. "If grub short, you come back," he told them. "Don't wait too long. If you find Indian, then you all right. He help you. You short grub, don't find Indian, that bad. Don't wait till grub all gone. Come back."

Wallace promised to exercise all prudence. He would not endanger their lives.

Stanton asked, "We're going with you as far as Michikamau at least, aren't we?"

"You've got to let us go to Michikamau," said Richards.

And so it was decided. They spent the rest of that day caching materials and food for the three men to recover on their return from Lake Michikamau. There was another cache eight days back on the Naskapi, Stanton's beloved pemmican. Richards gave Wallace a new shirt, a heavy one to help keep him warm in the cold weather ahead. He also presented him with a package not to be opened until the sixteenth of September, Richard's birthday. Wallace and Easton, it was decided, would keep the tent as well; the others would sleep under the tarpaulin.

And all that day and all through the night Wallace kept remembering another painful separation, when he and George Elson had bid goodbye to Hubbard along the banks of the Susan River. Nobody had ever described that parting more poignantly than Hubbard had in his journal:

*Sunday, October 18, 1903. Our past two days have been trying ones. I have not written my diary because so very weak. Day before yesterday we caught sight of a caribou, but it was on our lee, and, winding us, got away before a shot could be fired.*

*Yesterday at an old camp, we found the end we had cut from a flour bag. It had a bit of flour sticking to it. We boiled it with our old caribou bones and it thickened the broth a little. We also found a can of mustard we had thrown away. I sat and held it in my hand a long time, thinking how it came from Congers and our home, and what a happy home it was. . . .*

*This morning I was very, very sleepy. After the boys left—they left me tea, the caribou bones, and another end of flour sack found here, a rawhide caribou moccasin, and some yeast cakes—I drank a cup of*

*strong tea and some bone broth. I also ate some of the really delicious*
*rawhide, boiled with the bones, and it made me stronger—strong to*
*write this. The boys have only tea and one-half pound pea meal. Our*
*parting was most affecting. I did not feel so bad. George said, "The*
*Lord help us, Hubbard. With His help I'll save you if I can get out."*
*Then he cried. So did Wallace. Wallace stooped and kissed my cheek*
*with his poor, sunken, bearded lips several times—and George did the*
*same, and I kissed his cheek. Then they went away. God bless and*
*keep them.*

Wallace wished now, of course, that he had remained with
Hubbard. How many hundreds of times had he chastised himself
for ever leaving his best friend's side? He knew that had they all
stuck together, forged on somehow, carried Hubbard on a litter if
necessary, within a week they would have made it out. They had
been stronger together, but too weak alone.

But if he knew this, why was he choosing again to separate? Well,
he told himself, the situation is different now. The others are strong
enough to make it back, plenty strong enough. Nobody is sick. And
Easton and I are strong enough to continue. It is important that we
do so, vitally important. I must continue on. Hubbard asked me to,
after all. He made me promise to see this through.

Still, it was a long cold night that Wallace spent with his
thoughts and doubts. He could smell winter closing in on them.
The chill in his nostrils smelled like death. He was not afraid of
death, not any more, but he did not want to take anybody else down
with him. He wished he could send them all back to safety, Easton
included. He wished he could take them all with him to Ungava.

Most of all, he wished that he and Hubbard had never said
goodbye.

Next afternoon, Wallace was still thinking of goodbyes. As he
pushed through a stand of brush on their march to Michikamau,
following Pete Stevens, with the other men several minutes behind,

it seemed to him that all the important moments of his life, ever since his wife's death, had been marked by sad goodbyes. Hubbard had gotten Wallace moving after Jennie's death, gotten him into the woods and the wilderness, out of his misery. Except that there was no end to misery, was there? Not really. Even a beautiful, clear day like this one, this warm, still Sunday, even this perfect day could not be enjoyed for itself. Because the end of this march would mean the end of his companionship with Stevens and Richards and Stanton. The end of a brotherhood.

It had happened much the same way with Hubbard. That had been on a September day as well, a day just as beautiful as this one. Hubbard, looking so joyful, nearly transcendent, had come down off a ridge to announce that he and George had seen Lake Michikamau, that it waited for them just over the next ridge, waited there like salvation itself.

But they had never made it beyond that ridge, and that was why a beautiful September day could make Wallace's eyes sting, could make his heart ache. The smell of the soil, the rich scent of boot-turned moss—every nuance of this journey reminded him of the other one.

He came out of the brush with his head lowered, a scratch burning along his forearm. He straightened up, more to ease the ache in his chest than for any other reason, and he lifted his eyes to look ahead. And there he saw the great broad lake at last. Pete was standing at the shoreline, not twenty yards ahead, grinning from ear to ear.

Oh, Hubbard, Wallace thought, and the ache in his heart swelled, his eyes blurred. Oh, how I wish it were you standing there!

Wallace crossed slowly to the edge of the lake, as solemn as a penitent. Pete understood, and he was quiet too—no whoops of triumph, no wild laughter. After a few moments he took off his cap and knelt on the rocks. He bent his wide hat brim into the shape of a cup, dipped it in the water, filled the cup and handed it to Wallace.

"You reach Michikamau at last," Stevens said. "Drink Michikamau waters before others come."

Wallace raised the makeshift cup to his lips and tilted it up. The water was icy cold and dizzying. He felt himself wanting to swoon at the sweet, sorrowful taste of it, wanting to let go of everything. This would be a good place to let go, he thought.

But there was a long way to travel yet and he could not let go. He merely smiled and passed the hat back to Pete, who drank what was left in it and then stood there, not speaking, until they were joined by the others, who carried just one canoe this time, the one that would take Wallace and Easton away from them.

An hour or so later they pitched their camp—their forty-sixth camp, and their last one together—on a rocky point a few hundred yards farther north. The remainder of the day was conducted in hushed tones, all movements made lugubrious by the sad knowledge of what tomorrow would bring. They divided up the food, then Wallace and Easton wrote letters for Richards to carry out and post at the first opportunity. Each man wondered if he would ever see the men of the other group again. They thought of all the things that could go wrong for either party, all the things that already had. And each man felt inexpressibly alone.

After supper they built up the fire to a roaring blaze, laying on every piece of wood they could find, saving only enough for a small breakfast fire. The sky remained clear and vast and untroubled, the stars brilliant. The men talked for a while and made plans for where they would meet again when all had returned safely home. Wallace could not help but reflect on his and Hubbard's and Elson's similar conversations, of his and Hubbard's plans to buy a farm together, to show George all the sights of New York City, to live out long lives of fast friendship and unflinching loyalty.

Beauty and misery, Wallace thought. Beauty and sorrow.

Afterward he read a passage from the Bible. Then Pete sang a few songs for them. "Home, Sweet Home" was first, then "I'm Going for

Glory, My Heart Is Sore." When he sang "Pray for Me While I Am Gone," his soft voice quavered and broke, and the others squinted and cleared their throats as if the smoke were getting to them.

When he finished singing, Pete told Wallace and Easton, "I goin' to pray for you fellas every day when I say my prayers. Can't pray much without my book but I do my best. Pray best I can for you every day."

That night they all prayed—prayed themselves to sleep. Next morning, after breakfast, Wallace took out his Bible again to read aloud. This time he read John 14, the same chapter he had read to Hubbard on the morning of October 18, 1903, before heading out into the storm. He did wonder about the wisdom of reading that same chapter again, wondered if he was maybe calling up another disaster, invoking a repeat of tragedy. But no other chapter seemed appropriate.

"'Peace I leave with you,'" he read, "'my peace I give unto you; not as the world giveth, give I unto you. Let not your heart be troubled, neither let it be afraid.'"

Then the men shook hands, held them long and hard. They turned away finally, as men do, when tears filled their eyes. Wallace and Easton climbed into the canoe and took up their paddles. The other men shouldered their packs. And the single group became two, one gliding north, the other trudging south.

Wallace and Easton crossed the divide approximately a week later. They had little time to savour the accomplishment, however, for winter was upon them. The temperature at their first George River camp fell to twenty-two degrees that night and climbed only to thirty-five the next day. That day they advanced only a mile and a quarter, moving "in the teeth of a gale," Wallace wrote, "the snow so thick we could not see the shore."

On the sixteenth of September they celebrated Richards' birthday by opening the package he had given them. In it they found a portion of Richards' own rations, a piece of fat pork and a quart of flour.

All the men had agreed before parting that on Richards' birthday, at precisely seven P.M., each group should enjoy the best dinner they could provide for themselves, and in this way they might feel that the party was united again, if only for an hour or so. Wallace and Easton's feast began with a cup of beef bouillon made from capsules. Then came fried ptarmigan and duck giblets, then a roast of black duck, spinach prepared from the last of their dried vegetables, fried bread and black coffee. Later, beneath charcoal skies and frosty winds, they smoked their pipes and speculated on where the other party might be camped that night.

But the hope that all might feel reunited by the birthday celebration was in vain. "I must confess," Wallace later wrote "that with each day that took us farther away from them an increased loneliness impressed itself upon us. Solemn and vast was the great silence of the trackless wilderness as more and more we came to realize our utter isolation from all the rest of the world and all mankind."

*Mina Hubbard's expedition, last days of August 1905*

AFTER THE NEAR DISASTER on August 22, Job relaxed and no longer worried about his dream. Calamity had been thwarted and, unless he had another dream, he did not expect it to visit them again.

Mina almost wished that the men would grow sombre again, and apply all their energies to the task of paddling, for no matter how swiftly the canoes raced down the rapids she wanted more miles put behind them. The valley through which the George River rushed seemed to be closing in on her, the mountains like fortress walls.

George must have felt some of the same claustrophobia. After three days of shooting rapids and portaging around roaring cataracts, when the river began to widen and the suffocating mountains receded, he gazed back toward the high stone walls in the distance and observed, "It looks as if we just got out of prison."

The river remained wild until the afternoon of August 26, when finally the canoes glided onto smooth water. After a few hours of paddling, however, and much to Mina's dismay, George nodded toward a point of land not far ahead and announced that they would pull ashore there and set up camp.

"But the post is only seven or eight miles ahead!" Mina told him.

"It might be farther," George said. "We don't really know."

"I took a reading with the sextant at noon."

"Even so . . . it's going to be too dark soon. We've got smooth water now but there's no telling how long it will last."

"Didn't you say not long ago that if the *Pelican* is at Ungava it would try to get underway on Saturday night? Well, today is Saturday, isn't it? Or don't you trust the calendar any more than you trust my readings?"

He looked into the western sky. "There won't be enough light for us to see what's just under the water," he explained. "And I doubt we're through the last of the rapids yet. And anyway . . ."

Then he stopped himself. Mina, though, knew what he was thinking: *And anyway, the post is probably farther than you think.*

He had no confidence in her ability to navigate. None of the men had believed her earlier when she had predicted the appearance of the Naskapi camp. But she had been right then and she was right now; she could feel it in her bones. Still, she had to admit that George was correct about the danger of submerged boulders and more rapids. Better to arrive at Ungava a day late but dry and alive than to float there face down with their lungs full of water—that was George's implication.

For Mina's part, she would have been willing to risk drowning.

Consequently the night was a restless one for her. She fretted alone in her tent, read from Laddie's journal, wrote in her diary, reread her field notes, looked at flowers she had plucked and pressed inside the pages of her diary—the delicate blue cornflowers, the tiny violets, the sweet pink bell of the vining *Linnea borealis*, still fragrant, still evocative. She slept only fitfully, waking several times through the night to peek outside, anxious for the first rosy slivers of dawn to appear on the horizon.

When morning finally came it was all she could do not to shout at the men to move faster. Why did the simplest of tasks take such an inordinately long time? She gulped down only half a cup of tea for breakfast and, rather than give the men an opportunity to pour themselves a second cup, emptied what remained in the kettle into her water bottle.

"We can drink this as our celebratory toast when we reach Ungava," she said.

When she carried the water bottle to her tent to be packed with the other things, Joe whispered to the men, "It will taste good in camp at tonight's supper too." They laughed softly, grinning and nodding. Not one of them expected to reach the post that day.

A mile below their camp they encountered another set of rapids, too dangerous to run. After a short portage they emerged onto a kind of plain where the river spread out to over two miles wide. Again the canoes were put in the water. With the wind at their backs they were making good time again, the current strong and the men paddling in a steady rhythm.

The next rapid came upon them suddenly, with no rumble of warning. Both canoes were nearly on the brink of it, rounding a bend, before it was spotted, and only with desperate paddling did the men manage to pull ashore in time. Afterward they stood on shore for nearly half an hour, catching their breath and letting their racing hearts calm. Then George surprised Mina. "I think Job and I might try to run this rapid," he said.

Job said nothing, but his eyes lit up and a small smile creased his lips.

Joe and Gilbert decided to portage. As they were separating the loads they would carry, Mina, who had been studying the turn of the river ahead, approached George. "When you get out beyond those points of rock," she told him, "you should be able to see the island opposite the post. Wave back to me to let me know you saw it."

George smiled. "All right. I'll watch for it."

"I'm telling you, it's there."

"I'll watch for it," he said.

But she knew what that smile meant, and it infuriated her. She turned and marched back to the other canoe and sat down on a pack.

George and Job worked their canoe into position to take the rapid. But within seconds the current had them in its grip, pulling them away from their intended path. They paddled mightily, digging at the water, but they could not turn the canoe. Finally both men gave up and dropped down low in the craft, mere ballast.

Immediately the canoe swung around and shot stern-first down the rapids. Mina was on her feet now, straining up on her toes, breathless. Then she began to run along the shore, trying her best not to lose sight of them. The canoe was dancing, she thought, like a leaf on wild water. Job and George remained huddled low, riding it out.

For a few minutes they disappeared from Mina's view. Up ahead the river swung from west to north, and though she could hear what sounded like George's voice echoing over the water, she could not make out any words. Had they capsized? Was George calling for help? She ran faster, stumbling and lurching over the loose rocks. She could hear Joe and Gilbert coming up fast behind her.

A huge boulder blocked her path. She climbed over it, scraping an elbow. At the top, she shot a look downriver. There, sixty or so yards ahead, the canoe floated on calm water. And George was standing in the bow, facing her, waving his cap back and forth over his head, shouting at the top of his voice. It took her a while to understand what he was saying.

"I see the island!" he called. "I see the island!"

They could not paddle fast enough to suit her. "Do hurry a little," she told George. And for a minute or so he plied his oar more vigorously, but with the post itself not yet in sight his efforts and those of the other men struck Mina as altogether too leisurely. And how merrily the men chatted, as if out for a Sunday glide across a lake in a park. Thirty minutes earlier she had feared for George's and Job's lives. Now she wanted to knock their heads together.

At the same time, the thought of soon returning to her previous life made her weak with fear. Two nights earlier she had written in her diary: "Now that the work is so nearly done . . . I dread going back. . . . What am I going to do? I don't know."

But with the post so near, every minute seemed ten. By her calculations another hour passed before a white speck materialized on a distant point of land. Now five sets of eyes squinted hard, keeping the speck in sight lest it disappear again. And soon the speck grew into a dot of white, then gradually filled out until it took the shape of a small building. A few minutes later Mina's crew could make out several black specks moving around in front of the building—people walking! And there was a boat out in the open water—not the *Pelican*, unfortunately, just a rowboat. Manned, it soon appeared, by an Eskimo and his son, who were busy checking their nets.

Mina's canoe was the first to pull alongside the fisherman's boat. The father leaned over to shake George's hand. "Are we near the post?" George asked. "The Hudson's Bay post?"

The Eskimo nodded and smiled. He answered in his own language, which nobody in Mina's party understood.

"He seems to be saying yes," Mina said.

"Has the *Pelican* arrived?" George asked.

The same nod and smile, accompanied by slightly different words. "It has? The steamer has arrived? Has it departed already?"

The boy, who looked to be twelve or so, smiled and nodded too.

Mina said, "Let's just keep going, George. Thank you!" she told the fisherman. "Thank you very much!" Then, "Hurry, George, please. Please do try to hurry."

A few minutes later the post was sighted, deep in a cove on the right bank of the river, still far enough ahead as to appear microscopic against the background of mountains, with the vast Ungava Bay fanning out to the north. "There it was deep in a cove," Mina later wrote, "on the right bank of the river, a little group of tiny buildings nestling in at the foot of a mountain of solid rock." The tide was low and the cove held almost no water. A wide, boulder-strewn mudflat stretched between the canoes and the shore below the post.

Mina had been turning in one direction after another, scanning the water. Finally she said it. "The steamer isn't here."

"Maybe it hasn't arrived yet," George said.

"And maybe it's already gone." Oh, how she wanted to upbraid George at that moment! How she ached to cry out, *Why didn't you listen to me last night when I wanted to go on?* But then she remembered the last set of rapids and how close her party had come to being sucked into them. If the canoes had entered that rapid last night, when the light was dim and visibility poor, there was small chance any of them would have survived. So yes, she had been right about the post. But George had been right about the rapids.

Where the mudflats began, the men stowed their paddles and reached for the poles. To Mina's surprise the canoes were poled along quite smoothly, slipping over the mud with only an inch or so of water beneath the hulls.

A man in hip waders was coming toward them across the mud. A white man. He was trailed by six Eskimos. "That must be Mr. Ford," Mina said.

She could not wait until he closed the last twenty yards. She stood in the canoe and shouted, "Has the ship been here?"

"Oh, yes!" he called back. "Yes, indeed!"

"And gone again?"

"Yes, indeed!" he answered.

She dropped down onto her seat. What she wanted was to bury her face in her hands, weep herself into oblivion. Instead she sat stone-faced. They had come so far, had done so much, only to fail in the final objective. Now she would be forced to spend a long, idle winter here, all of them would. And she would have to keep four men on her payroll all the while. How could she possibly afford it?

The post agent came trudging up to her, his boots sucking mud. "What ship do you mean?" he asked with a smile. "Is there any other ship expected here, other than the company's ship?"

"No, that's the one I mean," she told him. "The *Pelican*. Has she been here?"

"Oh, yes," he said, reaffirming her worst fear. Then, after a pause, he added, "She was here last September. I expect her in September again. Another two weeks or so."

George turned to look at her. His grin was the widest she had ever seen.

But Mina, for a reason she could not yet articulate nor barely understand, continued to sit there with no expression on her face. She knew she should be joyful at that moment, should be exultant. Instead she felt empty of all emotion, peculiarly drained. "My heart should have swelled with emotion," she wrote, "but it did not. I can not remember any time in my life when I had less feeling."

George misinterpreted her response. He asked Mr. Ford, "Have any others arrived before us? Another party?"

"You are the first," the agent said. "Congratulations, Mrs. Hubbard. You are Mrs. Hubbard, are you not? I don't see how you could be anybody else."

He held out his hand to her. She took it, suddenly weak, suddenly hollow, and forced a smile. But she felt no happiness. Distantly, as if she had become separated from her body, she felt slightly nauseated. And as Mr. Ford helped her to her feet again, she could only wonder at this sense of detachment. Something was over, that was why she felt as she did. That was what sickened her. Something monumental had come to an end. And for the life of her she could not decide whether she had succeeded or failed.

"Wait," George said before she stepped out of the canoe. "You can't wade through the mud in your moccasins." He rummaged through a pack until he came up with a pair of sealskin boots. Mina leaned on Mr. Ford's arm and raised one foot to George, then the other, so that he could pull off her moccasins and push on the boots.

Properly shod, she used a paddle as a walking stick and, holding Mr. Ford's arm with her other hand, she stepped onto the mud and waded toward shore. He tried to make conversation but she found even the simplest of responses an ordeal.

"I can only imagine the adventures you've had," he told her.

"Yes," she said. "Many."

"Fraught with hardships, I would imagine."

"Only a few."

"Amazing, considering the journey you've made. Did you happen to come across the caribou?"

"We did, yes."

"You did? And the Indians?"

"Yes."

"You visited their camp? Was it the Montagnais or the Naskapi?"

"Both," she said. "We saw both."

"I can only imagine," he told her. "A woman. What a wonderful accomplishment you've made!"

She smiled. The effort all but drained her. She felt very tired, very sleepy. With each blink of her eyes she wondered if she could get her eyelids open again. She wished she had her tent to go to

now. Or Laddie's tent. If only she could join her Laddie in his tent
where he waited for her . . .

She realized then that Mr. Ford was escorting her onto solid
ground. They were moving up the hill toward the main building, a
small white house some fifty yards away. She could see a white
woman, Mrs. Ford, waiting at the bottom of the porch steps, beaming, a large, rather plump woman, hands clasped above her chest.

But Mina could not breathe. She could get no air into her lungs.
She let the paddle fall from her hand, let her hand slip off Mr.
Ford's arm. She turned toward the river, looked back across the
mudflats with the gulls and plovers flying about, squawking. She
was shivering now, freezing, and though not a drop of rain was
falling she could feel icy pricks of rain stinging her face and hands,
blurring her vision.

She had been thinking about Laddie's tent, his last camp, the one
he had described in his journal. She knew that entry so completely,
knew every word of it by heart. She had carried the image in her
mind all summer long and could see the tent now as clearly as if it
existed not twenty yards from where she stood, could feel the icy
rain, the cold tingling of her cheeks. The October wind was whipping the canvas of Laddie's small tent, the fabric snapping. Laddie
was lying on his side just inside the open flap, a blanket wrapped
about his thin shoulders as he wrote in his diary:

*My tent is pitched in open tent style in front of a big rock. The rock
reflects the fire, but now it is going out because of the rain. I think I
shall let it go and close the tent, till the rain is over, thus keeping out
wind and saving wood. To-night or to-morrow perhaps the weather
will improve so I can build a fire, eat the rest of my moccasins and
have some bone broth. Then I can boil my belt and oil-tanned moccasins and a pair of cowhide mittens. They ought to help some. I am
not suffering. The acute pangs of hunger have given way to indifference.
I am sleepy. I think death from starvation is not so bad. But let no one*

*suppose that I expect it. I am prepared, that is all. I think the boys will*
*be able, with the Lord's help, to save me.*

He was too tired to write any more. He laid the pen aside, laid
his hand atop the book, spread his fingers across it. He would rest
for a while and maybe write some more later. Or he would write
tomorrow. But first he would sleep. Yes, sleep was so lovely. Such an
easy thing. He thought he could sleep for a long time now. It was
the easiest thing in the world to do, to go to that place where the
pain disappeared, just to close his eyes and sleep . . .

Even after the image faded away and the rain stopped and it was
again a bright, clear day in August 1905—when Mina was again
standing in Ungava with Mr. Ford below the Hudson's Bay
Company house, with Mrs. Ford waiting on the bottom porch
step—even then she could not bring herself to climb the last fifty
yards to that house. She stood looking out across the mudflats, staring at the two canoes still beached out there, the two men sitting
motionless in each canoe.

"Mrs. Hubbard?" Mr. Ford said, and touched her gently on the
shoulder. "Shall we continue now? Mrs. Ford is so anxious to meet
you, you know. She's been watching for you every day. You will be
the first white woman she's seen in two long years."

And something in Mr. Ford's words, something in his voice,
brought Mina back to reality. She realized suddenly, with the abrupt-
ness of a slap, why George and Joe and Job and Gilbert had not followed her up the hill, why they had not moved from the canoes.

Because she was white and they were not. And they were back in
civilization now, at a white man's post. They were her charges here,
she was responsible for them. They did not own this place as they
owned the wilderness. They could not act without her consent.

Her body flushed with shame. How could she have been so neg-
lectful? Those four men had brought her here safely, triumphantly,

protecting her every step of the way, and she had walked away from them without a word. Laddie would never have been so selfish. He had been thinking of others to the very last, at the hour of his death, thinking only of his companions and their comfort.

"We were like Light and Darkness," she later wrote, "and with the light gone how deep was the darkness. Once I had thought I stood up beside him, but in what a school had I learned that I only reached to his feet. And now all my effort, though it might achieve that which he would be glad and proud of, could never bring him back.

"I must go back to the men at once."

She pulled away from Mr. Ford and strode down the hill, her muddy boots slapping the ground. "Mrs. Hubbard?" he called. "If there's something you need from the canoe I'll have the Eskimo boys bring it in!"

She gave no answer, did not look back. She marched toward the canoes, out across the mud, scattering the gulls. She came first to Job in the bow of the canoe and reached out and seized his hand in both of hers. "Thank you, Job, thank you so very much. For all you've done. I can never thank you enough."

She did the same with Joe. Then Gilbert. Then George. Her cheeks were streaked with tears. "We will all walk up together," she told them. "The final hike together. I'm so sorry I went ashore without you. Please forgive me, please. I would not even be here were it not for each of you."

The men wanted her to walk in front of them but she refused. "That's not the way it's been, is it?" she asked. "You led me everywhere. And now you shall lead me home."

It made her feel a little better to see how the men beamed, how proudly they strode across the mud, Job and Joe and Gilbert side by side and leading the way. George, as always, walked beside her. She moved close and took his hand. Immediately his eyes flared with panic and he tried to pull his hand from hers before Mr. Ford could see. But she held tight. "Don't let go," she told him.

"But missus . . . you don't understand. It's not like before. It could get me in trouble."

With that she released him. "Then give me your arm. The mud is so slippery, anyone can understand that."

She laid her hand on his arm and for a moment they walked like that, like a gentleman and his lady. But then he felt the pressure of her hand on his arm increasing, realized that she had slowed, was reluctant to go on.

"There's nothing beyond this for me," she said. She came to a stop. Her hand squeezed his arm. "Can't we just turn around, George? Can't we pretend we've never come this far?"

George gazed out into the bay. Gently he asked, "Is that why you did all this?"

"It's so unfair. It isn't right that I should succeed, and live, when he did not. He was so much better than I can ever hope to be."

"In that case," George told her, and laid his hand atop hers for just a moment, "maybe what's best for you and me now is if we both try to be a little more like him."

It hurt so much to nod, to smile, to admit that George was right. It would all hurt from now on, every step and every breath. But she would do it. She would walk up that hill, she would greet Mrs. Ford. She would live and do what needed to be done, but she would never forget. And she would march to the front like a soldier.

*Dillon Wallace's expedition, the final leg, 1905–06*

AFTER TWELVE WEEKS ON THE TRAIL, Wallace finally encountered the Labrador Indians. A small hunting party of four men and a boy waved from a hillside one afternoon, calling Wallace and Easton ashore. Wallace shared his tobacco and tea with the men, who then invited the two white explorers, by way of gesticulation and arm-pulling, to visit the Indians' hunting camp three miles downstream. They were delighted to do so.

The entire population of the camp turned out to greet the white men. Their tent was pitched between the Indians' two deerskin wigwams, the camp stove was lit, and soon eleven Indians crowded inside the little tent with Wallace and Easton, where more tea and tobacco were served.

Although the two groups could understand almost nothing of each other's language, Wallace was made to understand that this was a band of Montagnais. Once or twice each year they travelled to the Hudson's Bay post at Davis Inlet to trade their furs for ammunition, clothing, and other necessities. Unlike the Indians Mina Hubbard had encountered, this band had been coming across small herds of caribou with some regularity. Hindquarters and other cuts were now hanging all over the camp, being dried for winter use.

Wallace and Easton remained with the Indians until the following afternoon. Before departing they were warned to be on the lookout for dangerous rapids and waterfalls ahead. For two days after coming onto a "big, big river," the Indians told them, travelling would be good. Beyond that, "*Shepoo natchi, shepoo natchi.*" No translation was needed other than the look of fear in the Indians' eyes.

The entire camp assembled along the shore to see the pair on their way. It was the Indians' custom to pitch small stones at departing visitors; to be struck by a stone was supposed to ensure good fortune. Wallace and Easton sailed away unscathed.

Even so, their luck held a while longer. The next day Wallace dropped two caribou with two shots from his .33 Winchester, from a distance he calculated at three hundred and fifty yards. With more meat than they could carry, he and Easton spent the next four days curing the venison and caching a portion of it in case they might need, for whatever reason, to turn back. Along with their remaining pemmican and other rations, they now had provisions for eight weeks or so, and felt confident that their days of privation were behind them.

They spent another day travelling, and easily discovered the portage trail the Montagnais had told them to look for. But here their sudden change of diet caught up with them. Having overindulged on fresh venison for several meals in a row, both men became almost too ill to travel.

They pressed on despite their gastrointestinal agonies, even running several rapids during a blinding snowstorm. When visibility became so poor that the man in the stern of the canoe could not even see the man seated in front, they decided that further travel would be foolhardy. For two days they were snowbound on the rocky shore. The wind drove waves against the boulders with such force that the spray flew thirty feet into the air. By the second day of their forced encampment, the ground was covered by a half-foot of snow and the rocks along the shore were encased in ice.

On the morning of September 29 Wallace thought he detected a subsidence in the force of the wind. "If we don't move now," he told Easton, "before the river freezes up, we might have to leave the canoe behind for good." It proved to be a near-fatal decision.

As the men paddled downriver, the spray coming off the water froze in their beards and moustaches and numbed their faces. Their clothes were heavy with ice, as were their paddles and all exposed surfaces of the canoe. Before they knew it, they were in the midst of a stretch of white water. But because their speed was good and the course ahead seemed clear, they did not pause to reconsider the situation.

Moments later the canoe struck a submerged rock and swung broadside in the fierce current. They did not even have time to call out to one another before they were thrown into the icy water. Wallace was immediately pulled down, fully submerged and dragged along the river bottom, scraping between the rocks. Lungs burning, he was able finally to plant his feet on a rock and push to the surface in a relatively clear stretch of water. Some twenty feet away, the capsized canoe floated toward him. Easton was attached to the side of it, struggling to free himself, his jacket caught on a bolt.

As Wallace swam toward him, Easton worked his hunting knife free and managed to cut himself loose. But their hands were so numb that neither man could get a grip on the slippery canoe, and no matter how deeply they gasped they could not pull a full breath into their lungs. Their legs seemed distant and useless, dead with cold, and their brains could not hold a thought for more than a few seconds.

Somehow Easton found the presence of mind to take hold of the canoe's tracking line. He clamped it between his teeth and swam toward shore. Wallace swam alongside the canoe, one hand kept underwater to hold in place the packs still trapped under the thwarts. In the meantime all the lighter packs and paddles were floating downstream. The heaviest packs—none of them tied down—had sunk irretrievably.

For most of thirty minutes Wallace and Easton struggled to get the canoe ashore. When they reached solid ground, their legs would barely hold them up. Still, they managed to heave the canoe over on dry land and drain out the water.

"F-fire," Wallace stuttered. A full minute had seemed to pass between the time his brain conceived of the word and his mouth could express it. He and Easton both hobbled along the shoreline searching for wood, but not a stick was to be found. Reluctantly they dragged the canoe back into the water, climbed in and, using their frozen hands as oars, paddled an eighth of a mile to a wooded shoreline behind a little bay. By now all colour had drained from Easton's face. His windburned and sunburned skin was deathly white.

While Easton feebly tried to gather wood, plucking uselessly at low-hanging branches, Wallace attempted to find the waterproof matchbox in his trouser pocket. But his hand would not work right and he could not get his fingers to slide into his pocket. He could not think what to do. Convulsing in shivers, brain and body rattling, he loosened his belt, unbuckled his trousers. Finally, after much manoeuvring, he was able to work a hand down into the ice-stiff pocket. He brought out the matchbox, fumbled to get it open, struggled to pick out a match. Only by holding his hand very close to his face and squinting through the ice on his lashes could he tell whether a match was clutched between his fingers.

When at last he had secured one, he struck it across the bottom of the box. But the box was wet and the match broke in half. He struggled again to get another match between his finger and thumb.

Wallace looked up then at Easton, who had stopped plucking at branches and was standing not far away, swaying back and forth, his face pale and waxy, eyes blank. "Run!" Wallace shouted at him. He did not recognize his own voice; it sounded choked, distant and strange. "Run, Easton! Run!"

They both tried to run, but their legs collapsed and they fell side by side. Wallace staggered and lurched climbing to his feet, took a few steps back toward Easton and fell over. Now he crawled to Easton, who lay there groping blindly with his hands, staring into space, seeing nothing.

Wallace knew that only a fire could save them. Again he fumbled with the matchbox, got hold of a match, tried to light it and failed. Again and again he tried, until only three matches remained. Three matches, he told himself. Three matches and then death.

The first of the three flared, but his fingers could not hold onto it, and he dropped it in the snow. It hissed out. The second match lit too, and before he could drop this one he carefully laid it on a handful of dry moss at the base of a tree. The moss smoked and then caught fire. As quickly as he could, Wallace gathered up every twig within reach and laid them on the flames. When the fire seemed strong enough he reached for a larger piece of dead wood. Then another. Another. The blaze grew and warmed his face and hands. He hobbled to his feet again, stumbling about among the trees, and dragged one dry limb after another back to the fire. The wood crackled and spat. Easton, crawling on his hands and knees, dragged himself close to it. Wallace piled on more and more wood, his body warming as the blaze grew. Finally he laughed out loud.

Later, when he wrote about the incident, Wallace observed that their firearms had all been lost in the river, "our clothing, nearly all our food, our axes and our paddles, and even the means of making new paddles were gone, but for the present we were safe. Life, no matter how uncertain, is sweet, and I laughed with the very joy of living."

The remainder of the expedition proved not much easier. After nearly losing their lives to hypothermia, Wallace and Easton were able to thaw out by the fire, but their situation was bleak indeed. They eventually managed to recover their paddles and a few other supplies that had floated downstream to an eddy, but their guns, axes, all cooking utensils, plus 350 unexposed photographic films were lost forever. Among the items salvaged were their blankets, clothing, tent, a supply of matches, tea, caribou tallow and fifty pounds of pemmican. They had no choice but to press on and hope that the current would carry them out of this hell.

With the coming of October, winter cinched its noose tighter and tighter. Equipped with only summer clothing, and in an area where little wood was to be found—and when it was, it was usually wet—the men stayed cold day and night. With only pemmican and a few wild berries to sustain them, they suffered constantly from gnawing hunger. They saw flock after flock of ptarmigan, ducks, and geese, but they had no guns or ammunition.

They also encountered numerous Indian signs, but the hunting camps were all abandoned and nothing had been left behind. Storms raged and winds howled. The men fell into a tedious routine, moving during the daylight hours and camping at twilight.

Most days they were drenched by rain or blinded by snow. They seldom spoke to one another, too deep in their misery for any but essential conversation. Easton had been so traumatized by his icy submersion that he no longer washed or bathed and refused any contact with water except for what he drank.

Not until the evening of October 16 did Wallace and Easton spot the lights of the Ungava Bay post. Because the tide had left the bay drained of everything but mud, leaving no approach by canoe, they dragged their belongings to the safety of higher land, then started to pick their way along the face of a clifflike hill in hopes of reaching the post on foot. But their footing was dangerous and the light was receding rapidly. They found a niche a hundred feet or so above the mud and there piled up all the brush and loose wood they could find, meaning to light a signal fire at the first sign of life from the post.

It wasn't long before a lantern light appeared and began to move down toward the mudflats below the post. Wallace and Easton ignited their signal fire, then jumped up and down, waving their arms and shouting. In time the lantern light turned in their direction, seemed to be approaching them. Then it disappeared.

Resigned to spending a cold night on the cliff, the men smoked their pipes and watched their signal fire slowly dying. "When all at once," as Wallace described it, "there stepped out of the surrounding darkness into the radius of light cast by our now dying fire, an old Eskimo with an unlighted lantern in his hands, and a young fellow of fifteen or sixteen years of age."

The boy, who turned out to be the grandson of John Ford, the post agent, explained that the Eskimo had seen Wallace and Easton striking matches earlier to light their pipes, even before the signal fire was set ablaze. Since there were no matches left within a hundred miles of the post, Mr. Ford assumed that there were strangers stranded on the hill, and sent his grandson and the Eskimo to investigate. Their lantern had blown out along the way.

With the relit lantern to guide them, Wallace and Easton were escorted to the agent's house. Mr. Ford promptly treated them to a supper of fried trout, bread, jam and tea. There Wallace was informed of what he already suspected—that Mina Hubbard and her entire party had arrived in good condition, with provisions to spare, a full six weeks ahead of him. The only good news was that the *Pelican* was experiencing one of its typical delays and had not yet arrived.

Whether to spare himself the humiliation of having to return on the *Pelican* with Mina Hubbard or, as he claimed in his book, because the post's storehouse was virtually depleted and he did not wish to burden Mr. and Mrs. Ford with two more mouths to feed until the steamer arrived—or because he hoped to salvage his reputation as an explorer, which would now be brought into question—Wallace decided, in spite of Mr. Ford's caution that such a plan would be unwise, that he and Easton would continue to Fort Chimo, the most isolated station in northern Labrador. From there they would "travel across the northern peninsula and around the coast in winter and learn more of the people and their life."

Wallace and Easton spent three days at the post—with Wallace avoiding Mina Hubbard all the while—as they waited for the ice to form, to make a dogsled trip to Fort Chimo feasible. On the third day the *Pelican* came steaming into the bay. From the ship's commander Wallace received satisfying news: Richards, Stevens, and Stanton were all safe and sound at the North West River Post. Now, with transportation at hand, Mr. Ford again advised against Wallace's proposed dogsled expedition. But Wallace would not be swayed.

On October 22 the *Pelican* weighed anchor with both the Hubbard party and, briefly, the remains of the Wallace party aboard. Wallace and Easton, still in their threadbare summer clothing and meagrely provisioned, disembarked just twenty miles later, at the mouth of the George River. There they boarded a small boat manned by Eskimos and began their trip to Fort Chimo, 150 miles away.

The ensuing journey proved to be every bit as perilous as the one to Ungava Bay. Six days after leaving the *Pelican*, Wallace, Easton, and their Eskimo guides were forced to seek refuge on an island from a gale that raged for three days and transformed Ungava Bay into a minefield of pack ice. With their small boat now useless, the party had no option, when the storm finally subsided, but to set off on foot, without snowshoes, across the drifted snow and cracked ice.

Three days later another storm hit. This time Wallace and Easton hunkered down in a log hut while the Eskimos continued on. Six days later, with Wallace and Easton again out of food, rescuers pounded on the door of the hut. They had arrived with a dogsled team, deerskin clothing, and boots.

On November 28 the two white men finally reached Fort Chimo. There they remained until early January, when they returned to Fort George by dogsled and resumed their journey down the eastern coast of Labrador.

On April 17, 1906, their Labrador adventure came to an end at the southern coastal town of Natashquan. All told, Wallace and Easton had explored a thousand miles of Labrador's interior and had travelled another two thousand miles along the coast.

# PART III

*Afterword*

BOTH MINA HUBBARD AND DILLON WALLACE went on to write books about their expeditions. Neither book makes a single mention of the rival expedition nor once acknowledges the competitive nature of the race to Ungava. The name and spirit of Leonidas Hubbard Jr., however, haunt both narratives.

Wallace's book, *The Long Labrador Trail*, was the more popular of the two accounts and went through numerous printings. First published in 1907, a year before Mina's *A Woman's Way Through Unknown Labrador*, its prose is distinctly more lively, more calculated to emphasize the dangers and tribulations of the ordeal. Indeed, Wallace's crew experienced far more mishaps and missteps than did Mina's. His journey, in comparison to hers, seems to follow a blunderer's route to Michikamau, with the Wallace party more often lost than not. Also, whereas Mina accorded full credit for the success of her mission to her crew, Wallace's various accounts accentuate his own role as decision-maker and leader, and sometimes offer contradictory explanations for the choices he made.

In *The Long Labrador Trail*, for example, Wallace claims that he decided to continue from Ungava to Fort Chimo because too few provisions remained in the Hudson's Bay Company's stores. But in an article in *Outing Magazine* dated February 1906, he wrote:

> I have decided that instead of returning with the *Pelican* I shall go to Ft. Chimo at the earliest possible moment and endeavor to get into the deer killings with the Indians, and get, if possible, photographs of the spearing and the general slaughter that will take place. . . . Then with dogs I shall return home as quickly as possible via the coast. . . . The long journey with Eskimos and life in snow igloos offer little pleasure—but will give good material.

In other words, he was willing to sacrifice his own comfort for the sake of his readers. He had by now thoroughly adopted the pose of a bold adventure writer, a persona that, in his publications at least, supplanted that of the soft-spoken lawyer whom Leonidas Hubbard had had to coax along to a place called Labrador.

In that same *Outing* article, the next to last paragraph contains this almost grudgingly offered information, more revealing in its brevity than a dozen sentences could have been: "Mrs. Hubbard and her four Indians are here [at Ungava] and return by the *Pelican*."

Having discovered a flair for storytelling, Wallace eventually gave up his law practice for the life of a writer. He wrote on assignment for *Outing* and other magazines, and authored a total of twenty-eight books, many of them fiction and most aimed at a youthful audience. The last would be published in 1936, three years before his death at the age of seventy-six.

In 1913 Wallace went into Labrador once more, this time accompanied by a friend and four guides—one of whom was Gilbert Blake—for the purpose of marking Hubbard's final campsite with a plaque. Unfortunately the plaque was lost when the party's canoe capsized. Wallace continued, however, and on a large rock near the site where his friend had died he chiselled this inscription:

LEONIDAS HUBBARD JR.
INTREPID EXPLORER
AND
PRACTICAL CHRISTIAN
DIED HERE OCTOBER 18 1903

By all accounts, George Elson's two expeditions with the Hubbards had a profound effect on his life. He frequently regaled his friends with stories of those adventures, though he did not write his stories down and publish them, as Mina had encouraged him to do. And perhaps the most revealing story was one he did not share.

Early in September 1905, while awaiting the *Pelican's* arrival at Ungava Bay, he wrote this in his diary:

> *I am very sure could write a nice little story. I am sure someone would be good enough to help me in doing so. Another thing in my mind. I would like now to get married this fall, if I was lucky enough—if I could strak luck and could get a white girl that would marry me and especially if she was well learnt we then could write some nice stories because she would know lots more than I would but not likely I will be so lucky.*

A week later he wrote:

> *In the afternoon Mrs. Hubbard and I working and talking about some things great importance. Great afternoon. . . . I could not sleep last night awake all night, thinking lots of new things. Was up at 3 A.M. What a happy life it would be if it would really happen. New plans so good of her to think so kind thoughts of me. She is more than good and kind to me.*

Whatever plans were made, they did not come to fruition. George Elson moved to Moosonee in northern Ontario after the expedition and went to work for Revillon Frères, the Hudson's Bay Company's French rival, eventually assuming the position of manager at the Rupert House Post. There he met a sixteen-year-old Cree girl named Ellen Miller, whom he married in 1912. They had one child; it died in infancy.

George continued to work for Revillon Frères, transferring from Rupert House to Fort George and back to Moosonee, until 1936, when the company was taken over by the Hudson's Bay Company, which kept him on until his retirement at the beginning of the Second World War. He died on November 15, 1944, and was buried on Moose Factory Island.

Mina's return from Labrador, and in fact the first reports of her success there, were met with skepticism in the press. The North Adams *Evening Transcript*, published near her home in Williamstown, Massachusetts, speculated that "she cannot have carried out her original intentions. She was to have proceeded to Ungava, which would take her on a much longer journey than she has apparently made."

Her public appearances, on the other hand, beginning with those organized by friends in Williamstown, were an immediate success, and in time her speaking engagements took her over much of North America and England. She wrote at least two articles about her expedition, one for *Harper's Magazine* and the other, a more objectively phrased piece meant to outline the scientific accomplishments of her journey, for the *Bulletin of the American Geographical Society*.

Although Mina's book did not enjoy the popular success of Wallace's, her accomplishments were recognized by the scientific community. Hers were the pioneer maps of the Naskapi and George River systems, and the first map to indicate that Seal Lake and Lake Michikamau were in the same drainage basin and that the Naskapi and Northwest Rivers were not two distinct rivers, as had been generally assumed, but one and the same. In addition she provided detailed field notes and observations about the area's flora and fauna, plus invaluable photographic and written descriptions of the Montagnais and Naskapi natives.

While on a lecture tour in England in 1907, Mina met Harold Ellis, the son of a wealthy Quaker family. A year later, they married. They had three children. In 1926 the couple divorced.

Over the years Mina and George Elson maintained a correspondence, and during her visits to Canada the explorer and her guide often got together. In 1936, when Mina was sixty-six years old, she made an impromptu detour from her planned itinerary, travelled to Moosonee and surprised George with a visit, then persuaded him to take her on a canoe trip up the Moose River. Neither left any record of the details of their final day together.

Mina remained adventurous to the end. On a clear spring morning in 1956, she called out to the friend she was visiting, "I am going to explore!" and went off hiking into the unknown. The *Purley and Coulsdon Advertiser* of Friday, May 11, described the incident like this:

> A former woman explorer in Labrador, who still liked to explore the district where she was staying, was killed when crossing the railway line near Coulsdon South station. She was 86-year-old Mrs. Mina Adelaide Benson Hubbard Ellis, who was staying with friends at Fairdene Road, Coulsdon.
>
> Her daughter, Mrs. Margaret Russell, of Mirfield Common, Reading, told a Croydon inquest on Tuesday that her mother had gone out to Labrador many years ago to explore a river—a task which her first husband had left uncompleted when he had died from starvation on an exploration there.
>
> Later an *Advertiser* reporter was told there was a mountain in Labrador called Mount Hubbard and that Mrs. Ellis, who had travelled with her first husband's guides, had written a book called *A Woman's Way Through Unknown Labrador*.

Evidence was given that Mrs. Ellis had become very forgetful and often had to be brought home by strangers as she had forgotten where she was staying.

A verdict of accidental death was returned, and the coroner, Mr. J. W. Bennett, said he did not think there was anything in the history of Mrs. Ellis, or the circumstances surrounding what happened to indicate a suicidal act on her part. She had no right to be on the track—it appeared that she was just wandering about and did not know where she was.

A schoolgirl and two schoolboys saw the accident. The girl, 14-year-old Jill Foster of Coulsdon Road, Old Coulsdon, said she was on the platform at Coulsdon South station when she saw an elderly woman walking on the top of a grass bank near the railway.

After walking by the railway the woman started to cross the lines, walking slowly and carefully and stopping for a while between the two tracks. When the woman was crossing the last line of the second track, she was struck by a train.

Fifteen-year-old Roger Aslin of Chaldon Way, Coulsdon, and his schoolboy friend had shouted to the woman that a train was due, but he did not think she had heard.

Whether Mina did or did not hear the warning calls will never be known. What is known is that her success in Labrador failed to bring the peace she had hoped for. On Christmas Eve in 1906, after attending a church service and listening to a concert of hymns, she wrote in her diary, "Some of it very sweet. Made me feel so lonely and sad in a way I do not altogether understand."

Later she paused to look up at the night sky, then turned to her diary again: "Stars so beautiful. Heart so hungry, so hungry. Oh so hungry. How his eyes would shine if he could stand by me now to tell me how proud he was of my success. Oh Laddie, dear precious beautiful Laddie, I want you. Oh I want you this beautiful Christmas eve."

# AUTHOR'S NOTE

I FIRST HEARD THE STORY of Leonidas and Mina Hubbard's expeditions to Labrador in the early fall of 1995, after my return from Alaska's Arctic Circle, where the Discovery Channel had sent me to find the Porcupine caribou herd. "Another place you might enjoy," an acquaintance told me, "is Labrador. Just be careful you don't end up the way a writer named Hubbard did back at the turn of the century."

Like Dillon Wallace, the man who became Mina Hubbard's nemesis, I had a vague idea of where Labrador is located and, after some difficulty, finally found it on one of my maps. Even modern maps often fail to identify Labrador as such, and blend it into Newfoundland. But my frustration in trying to locate Labrador only whetted my interest.

From the very beginning the Hubbards' story intrigued me. I read everything I could find on the subject—and there was a great deal to find, most significantly the books and journals authored by the Hubbards and their colleagues. But despite the wealth of primary and secondary source material about these three expeditions conducted by the Hubbards and Dillon Wallace, I came to feel that a significant aspect of their story had not yet been told. For me, what existed of the literal truth of their story was insufficiently illuminating. I craved a deeper truth—a dramatic and emotional truth. Still waiting to be revealed, it seemed to me, was the *interior* story—and Mina Hubbard's most compellingly, for of all the participants in this drama, she has the richest and most complex story, the most heartfelt and the most heart-driven.

I was drawn to the story through Mina herself, particularly her unflinching devotion to her husband and her resolve to preserve his reputation no matter what the consequences. Several characters in my novels have exhibited a fanatical attachment to an ideal, so, I suppose, given my interest in characters whose excesses are poured out on the page, it was only natural that Mina Hubbard should haunt and enchant me.

But how to tell her story? Facts, like beauty, are only skin deep. Especially when the "facts" themselves are subject to interpretation.

The first book written about the first Hubbard expedition, the book that so outraged Mina Hubbard, was Dillon Wallace's *The Lure of the Labrador Wild*. But it was composed with the help of a ghostwriter who had not accompanied Wallace on the journey. So the question arises: How much of the tale was embroidered by the ghostwriter, and how much by Wallace himself? Wallace's and Mina's books about their 1905 expeditions did not appear until 1907 and 1908 respectively; we can logically assume that both authors, after much reflection and revision, added and omitted information from their accounts so as to further their individual aims. They had their field notes and diaries as guides, yes, but the books were ultimately crafted from memory and intention passed through the filter of subjective experience. No tape recorders were used to capture conversations; any dialogue that appears in Hubbard's and Wallace's books can be assumed not to be verbatim, but imperfectly remembered re-creations. The same can be said of descriptions of settings, individuals, and events.

Additionally, neither book makes a single mention of the rival expedition. Are we to assume from this that neither explorer gave a thought to the progress of the other? Hardly. It seems far more likely that the members of each crew discussed their rivals frequently, and wondered, all along the way, about their relative locations.

And what are we to make of George's and Mina's carefully worded references to one another in their diaries? So much more is said by a deliberate silence on certain matters than any number of words could disclose.

Still, these books are the accounts closest to factual because they were written by the participants themselves: the journal of Leonidas Hubbard Jr.; Mina Hubbard's unpublished diary and her book, *A Woman's Way Through Unknown Labrador*; George Elson's unpublished diary, plus the narrative he composed at Mina's request—the latter included, along with portions of her husband's diary, in Mina's book; Dillon Wallace's books, *The Lure of the Labrador Wild* and *The Long Labrador Trail*; and the diary of Leigh Stanton, a crew member on Wallace's second expedition. Working from these primary sources alone and putting secondary sources aside, I attempted to weave together a chronicle that would illuminate all three expeditions, and especially Mina's.

But I soon found myself unable to move beyond a basic outline of known "facts." I was paralyzed by what I did not know—all the conversations not recorded; all the emotions suffered alone through cold, grey nights; all the fears and doubts never uttered; all the secrets never shared. The novelist in me longed not only to observe the characters in this drama but to inhabit them. But I was writing a nonfiction book this time. How could I do so without observing strict fidelity to the facts?

I agonized for months. I read and reread the primary sources. And somewhere along the line the import of the various authors' omissions and contradictions dawned on me. I realized that even these primary sources, whether composed mere minutes after the events described or after months of reflection, were, by their very nature, highly subjective accounts. Diary entries, for example, are sometimes scribbled in haste while waiting for the bacon to fry, and are sometimes pondered over long and hard, with full knowledge that a later generation may read and judge those words. Published books are subject to even greater artifice.

So what does this mean?

It means that Norman Mailer is correct. All writing is fiction.

As Simon Schama points out in the afterword to *Dead Certainties*, " . . . even in the most austere scholarly report from the archives, the inventive faculty—selecting, pruning, editing, commenting, interpreting, delivering judgments—is in full play." Mina's and Wallace's books are not austere scholarship but subjective retellings of their adventures. In choosing to avoid any mention of each other—hardly an inconsequential omission—both Mina and Wallace chose to turn the corner from unedited fact to something much closer to fiction. Additionally, George Elson's narrative of the 1903 expedition, written well after the fact, was surely affected not only by his own sense of guilt and grief, but by Mina's fervent plea that he compose his account in order to assist her in vindicating her husband.

We can assume that each of the authors of the Labrador diaries and books believed that he or she was writing a full and truthful account of their experiences. But, as R. V. Casill observed in his novel *Clem Anderson*, "The end of every quest to know the truth is speculation."

If I wanted to know the truth underlying Mina Hubbard's story, I too would have to speculate. "Begin with a fact," said Thoreau, "and hope it will flower into a truth."

It was this admonition that gave me the freedom I needed to begin writing. From the primary sources I culled the most interesting scenes and fitted them together like pieces from five or six different jigsaw puzzles. Between the joints I added a good bit of glue in the form of speculation—description of setting and physical action, dialogue, emotional response, thoughts and feelings never recorded. In short, I dramatized.

Dramatizations are, by their very nature, speculations on how a scene might have played out. As Schama observes, the original meaning of the Greek word *historia* was "inquiry." "But to have an inquiry . . . ," he says, "is surely to require the telling of stories. And so the asking of questions and relating of narratives need not, I think, be mutually exclusive forms of historical representation."

I think so too.

The best I could hope to do, I realized, when working a hundred years after the incidents described, was to produce, through my own imperfect and subjective response to the materials, an authentic portrait of a time, a place, and a group of individuals who once engaged in a compelling drama that embodied every flaw and virtue of the human heart.

When I was writing nonfiction articles for the Discovery Channel magazines, I was encouraged by a very talented editor to put myself into every story. She did not mean by this that every story should be a first-person narrative, but that the writer should inhabit every story as if he had been on site.

For *North of Unknown* I edged close to every campfire so as to hear what Mina, George, Job, Joe, and Gilbert might say to one another, and to see how their facial expressions and body language confirmed or refuted what was said. I tucked myself into a corner of Mina's tent each night. I placed my feet in her footsteps as she hiked through the brush. From time to time I peeked in on Wallace and his party, saw and heard what I needed so as to know those men better, and hurried back to Mina.

It was impossible for me to keep any emotional distance from those brave souls. I saw them through my eyes—eyes educated in a world a century distant from theirs. I experienced them through my sensibilities, my own abilities and fears and desires. Still, I strove at all times not to betray any of them with a depiction that was inherently false.

Throughout the writing of this book, I often wondered what it was about Mina Hubbard that I, a male writer in the twenty-first century, found so alluring. It is true that, like most men, I would love to be adored as completely as Mina adored her Laddie, would love to be viewed as a god. Others of Mina's qualities are just as endearing: she was strong and brave and resourceful, an adventuresome woman, intelligent and loyal and resolute. But perhaps what fascinates me most about Mina Hubbard is that I know I would be a better man if I could be more like that shy nurse from Ontario. What she accomplished she did not for her own benefit but for another. And that, among our entire pantheon of explorers, is a rare thing indeed.

## SOURCE MATERIAL

Elson, George. Narrative of 1903 Labrador expedition, published in *A Woman's Way Through Unknown Labrador* by Mina Hubbard. John Murray, London, 1908.

——Unpublished diary, microfilm copy. National Archives of Canada, Ottawa, reference #R1648–0-6-E, A-26.

Hubbard, Leonidas Jr. Diary of 1903 Labrador expedition, microfilm copy. National Archives of Canada. Portions published in *Outing Magazine* (March 1905, pp. 648–89) and *A Woman's Way Through Unknown Labrador* (pp. 239–85).

Hubbard, Mina. *A Woman's Way Through Unknown Labrador*. John Murray, London, 1908.

——"Labrador, from Lake Melville to Ungava Bay," *Bulletin of the American Geographical Society,* 38:9, 1906, pp. 529–39.

——"My Explorations in Unknown Labrador," *Harper's Monthly Magazine,* May 1906, pp. 813–23.

Hubbard, Mina. Unpublished diary of 1905 Labrador expedition, microfilm copy. National Archives of Canada, Ottawa, reference #R1648-0-6-E, A-26.

Stanton, Leigh. Unpublished diary of 1905 Labrador expedition. Transcript copy prepared and edited by Craig Monk. Centre for Newfoundland Studies Archives, Memorial University of Newfoundland, St. John's. Collection 244, 3.02.006.

Wallace, Dillon. *The Lure of the Labrador Wild.* Fleming H. Revell Company, New York, 1905.

—— *The Long Labrador Trail.* Outing Publishing, New York, 1907.

—— "Dillon Wallace Succeeds," *Outing Magazine,* February 1906, pp. 659–60.

RANDALL SILVIS is the author of eight books of fiction. A Senior Fulbright Fellow and Thurber House writer-in-residence, his many awards include the prestigious Drue Heinz Literature Prize, three National Playwrights Showcase Awards and two fellowships from the National Endowment for the Arts. He lives in Pennsylvania with his wife and their two sons.

The text of *North of Unknown* has been set in Antique Jenson, a modern face which captures the essence of Nicolas Jenson's roman and Ludovico degli Arrighi's italic typeface designs. The combined strength and beauty of these two icons of Renaissance type result in an elegant typeface suited to a broad spectrum of applications.